Conversations with Derek Walcott

Literary Conversations Series

Peggy Whitman Prenshaw
General Editor

Conversations
with Derek Walcott

Edited by
William Baer

University Press of Mississippi
Jackson

Library of Congress Cataloging-in-Publication Data

Walcott, Derek.
    Conversations with Derek Walcott / edited by William Baer.
        p.   cm. — (Literary conversations series)
    Includes index.
    ISBN 0-87805-854-0 (cloth). — ISBN 0-87805-855-9 (paper)
    1. Walcott, Derek—Interviews.   2. Authors, West Indian—20th
century—Interviews.   3. West Indies—Intellectual life—20th
century.   I. Baer, William.   II. Title.   III. Series.
PR9272.9.W3Z477   1996
811—dc20   95-44262
                                                              CIP

British Library Cataloging-in-Publication data available

Books by Derek Walcott

Twenty-Five Poems. Port-of-Spain, Trinidad: Guardian Commercial Printery, 1948.

Epitaph for the Young: A Poem in XII Cantos. Bridgetown, Barbados: Advocate, 1949.

Poems. Kingston, Jamaica: Kingston City Printery, 1953.

In a Green Night: Poems 1948–1960. London: Cape, 1962.

Selected Poems. New York: Farrar Straus, 1964.

The Castaway and Other Poems. London: Cape, 1965.

The Gulf and Other Poems. London: Cape, 1969, as *The Gulf: Poems,* New York: Farrar Straus, 1970.

Dream on Monkey Mountain and Other Plays. New York: Farrar Straus, 1970.

Another Life. New York: Farrar Straus, and London: Cape, 1973.

Sea Grapes. London: Cape, and New York: Farrar Straus, 1976.

The Joker of Seville and O Babylon!: Two Plays. New York: Farrar Straus, 1978, and London: Cape, 1979.

The Star-Apple Kingdom. New York: Farrar Straus, 1979, and London: Cape, 1980.

Remembrance & Pantomime: Two Plays. New York: Farrar Straus, 1980.

The Fortunate Traveller. New York: Farrar Straus, 1981, and London: Faber, 1982.

Midsummer. New York: Farrar Straus, and London: Faber, 1984.

Collected Poems 1948–1984. New York: Farrar Straus, and London: Faber, 1986.

Three Plays. New York: Farrar Straus, 1986.

The Arkansas Testament. New York: Farrar Straus, 1987, and London: Faber, 1988.

Omeros. New York: Farrar Straus, 1989.

Odyssey: A Stage Version. New York: Farrar Straus, 1993.

Antilles: Fragments of Epic Memory (Nobel Address). New York: Farrar Straus, 1993.

Contents

Introduction

In 1992 Derek Walcott, Caribbean poet and playwright, was awarded the Nobel Prize for Literature. The formal announcement by the Swedish Academy came as no surprise to literary critics and readers. As Peter Balakian had written six years earlier in *Poetry* magazine, Walcott's verse had "already taken its place in the history of Western literature."

Walcott's unique literary achievements have naturally been affected by what the Swedish Academy referred to as "the complexity of his own situation." Born on the small island of St. Lucia in the Lesser Antilles, Walcott was nevertheless the beneficiary of an excellent "English" education with its many British traditions. Of mixed ancestry—both English and black West Indian—Walcott has expressed the consequent internal difficulties in his poem "A Far Cry From Africa": "I who am poisoned with the blood of both,/Where shall I turn, divided to the vein?" Even linguistically, Walcott is heir to conflicting traditions since he speaks English, French, and Creole patois. Finally, there is also the writer's complex relationship with other nations and regions beyond the island of St. Lucia, especially the United Kingdom, Africa, other Caribbean countries (such as Jamaica and Trinidad where he's lived at various times), and the United States (where he's taught almost every year since 1981).

Out of this unique situation, Walcott has managed to create what James Dickey once described in the *New York Times Book Review* as "a highly colored, pulsating realm of his own." Certainly Walcott's poems and plays reveal a great deal about the creative figure behind this literary "realm," but it's in the author's various interviews that Walcott is most clearly able to "explain" his background and express his singular opinions on a wide range of subjects—all of which are pertinent to his writings.

Fortunately, Derek Walcott is an extremely articulate conversationalist who's always willing to express his forthright views in depth. As

Edward Hirsch has remarked in *Contemporary Literature,* Walcott
"has the unique ability to be able to respond in remarkably full and
complex sentences to the most diverse kinds of questions," and, in
the literary conversations that follow in this book, Walcott's ability is
clearly facilitated by the fact that most of his interviews have originally appeared in academic journals rather than in more space-con-
scious newspapers.

Within his various interviews, Walcott addresses numerous inquir-
ies about his St. Lucian background, his painting, his founding of the
Trinidad Theatre Workshop, the contemporary status of the Caribbean
theater where "Some of the finest Shakespeare I have ever heard was
spoken by West Indian actors" (Hirsch), and his opinions about the
work of such Caribbean writers as Claude McKay, Edward Brathwaite, C. L. R. James, and the controversial V. S. Naipaul. Regarding
the last, Walcott concludes, "Certainly anyone can say what they
want about Naipaul, in terms of his philosophy or his attitude to
Trinidad, but it is impossible to degrade him as an artist" (Milne).

Throughout his interviews, Walcott also enthusiastically recalls his
own literary influences, including Hardy, Eliot, and, most signifi-
cantly, Auden—whom, Walcott claims, wrote with a "technical daring
that goes beyond, I think, Eliot and Pound." At other times, Walcott
carefully discusses the use of folk materials in his work, the problems
of racial prejudice, Caribbean and world politics, his feelings about
craft and creativity, his friendships with Joseph Brodsky and Seamus
Heaney, his disappointment with contemporary American verse, and
many other subjects.

The varied works of Derek Walcott all clearly aspire to a peaceful
harmony among diverse peoples, and his famous poem "Eulogy to
W. H. Auden" expresses the hope "that the City may be Just,/and
humankind be kind." But Walcott, having grown up in a part of the
world inhabited by descendants of Africans, Asians, and Europeans,
is fully aware of the legacy of human racism. Nevertheless, he advises
against belligerence or even a sense of historical sullenness. As he
explains in *The Paris Review* interview, "what I'm saying is to take
in the fact of slavery, if you're capable of it, without bitterness,
because bitterness is going to lead to the fatality of thinking in terms
of revenge." Thus Walcott is opposed to bellicose "Black Power"

solutions, while at the same time rejecting the concept of "affirmative action" as demeaning "patronage."

Speaking of his poetic writings in *The Paris Review* interview, Walcott admits that "I have never separated the writing of poetry from prayer. I have grown up believing it is a vocation, a religious vocation." Having such a serious attitude about his creative endeavors, Walcott is particularly interested in matters of craftsmanship and is naturally concerned that younger writers are often encouraged to express themselves in undisciplined literary modes. He points out that "the universities encourage laziness in the sense that they encourage the individuality of the young writer, and they don't include the scholarship and history of poetry." He's clearly disturbed that young writers don't take rhyme and meter more seriously, and he's astonished when their teachers complain that there's "too much rhythm" in the students' poetry. Walcott responds firmly, "I don't know any other culture in the history of the world that has ever said that to anybody—that poetry has too much melody!"

Walcott is similarly concerned about the dangers and debilitating effects of the ego in contemporary poetry, and he strongly discourages "individualism" and "experimentation" in the work of young writers: "Originality is the obsession of ambitious talent. Contemptible from early on and insufferable in the young" (Sjöberg). As a result, Walcott concludes that "all you can really do at a young age is apprentice yourself to the craft," and when this mode of poetic development is abandoned, as it usually is in the United States, the consequent poetry is inevitably unsatisfying, both "egotistical" and "boring."

As his various interviews show over and over, Derek Walcott is an extremely honest, yet generous and appealing man of prodigious and broadminded intelligence. He's also a consummate artist, endlessly fascinated with the sound-charged possibilities of language and literature. But unlike so many other poets and playwrights of lesser talent, Walcott is not obsessed with matters of personal vanity. As he explains in one of the interviews, "I think every poet of any modesty hopes to make just a small contribution to the sound of the world's hum, and does not by any means wish to be individual or be praised for his style or whatever." Clearly Derek Walcott has already made that contribution, and much more, to the body of the world's literature.

*   *   *

As with the other books in the Literary Conversations Series, the
following interviews are presented chronologically in the order in
which they were conducted and reproduced in their entirety. Obvious
typographical errors have been silently edited. Given that these interviews cover a span of nearly thirty years, there is naturally some
repetition of subject matter, but Walcott consistently adds new information and examples in his thoughtful responses. As both a Nobel
Prize-winner and the most important literary figure to emerge from
the Caribbean, Derek Walcott's literary, social, and political opinions
are always of interest and significance, and they are of particular
value to the student of his poems and plays as well as the professional
literary scholar.

Concerning the brief "Chronology" of Derek Walcott's life and
work which follows this introduction, I've made no attempt to list the
countless worldwide productions of the author's plays and have,
instead, cited only the publications of his dramas as well as the
various awards he's received for his plays.

I would like to sincerely thank a number of people who have
generously helped me with this project: Arthur Miller, Wyatt Prunty
and the Sewanee Writers' Conference, Rachael Wiegand, Mike Car-
son, Jennifer Condon, Seetha A-Srinivasan, and, of course, Derek
Walcott.

WB
July 1995

Chronology

1930   Derek Alton Walcott born 23 June in Castries, St. Lucia, British West Indies, to Warwick Walcott, a civil servant, and Alix Walcott, a schoolteacher. The family also includes his twin brother, Roderick Alton, and an older sister, Pamela.

1931   Death of his father, Warwick Walcott

1941–47 Attends St. Mary's College, Castries, St. Lucia

1947–50 Assistant Master, St. Mary's College, Castries, St. Lucia

1948   Publication of *Twenty-Five Poems*

1949   Publication of *Epitaph for the Young: A Poem in XII Cantos*

1950–54 Receives scholarship to attend the University College of the West Indies, Mona, Jamaica, where he earns a Bachelor of Arts Degree

1950   Co-founds the St. Lucia Arts Guild with Maurice Mason

1951   Publication of *Poems*

1953–54 Teacher, Grenada Boys' Secondary School, St. George's, Grenada

1954   Marries Faye A. Moyston (one son, Peter. Divorced); Teacher, St. Mary's College, Castries, St. Lucia.

1955   Teacher, Jamaica College, Kingston, Jamaica

1956–57 Feature Writer, *Public Opinion,* Kingston, Jamaica

1957   Jamaica Drama Festival Prize for *Drums and Colors*; First visit to the United States.

1958–59 Rockefeller Foundation Fellowship, to study theater in the United States under José Quintero at the Circle in the Square Theater in New York City and Stuart Vaughan at the Phoenix Theater in Arizona

1959   Founds Little Carib Theatre Workshop (later the Trinidad
          Theatre Workshop)

1960–62   Feature Writer, *Trinidad Guardian,* Port-of-Spain, Trinidad

1960   Arts Advisory Council of Jamaica Prize

1961   Guinness Award for Poetry for ''A Sea-Chantey''

1962   Marries Margaret Maillard (two daughters, Elizabeth and
          Anna. Divorced); Publication of *In a Green Night: Poems
          1948–1960;* Ingram Merrill Foundation Grant.

1963–68   Drama critic and freelance writer, *Trinidad Guardian,* Port-
          of-Spain, Trinidad

1964   Publication of *Selected Poems;* Borestone Mountain Poetry
          Award for best poem of 1963, ''Tarpon.''

1965   Publication of *The Castaway and Other Poems*

1966–68   Rockefeller Foundation Grant for the Trinidad Theatre
          Workshop

1966   Second Place Prize for Poetry, First World Festival of
          Negro Arts, Dakar, Senegal; Founds the Basement Theatre,
          Port-of-Spain, Trinidad; Royal Society of Literature Heine-
          mann Award for *The Castaway and Other Poems;* Fellow,
          the Royal Society of Literature, England.

1969   Audrey Wood Fellowship Award; Cholmondeley Award for
          ''The Gulf''; Gold Hummingbird Medal, Trinidad; Eugene
          O'Neill Foundation—Wesleyan University Fellowship for
          Playwrights Award.

1970   Publication of *The Gulf and Other Poems;* Publication of
          Dream on Monkey Mountain and Other Plays.

1971   Obie Award for the most distinguished Off-Broadway play,
          Dream on Monkey Mountain

1972   Order of the British Empire

1973   Publication of *Another Life;* Honorary Doctor of Literature,
          University of the West Indies.

1974   Jock Campbell *New Statesman* Award for *Another Life*

1976   Publication of *Sea Grapes;* Resigns as director, Trinidad
        Theatre Workshop.

1977   Borestone Mountain Poetry Award for best poem of 1976,
        "Midsummer, England"; Guggenheim Award.

1978   Publication of *The Joker of Seville & O Babylon!: Two Plays*

1979   *American Poetry Review* Award; Honorary Member, Amer-
        ican Academy of Arts and Letters, New York; Publication
        of *The Star-Apple Kingdom.*

1980   Publication of *Remembrance & Pantomime: Two Plays;*
        International Writers Prize, Welsh Arts Council.

1981   Visiting Professor, Columbia University; Visiting Profes-
        sor, Boston University; John D. and Catherine MacArthur
        Foundation Grant.

1982   Publication of *The Fortunate Traveller;* Marries Norline
        Metivier; Visiting Professor, Harvard University.

1983   Royal Society of Literature Heinemann Award for *The
        Fortunate Traveller*

1984   Publication of *Midsummer*

1985–   Visiting Professor, Boston University

1986   Publication of *Collected Poems 1948–1984; Los Angeles
        Times* Book Review Prize for *Collected Poems 1948–1984;*
        Publication of *Three Plays;* National Writer's Council Prize,
        Welsh Arts Council.

1987   Visiting Professor, Harvard University

1988   Publication of *The Arkansas Testament;* Queen's Gold
        Medal for Poetry.

1989   Publication of *Omeros*

1992   Nobel Prize for Literature

1993   Publication of *Odyssey: A Stage Version;* Publication of
        Antilles: Fragments of Epic Memory (Nobel Address).

Conversations with Derek Walcott

There's No Bitterness in Our Literature

Carl Jacobs / 1966

From *Sunday Guardian* (Trinidad), 22 May 1966, 9. Reprinted by permission of the *Guardian* and Carl Jacobs.

West Indian poet Derek Walcott, who has just been awarded a $960 prize by the Royal Society of Literature and has also been invited to become a Fellow of the Society, speaks of West Indian literature with *Sunday Guardian* writer Carl Jacobs.

Having remained in the West Indies and having seen so many other West Indian writers emigrate to England, don't you feel somewhat isolated?

Occasionally, but I have been getting in a few trips over the last few years. Two years ago, for example, I attended an international Congress of Poets in Berlin, and I also visited London, New York, Boston and Texas.

These trips keep me in touch with other poets. Because of them, I have made friends with several writers in England and America.

I don't feel as isolated and frustrated as I used to, in that sense. But there is still an isolation in the sense that, as West Indian writers, whether we live in London or the West Indies, we are both cut off from and are a part of a tradition.

What tradition is this?

It is the body of writing in English that we were brought up in. Call it the English literary tradition.

West Indian writers in London, I believe, would feel a greater isolation than I do because they are also living on another kind of island.

An Area of Darkness by Naipaul, which deals with India, is all about that sort of anguish.

We are still provincial or regional writers because we retain powerful attachments.

3

Could you define our particular provincialism? Do you mean that our outlook is insular or restricted?

I didn't mean it in that narrow sense. What I meant was a deeper communion with things that metropolitan writers no longer care about, or perhaps cannot care about. And these things are attachments to family, earth and history.

What particular quality do these attachments give to our writings?

I think the great thing about West Indian writing, especially in the novel, is that its spirit is tragic-comic. It has a self-amusement, a sense of irony, that is more robust than most novels written anywhere else today.

It is the same sort of element you find in Chekhov, Dickens or Shakespeare.

This is the distinctive quality of our writing. This is what makes it so alive.

Any people whose artists have this sense of tragic-farce have great strength. There is really no bitterness in West Indian writing, even if our history is so degrading.

Why have our writers been so productive in prose as compared to poetry?

We used to be more productive in verse. Maybe that was a young man's thing, because every novelist, especially in the early phases of his work, is something of a poet.

Lamming, Hearne, Wilson Harris, Mittelholzer, Jan Carew, all used to write poetry.

Probably they became novelists because most publishers still want poets to write prose or prose books. Or maybe a kind of adolescence was over for them once they went to England.

Or perhaps it was first the necessity of making a living that made them novelists.

Also, there was so much social ferment and change and so much to say that they must have felt that poems could not contain everything they wanted to express.

But, in a sense, writers like Lamming and Harris particularly are still poets; their books certainly have a poetic structure.

One must also remember that West Indian literature had its beginning in poetry. Jamaican Claude McKay is the best example of that.

How is a poem born within you?

I don't think anyone knows precisely how or where a poem originates.

It might have something to do with a built-in subconscious computer that assembles previous reading in terms of an experience, but generally I find that what Graves has said about the beginning of a poem is true for me.

Graves said that a poem comes in one line and a half and that line and a half, whatever length the syllables may be, dictates the structure of the poem and that, perhaps, everything else around that line and a half is artificial.

For instance, the Japanese don't go further than the seventeen syllables of their Haiku.

That first line and a half may be an image or a metaphor and, if the spirit is on you, you find yourself writing an entire poem that is a revelation to you line by line, and you just watch your hand work until it stops.

But at the same time a hell of a lot of antennae are working because you are both creating and rejecting at the same time; your own critical faculties seem to be suspended but, in fact, they are very hard at work.

Sometimes you postpone the act of a poem and try writing it later, but then the slightest shift of meter makes whatever you write a fake.

Most of the time you write bad poems. And you even have to publish them to your embarrassment.

Pound once said that there are very few poets who can show more than twenty pages of any absolute validity.

Poetry, I think, is the toughest bloody art in the world.

Do you think anything can be done to stimulate poetry?

I don't think anything should be done to stimulate poetry because a poet does not need any public stimulus.

Whether poetry is read by a lot of people or not, it eventually doesn't matter.

Would you say that poetry is a useless exercise?

At the Berlin Congress somebody made that point and, although I did not say it, I thought to myself that poetry may be useless but it is inevitable.

It has nothing to do with social unhappiness because poetry can celebrate perfection as easily as it can celebrate deprivation.

How do you view the local poetic horizon?
There are signs that a few young people are writing poetry as keenly as other people once wanted to be novelists.

There are poets of promise here like Wayne Brown, Roger McTair, Judy Miles, and, in fact, most of Cliff Sealy's "Voices" group. They are a young generation of very talented poets who can be as good as our novelists.

Bajans Are Still Very Insular and Prejudiced

Carl Jacobs / 1967

From *Trinidad Guardian,* 23 July 1967, 5. Reprinted by permission of the *Guardian* and Carl Jacobs.

In mid-August, the Basement Theatre Workshop leaves from Toronto where they have been invited to take part in Canada's Centennial Celebrations during Caribbean Week.

The Basement Theatre thus becomes the first West Indian drama company to perform outside the region. Recently, they returned from a successful trip to Barbados, which made them the first Trinidad drama group to "export" their talent.

Sunday Guardian writer Carl Jacobs speaks to Derek Walcott, poet-playwright and director of the Basement Theatre.

You have just returned from Barbados which is the company's first trip overseas. What was the reception like and what are your impressions of the theatre in Barbados?

Probably the most successful of the three plays we took was Eric Roach's *Belle Fanto.* The other two were *Joumard,* a comedy by me, and *The Zoo Story.*

There was something in Roach's play that appealed strongly to Barbadian audiences, although we thought that there might have been some difficulty with the dialect which is very rural Trinidadian.

We have now done this play seventeen times, and it still seems to be fresh and appealing to all sorts of audiences.

The theatre in Barbados is not as alive as it is down here. There does not really seem to be a native theatre, and the Bajans do not seem aware of the fact that there are a lot of West Indian plays available. I believe that contributed to their enjoyment of *Belle Fanto.*

What effect did this first overseas tour have on the company?

I am sure that it increased the standard of their performances and, because of this, we hope to make these tours a regular thing every year. If we did not have to go to Toronto and Guyana, the trip could have included St. Lucia and Grenada.

It has made us realize that we have potential audiences throughout the West Indies.

Could you say more about your trip to Toronto and Guyana?

The first invitation we got came from Guyana where there is a very active company called The Theatre Guild. We are to go there in mid-August. During the run of *Moon on a Rainbow Shawl* earlier this year, we received an invitation from Toronto to come and take part in Canada's Centennial Celebrations there during Caribbean week.

We will present the same bill plus a full-length play called *Dream on Monkey Mountain.*

This is your latest play, isn't it?

Yes. It is an attempt to cohere various elements in West Indian folklore, but it is also a fantasy based on the hallucination of an old woodcutter who has a vision of returning to Africa.

It will be premiered in Canada, but we will do it in Trinidad as part of our second repertory season later this year.

What does your repertory comprise now?

Since we opened at the Basement in January last year, we have done *The Zoo Story, Sea at Dauphin, Belle Fanto, The Blacks, The Road, Moon on a Rainbow Shawl,* and *Joumard.*

Instead of doing ephemeral little plays quickly, the plan is to establish a repertoire that we can always draw on and revise.

This means that none of these plays have really been shelved. We can always take *Moon on a Rainbow Shawl* to the other island, for example.

They want us to do *The Blacks* in Barbados, probably to jolt the Bajans a bit. I am not too sure how it would have gone down there. Barbados still seems to me very prejudiced and insular. They need a theatre that is bold and tackles their particular problems.

Why did you revive The Zoo Story?

When we began, we had a theatre that seated sixty people and ran for six nights, but an audience developed for our work and by the time we had finished our 26-night season at the Basement, plus our five-night run at Queen's Hall with *Moon,* we knew that we now had a sizable following. Although people have said that the Basement Theatre caters to a special section of the community, we have proven that this is definitely not so, and it has never been like that.

We have no special seats, no snob section, and if more than 2,000 persons saw *Moon* at Queen's Hall and Naparima Bowl, this should be enough evidence that our work is not addressed to any intellectual elite and that we harbor no prejudices whatever.

We try to mix our bill as much as possible. We have done Theatre of the Absurd, naturalistic plays and farce. This presents a great challenge to the actors. Some, for instance, have played six different roles in a year.

What is the financial position of the company now?

The money we made on *Moon* is going to help finance our trip to Guyana. Generally, the actors are paid honorariums after the run of a play, and this is done after paying royalties and clearing expenses.

We received last year a donation from a friend of the company of $1,200. We have been helped a lot by India Overseas who let us use the Astor Cinema on Sunday mornings for rehearsals.

We recently received $500 from the St. Augustine Players when their group went out of existence. We have never made any application to the government for assistance, but I hope that when the Company has more fully established its reputation, we would be able to ask for a subsidy towards getting a theatre and grants for actors to study abroad.

Walcott on Walcott

Dennis Scott / 1968

From *Caribbean Quarterly* (Jamaica), Vol. 14, No. 1&2 (1968), 77–82. Reprinted by permission of *Caribbean Quarterly*.

Scott: Derek, you are a poet as well as a playwright. The two things, the two activities, combined in one talent, so to speak, must affect the way in which the artist performs in either capacity. How do you find that your concern with poetry changes the way in which you approach writing a play?

Walcott: Dennis, I would say that the stress would be to try to preserve the verse at the expense of anything else. So that in terms of performance—(and that's a subtle word because the content in the word 'performing' means that you *can* write poems if you work in the theatre)—you can be too attracted towards the poem that is dramatic in expression. The other thing is that you have to watch out as a playwright that you don't write, or that you cut out lyrical or sweet or, you know, 'nice sounding' stuff. You may feel that as a writer it sounds good but you know how much you have to excise, and in my own particular case, you know, people do ask questions. They say, I know you wrote a play in verse but what have you been doing lately in poetry? You know what I mean? Well, the thing is that I *do* write my plays in verse and I hope that there is a moment, or there are moments, when the thing becomes a poetry on stage; and I would prefer to eventually write a play which would be a poem. And if that happens I would be satisfied.

Scott: Yes, but I am going to needle you on this point, you see, because I have felt sometimes in the case of your early plays like *Christophe* or *Ione* for instance that there are times when the verse takes over and what we get is not so much a poetic drama as a dramatic poem.

Walcott: Yes.

Scott: How do you react to this kind of accusation?

Walcott: Well, I think that a play is a dramatic poem. I think that any play that has any stature—and I am not talking about whether my plays have stature—I think that any play that works completely is a poem; and the components of that particular poem are physical: there is an actor saying certain things, lights, all the rest; (and I am not talking about playwriting a kind of play that is, you know, overtly metaphorical or is overtly symbolic. I am talking about something which is like a functioning unit) and once you have a complete concept of any play whether it's lights or you are cueing in with the cameraman, (sorry, but I mean it's true about the film too) it is a poem in the sense that it is conceived as a structure and it works metrically as finely as a poem does. And if you happen to write in verse then that's all the better.

Scott: Roughly then, you want the whole work to be a metaphor in itself, a totality.

Walcott: Exactly.

Scott: Let's talk more about your poetry. Are you aware of any particular direction in which you are moving?

Walcott: Well, I think—this is not being glib or fancy—my poetry is getting worse in the sense that it is becoming terrifyingly plain to me, and I am afraid that I am writing—you know that I have a nostalgia for obscurity in a way—I find myself at 38 writing almost so directly that I wish I were younger in terms of . . . well, I wish I were more "important" or complicated. Now this is much better for me as a poet but it's terrifying as a person—you know what I mean?

Scott: Yes, but I think it's much better for you as a poet as you say. Why do *you* think this is so?

Walcott: The answer is that I am probably a serener person sometimes. And then for instance what one might want to say is that happiness is not a theme for poetry these days. You know, domesticities, ordinary things . . . we are just talking glibly. I am very keen on the painting of Bonnard and people like that. In other words I think that people after the impressionists are great painters in the fact that they concentrated on a sense of the intimacy of an object, you know, the painters like Vacquery who go beyond the sentimental. Degas has a woman bathing or a table with flowers or something, well, I don't mean sentimental. And I think that this is something that has happened to me personally and it's something that *is* happening to me. And I find that my stuff is getting so plain that I am scared. You know, it simply becomes like a vase or a glass of water or something. This clarity is terrifying to me.

Scott: It's an interesting comment to have been made by a painter in a way. Perhaps that is one of the reasons. Do you paint as much now as you did earlier?

Walcott: I do a lot of painting now.

Scott: And might there be some correlation?

Walcott: Yes, yes.

Scott: And what about the film? You seem to be moving by your own admission more towards the visual, not the merely visual but the strictly visual.

Walcott: Well, when I say the visual I don't mean a visual thing that has the solidity of an object. It's a way of looking, you know, a concentration that is calmer. Now my personal life is calm and my poetry is not that involved or tormented. And everybody has a big yearning in a way, after a while, for being unhappy, but you can be professionally unhappy and this is what I am trying to avoid. I wouldn't like to be that!

Scott: Talking about being serene . . .

Walcott: When I say the word "serene," I don't mean that everything is swinging and fine.

Scott: I understand. Eddy Brathwaite, another poet, once said that you were a humanist poet as distinct from a folk poet. Put it this way and it seems, I think, fairly self-evident. What was your reaction at the time to this kind of statement?

Walcott: Well, I still don't like the division because that is a personal statement and that is a statement that means that Eddy and I come from different roots or different backgrounds. This is completely not true. It may be that Eddy is talking about a question of style, and the division is being made between a humanist and a folk poet in a small and intense and very dull kind of area, you know, in terms of political excitement, or very big kinds of meaning. I don't think the division can be made because there is so much access—and even to use the word "access" means that you are reaching a difference between somebody who is a poet somewhere and a guy who is, I don't know, cutting your lawn. And both Brathwaite and I would employ people, you know what I mean. And a man who cuts a lawn is not a "folk" person anymore than you are paying him to cut your grass. You know, this is a sociological statement that I am not interested in.

Scott: Might it not be more than a sociological statement? For instance, would you say that a regionalist poet was of less importance on a world scene . . .

Walcott: Absolutely not. I think one of the finest poets in the world—one of the finest poets not in the world, but one of the poets who has had one of the subtlest influences in terms of the content of anyone's work, has been Thomas Hardy; and you know, if you look at the intensity and the closeness and the privacy of Hardy's poetry as compared to some of the loudest statements made by some of the other kinds of poets, Hardy becomes every year I think a greater poet, simply because of the age, a kind of a prose age. The content of Hardy's poetry is so strong that everybody knows now that poets have to learn from novelists. I have been influenced now, and I hope that, I am glad that, I am still open to influence not by writers abroad but by West Indian writers.

Scott: I was just going to ask you this because there seems to me a greater sense of community among artists now than there ever was before. But at the same time I am not at all sure whether this community has drawn the poets themselves closer.

Walcott: Well, I think for instance, in the poem "Rights of Passage," the beautiful ending of Eddy Brathwaite's poem—you know—"The Dust," is a magnificent piece of timing. You know, an admirable thing.

Scott: In terms of the total rhythm of the work.

Walcott: And this is derived, obviously derived; I mean we couldn't have had that except that we had Lamming's novels, and we couldn't have had Eddy's section about the Rasta Man except that Roger Mais had already written that book *Brother Man*. And I couldn't have written certain things except that I had watched how closely the novelists used the language. I have been influenced as much by West Indian prose writers as I have ever been when I was younger as a poet.

Scott: What about the West Indian poets? Have you been influenced by them?

Walcott: No . . . I think . . .

Scott: You were about to say something—

Walcott: Well, I was going to say . . . really that a lot—it really sounds very affected but I mean, the bulk of West Indian poetry that we have is very, very bad. Don't you think so? I mean it's pretty poor!

Scott: Yes. Why?

Walcott: Well I believe the West Indian poet never approached the language as a construction problem, as a structure—which the novelist did. I mean Lamming and Naipaul and Hearne and even, not 'even', I am talking about more recent people, someone younger than I am, Michael Anthony for instance. They have a terrific sense of structure, as well as an elation in composing; something that the poets never bothered with. They depended a lot it seems to me on the 'Landscape' and 'Pain.'

Scott: Which coming from you is an interesting comment once again, since I could say fairly justly that *you* are dependent on landscape.

Walcott: No I am not dependent on landscape. I think I can't separate—I don't think anybody can separate—you can't separate your growth from your soil. You can have separate ideas but there is a way of looking at something. I mean, people look at the flowers and not at the trunk of the tree in West Indian poetry. You know, this sort of poinsettia and this sort of croton; but they don't know, they don't look at the ugliness of the bark. The strength that went down into the thing.

Scott: So selectivity then is possibly an over-simplified way of talking about the difference—

Walcott: No, I think they were provided with a language in which you could change daisies—you know, instead of putting 'daisies' you have 'poinsettia'—so the tree was there but the flowers were tacked on. That's what I mean.

I mean this was not happening in some of the younger poets—you know—in Wayne Brown, it's not there, in your poems, it's not there; but it used to be there. But I think what altered—what must alter the strength of West Indian poetry is what the prose writers have done with language, poetically. You know, whether it's Wilson Harris or Naipaul, the use of the language is—

Scott: Or Lamming, of course.

Walcott: Yes, yes. All of them.

Scott: There is another major factor which seems to inform any discussion on culture; in fact, on anything in the West Indies. And this is of course the old thing of identity. First of all, how have you approached this as a poet, and secondly how have you—where have you got to in this—forgive the word—quest.

Walcott: Well, I don't—I understand that you are asking me a question that is sort of set, you know, it's a conversation we are having, and when you use the word 'identity' I suspect you don't mean it in that sense. You know as a poet yourself that nobody sets out to resolve his identity because you know, if you come home drunk, you can't resolve your identity then, you see what I mean?

Scott: Yes.

Walcott: So this is personal—and to me poetry is an intimate and domestic thing. It gets more and more like that because the world outside is crushing and in terms of saying, you know, some character called Walcott is in search of a West Indian identity and everybody marks a question like a four-forty—I mean I am not interested in that! Because if an artist is resolving his identity then you are asking him private problems about friendship, and a lot of people who would ask about resolving your own identity would make very poor friends; so therefore they are not talking about character, they are insisting that you develop a style that they would like.

Scott: I take your point. But let's look at it after the event. After two books, two books of poems, a persona has emerged. Well, long ago, longer ago than that. A Walcott feeling has emerged.

Walcott: Well, I don't think so. I don't feel that. I feel that I remain, and I think that for the next generation or two of West Indian poets, I will be described as someone who broke ground, which is good enough for anyone to do. And that if anyone wants to call me—which will happen naturally, this is very good for poetry—a fake, it is because they would have assumed that I was assuming a mask—that I was hiding behind something—follow? I mean a lot of the poems have been about Robinson Crusoe and all that and that's a very easy mask to assume, but everybody hides behind some mask—something is built—something sets in the face, you know, and what is happening in the West Indies is like—since I have come to Jamaica—this character who is being interviewed and met and so on is not somebody I recognize. I don't know really who this person is, you know, and the role is played up to a certain point.

Scott: Okay. But you said yourself that one cannot—I think you said that one cannot avoid describing one's self in terms of masks . . .

Walcott: Yeats said that before, he said something about 'give a man a mask and he will talk the truth.'

Scott: And your own mask is your poetry—

Walcott: Well, this—it doesn't fit anymore. I mean two, three years ago I was very attracted to the Robinson Crusoe idea—the poems remain to me, if they are any good, they remain poems, but I am not interested in that idea anymore. I have written my last kind of Crusoe poem and now I am very keen on looking at how a table looks good in the morning—you know—across the table with your wife looking down on your children. This is what fascinates me now.

Scott: As well, I would imagine, as what you are reading at any particular time.

Walcott: Well you would tend to read those things that justify, endorse, underline the feelings that you have. You always justify your aesthetic by going to other people and saying, oh yes, Pasternak says that and Neruda says that. I will always remain, as long as I write in the West Indies, I will always seem to be a visible imitator, and superficially **I will** always be an imitator.

Scott: But at the moment who are you reading? Who do you read for pleasure among the English-writing poets?

Walcott: Well, I don't read poetry for pleasure. I read to be terrified in a way. And people who terrify me from their size and the grandeur of their imagination now are people like Pasternak and Neruda, a lot of Latin-American poets, Lowell—very few English poets—Ted Hughes a little . . . very few English poets now in fact, you know.

Man of the Theatre

The New Yorker / 1971

From *The New Yorker,* 26 June 1971, 30–31. Reprinted by permission; © 1971 The New Yorker Magazine, Inc.

Derek Walcott, author of the Obie Award-winning play *The Dream on Monkey Mountain,* is a tall, lithe West Indian of forty-one who has striking hazel eyes, longish hair (sideburns but no Afro), and a kind of casual, mussed elegance that stamps him as a man of the theatre. He has had two books of poetry published commercially, and one of plays (which includes the text of *Monkey Mountain*), and is the founder-director of the Trinidad Theatre Workshop, a group of twenty-odd actors who travel around the Caribbean presenting plays to audiences that often have very little contact with live drama. We met Mr. Walcott when he was here during *Monkey Mountain*'s successful run at the Negro Ensemble Company Theatre, on Second Avenue, and we arranged to have a talk with him one evening after a performance. We arrived at the apartment of a mutual friend with the sounds of Mr. Walcott's magnificent, almost Shakespearean sentences still ringing in our ears, and immediately asked him to explain some of the thinking behind the plot.

"On the surface, your play is the story of an old and ugly charcoal burner named Makak who comes down from his hut on the mountain to sell his wares, gets drunk, and spends a night in jail, where he has vivid hallucinations about Africa," we said. "But what are you really getting at? There seem to be as many theories as there are critics."

Mr. Walcott smiled gently and lit a cigarette. "*Monkey Mountain* is about many things," he replied, in the lilting cadences of the Caribbean. "It's about the West Indian search for identity, and about the damage that the colonial spirit has done to the soul. Makak and the people he meets in the play are all working out the meaning of their culture; they are going through an upheaval, shaking off concepts that have been imposed on them for centuries. They live in the West Indies because I live in the West Indies, but the basic situation is true of any society where man has been downgraded to a primitive, uninformed,

unpurposed existence. Makak is an extreme representation of what
colonialism can do to a man—he is reduced to an almost animal-like
state of degradation. When he dreams that he is the king of a united
Africa, I'm saying that some sort of spiritual return to Africa can be
made, but it may not be necessary. The romanticized, pastoral vision
of Africa that many black people hold can be an escape from the
reality of the world around us. In the West Indies, where all the races
live and work together, we have the beginnings of a great and unique
society. The problem is to recognize our African origins but not to
romanticize them. In the first half of the play, the concept of the
beginning of the world and the evolution of man is—shall we say?—
basically white. Then, when Corporal Lestrade, the brainwashed
colonial servant, retrogresses to become an ape and emerges as a man
to walk through the primeval forest, the play swings over to a black
Adamic concept of evolution. But the same sins are repeated, and the
cycle of violence and cruelty begins again. When the two criminals,
who are virtually brothers, fight, that's where the dream breaks for
Makak. He thought he was going to an Africa where man would be
primal and communal. Instead, it's back to original sin, with the tribes
killing one another. He ultimately rejects both insanities—the extremity of contempt for the black and the extremity of hatred for the white.
At the end, having made a spiritual trip to Africa and survived the
middle passage, he compares himself to a drifting tree that has put
down roots in the new world.''

"But at the end of the play, when Makak returns to his hut on the
mountain, isn't he rejecting both white and black societies?'' we said.

"You forget that Makak is a charcoal burner,'' Mr. Walcott said.
"He has to face reality, too. He has to come down to the market
every Saturday to make a living.''

While we were absorbing this piece of information, Mr. Walcott
added, with a grin, that the character of Makak, an elderly, poetic
alcoholic, was based on a man he'd known when he was a child in the
Windward Islands. "I was born in St. Lucia,'' he said. "A very green,
misty island, which always has a low cloud hanging over the mountain-
tops. When you come down by plane, you break through the mist,
and it's as if you were entering some kind of prehistoric Eden.
Monkey Mountain, where Makak lives, is really a peak called La
Sorcière, and the town where he is put in jail is Castries, where I grew

up. St. Lucia changed hands thirteen times during various wars. The people there speak the same Creole that people do in Haiti; we learn English in school almost as a foreign language, and perhaps that makes us value English the more. Islands are great places to live in, because the sea is close and there is the elemental feeling of things that are bigger than you are. And so, when I started to write this play, I remembered an almost inhuman man named Makak Rougier—I suppose his name meant 'Rougier's monkey,' because he worked for a man named Rougier—who used to come into town and get terrifyingly drunk. He'd roar up and down the main street, fling things around, and get arrested. At the same time, I was influence by Japanese Nō plays and the whole Kabuki thing. I thought that I could see in the truly ethnic West Indian dances—some of the surviving celebrating or warrior dances—the same kind of force you get in the Japanese theatre. We have a similar percussive feel—we use flute and drums—and we have a great oral tradition in the islands that gives us a reference for speech. So I tried to combine these elements into a play that could be done on a completely bare stage with just light, because we in the West Indies are also very poor.''

"How did you get interested in writing in the first place?" we asked.

"I grew up with a terrific mother in a house full of books," replied Mr. Walcott. "My father died when I was one, and my mother, a schoolteacher, who never remarried, loved to act. I have an older sister, and a twin brother who is also a playwright and lives in Canada."

By the time, Mr. Walcott was eighteen, he had written three books of poetry, which he published himself. "Shortly afterward, I got a scholarship to the University of the West Indies, in Jamaica, where I took a degree in French, Latin, and Spanish," he said. "I taught for a few years in Jamaica and Grenada, and in 1958 I was commissioned to write an epic pageant to celebrate the first meeting of the West Indian Federal Parliament. On the strength of that, I got a Rockefeller grant to study in New York, and it was here, twelve years ago, that I began thinking about St. Lucia and writing 'Monkey Mountain.' ''

At the present time, Mr. Walcott lives in Port of Spain, Trinidad, with his wife, Margaret, who is a psychiatric social worker, and two young daughters and a son. "Trinidad is a fantastic island," he said. "It's such an amalgam of races that it's perhaps the best place for the development of a genuine West Indian culture. And it's an enormously creative society; if you include all the people who work on Carnival, there are probably seventy thousand artists on the island. I could never become a Trinidadian, though, because there's also a basic irresponsibility in the Trinidadians' nature, which I, with my Methodist, St. Lucia bringing-up, find delightful but immoral. Last year, for example, we had a revolution, and right after it failed everybody said, 'Shoot those criminals! Hang them!' The government held a long, expensive trial, but the final judgment was suspended, because Carnival had begun. By the time it ended, the whole affair had started to bore the Trinidadians so much that public sentiment had changed to 'Well, give the boys a break.' So you have a whole country with not only compassion but a kind of shrug concerning a very serious political matter. In any Latin-American country, those boys would have been shot the next day.''

We asked Mr. Walcott if he had ever tried to capture the Trinidadian spirit onstage, and he replied that his latest play, *In a Fine Castle,* is the story of a bourgeois French Creole family who live in one of Port of Spain's elaborate Victorian mansions. ''When I began it, I was just interested in the characters,'' he said. ''But the revolution came along, and they got mixed up in it. Now I guess the play deals with the contrast between Carnival and revolution. Trinidad is a society where Carnival is regarded as a serious matter and revolution as fun. It's the ambiguity of this view that makes life there so interesting.''

Conversation with Derek Walcott

Robert D. Hamner / 1975

From *World Literature Written in English,* Vol. 16, No. 2 (November 1977), 409–20. Reprinted by permission of *World Literature Written in English* (Singapore).

My first meeting with Derek Walcott occurred on August 9, 1975, while he was in the middle of frenetic rehearsals for another run of his play *The Joker of Seville* (for which he was commissioned by the Royal Shakespeare Company in 1974). After viewing several late night rehearsals, I visited Derek in his home on the morning he was preparing to mail the final manuscript of *Sea Grapes* (his latest collection of poems) to his London publisher. The following conversation ranges over his interests in theatre, his own company (The Trinidad Theatre Workshop which he founded in 1959), poetry, literature, and criticism; the transcription has been edited for clarity and continuity but care has been taken to keep Derek Walcott's own words as nearly as possible to the form in which they were spoken.

Can you separate yourself into the categories of writer, director, and disinterested viewer?

As a matter of fact, I don't think that one ever honestly does it. There's a great suspicion on the part of people who say a writer should not direct his own work. But I think I have developed a kind of severity of judgment about cutting. For instance, I have had experiences where other directors have either told me, "You can't cut this because it works too well," or "It's too good to cut." So my attitude is to think in terms of excising what I think is superfluous or what I think is phony or whatever. Is that the positive or negative side? I suppose the dangerous thing in my case is the fact that I know the company very well, and the fact that I am used to their voices, their attitudes, their mannerisms. It's a cause for a lot of care. Because I have then, as a spectator, to have a completely blank mind in terms of what I am receiving. They know me; I know them; and so in conversational exchange they will relax you know, so I have to

keep on my toes to see that they have strength and clarity in what
they are saying.

But of course your personal involvement could lend to self-delusion.
Yes. That's right. On the other hand, there's another positive part
to it. It really is a case of communal creativity whenever we are doing
a play. Like last night, much to the annoyance of some of the actors I
saw something that had to be done that had bothered me for about
two years in the text for the Royal Shakespeare Company. Last night
in the middle of rehearsal I said, "Wait a minute. Stop! Let's try
this." And then I went up to a guy, made him carry the body of a
dead boy, and the whole scene was clarified by that action. I'm not
saying another director would not have suggested it to me, for instance. But that intuitive moment that says, "It's my work, right? I
see what they are doing; I know them; let us try this," has happened
many, many times in the creation of the plays. So I think that on the
positive side there are many more advantages than [disadvantages]
. . . even in terms of the theatre's concept of separate disciplines. In
fact, some of the most successful ensembles in history have come out
of a situation with a writer/director. I'm not just putting my name in
their class—Shakespeare working with his company, or say Molière
working with his company. I mean, many good things happen in terms
of what the actors do. I have been through enormous despair with two
or three plays watching a committee unable to handle any intuitive
moments and having plays actually, in terms of the text, very sincerely
butchered—I mean eviscerated by the kind of surrendering to the
imagination of the director. If you separate yourself, as in the professional theatre, you say, "Well, there's a hired writer, there's a hired
producer." What has happened in the American theatre, for instance,
is that as soon as a work is finished it is then given to some superman
(in their concept) called a director.

*Could it be that the system, or the industry, has elevated the
director to stardom?*
Right. I think that the system has got to the point now where the
writer provides his character outline for the director's imagination;
now I don't go with that. Certain writers you can't fool around with.
I think, for instance, Pinter would not allow it, because he had a
certain strictness. But, just to go back, I think emergencies that come

up in the actual working texts have provided some of the best dramatic moments out of pure necessity. These have happened to me. Sometimes we have put in a speech, right out of desperation because a guy has to go backstage and change. The pressure of that moment has made you create. You are saying, "I need something in here." And then you write it. I think that probably a lot of the soliloquies in Shakespeare are not there so much for dramatic necessity. Nobody knows what comes out of certain moments in the theatre.

You obviously care about the integrity of your own creation. If you were given the opportunity, how would you prefer that a critic approach the autobiographical element that figures prominently in your work? I think particularly of Another Life *and other poems. Will biographical critics read too much of you, the man, into your poetry?*

I suppose, in a sense, it is a matter of conclusions, a matter of conclusions rather than a psychological progression toward some portrait of the author.

Yes, right. A portrait of the author as a young man. I think, basically, I am asking how you view the relationship between art and the reality out of which you create your artistic world. Might one depend too much on biography, so as to detract from the more universal qualities of a poem such as Another Life*?*

Well, it would be hard for one to leave out the details of a person's life in a book of that kind. It is a particular experience. But in a sense it is a biography of an "intelligence," a West Indian intelligence, using it in the Latin sense of spirit. So, the biographical chronicle is not a physical one so much. Other intelligences are in the poem.

In the sense of a Stephen Dedalus, imaginary, literary, real?

You know I once wrote another thing called *Epitaph for the Young.* Well all the influences are there: I mean they are visible, deliberately quoted influences. There's Joyce, and *The Waste Land*, and Pound and it's all in there, I mean in terms of what one was learning. I wrote this at about nineteen. So this is sort of like an Urtext of *Another Life.* It was not a conscious thing. I realize that what I've done, in a sense, is not brought that life up to its own date, but sort of re-essentialized it, given it more of an essence in fact, made it more focal. In that sense, in terms of understanding your question and how

I would prefer to look at *Another Life,* I would say just what you're saying. I had a professor friend come in here and point out to me many errors of chronology, of place, of names that he had researched. So, you can go infinitely on in that direction.

Among the literary influences on your drama, I am interested in Synge and Yeats.

Certainly, *The Sea at Dauphin* is modeled completely on *Riders to the Sea.* I have to explain that. As a young writer coming out of the Caribbean, all those models which are obvious, self-evident models didn't bother me because what I had was the same thing Synge had: a totally new language, a totally new set of rhythms, a totally new people in a sense.

You were moved by parallels in environment, the entire milieu?

His example . . . you see; I don't think, for instance, there is resemblance in terms of the plot. But I learned a great deal from Synge, and a lot from Hemingway, Yeats, I think later.

Like you, Yeats was a poet/dramatist, influenced by the Noh theatre, using dance, mime, masks. Is there a difference?

Well, in Yeats there would not be any of the physical power I require out of plays in performance. The ritualistic elements of the dance and the chants are not literary because these things existed or still exist with my own environment. In the case of Yeats, that is a literary thing in a sense, forcing the material on to the contemporary stage. It is a nostalgic revival. The great thing about this is all these rites are authentic performances and one is simply absorbing what is physically existing in the country. That doesn't mean that I wasn't greatly influenced by Japanese theatre.

At last night's rehearsal you spoke of The Joker of Seville *as belonging to your company in style and spirit. Is there danger in working toward a regional kind of theatre that you might sacrifice artistic quality to provincialism?*

No, I think that in the real theatre no matter who the writer is, he is inevitably parochial and regional and very focal in particular things—whether it is Odets writing about people in Brooklyn or Pinter writing about his types. The more particular you get, the more universal you become.

Yes, in circles.

On a purely factual basis, *The Joker* was commissioned by the Royal Shakespeare Company and so it was their play. It gradually became absorbed into the spirit of the [Trinidad Workshop] Company, and it is very authoritatively now their play. Now, what I go after and what I really resent and resist a lot with them is any feeling of smugness that makes them say that we are the only ones who can do this well, because we are West Indians and because the play is by a West Indian writer. And that comes into universal areas of clarity of the character, clarity of the diction, clarity of the plot, and staging. The more intensely you can clarify with a feeling that this is you doing it, that this play was almost written for you, I think the quicker it is apprehended by anyone outside. It doesn't mean that nobody else can do it.

What is your response to the fact that writers in developing nations are constantly tempted to use their art as a vehicle for some cause or other, for a political platform?

I don't know. The best example we have had recently is Brecht, of course. Brecht's doing the classics over from a socialist viewpoint, or a communist one. I have not read his *Coriolanus,* but say *The Threepenny Opera* is played in capitalist countries as an entertainment, with sex, which as you know was not the correct response to what Mack the Knife was. What Brecht saw was a gangster character who was good at getting women. Whatever point he was making, the entertainment superseded the politics. That is what happened in the imagination; that is an example of one man setting out on a platform to do something. Every playwright who has a party or a thing that he wants done is political in a sense. If you're working in a Third World environment you see one's tendency of doing two things: you don't lower your sights and levels, but at the same time you are in what is called by other people looking on, "a semiliterate society"; that's in their terms. The definitions of literacy in the theatre are definitions of feeling and apprehension—not a matter of education. But at the same time one is going through a process of educating even by experience and not so much politically. So there is no writer in a virgin situation such as this who is not going through the process of platforming.

But insofar as he speaks to a situation and describes a problem he can still do it artistically.

Yes, the great danger is a smugness of authority that says I am the only writer in some certain society; then you absorb all those privileges and abuse them, at the cost of writing as you *should* do, when you create a work of art. I think that's what you're saying. The first principle is to create a work of art. Whatever it *says* simultaneously with its being is something else. In a political way, what is going to happen more and more in Third World countries is that the writer, although he may not wish it really, would prefer to see a government, even if it is a dictatorial-looking government—say a strong socialistic government—with a certain set of disciplines in terms of the general uplifting of the entire country. Now we're talking more in a sense of communist countries, socialist countries, countries that have new programs, sudden new junta countries as well. It is better (however negative and Fascist that sounds) to have a government that has a policy that says you may not criticize, and if you criticize, you will go to jail. I think a writer in the Third World would prefer to have a government that says this because what it means is that it is entirely up to the writer to say, "Look, I'm not going to write according to your policy. I am going to take the risk of jail or exile or whatever." You see, I think ultimately, Bob, a writer is not a selfish person, not a playwright anyway. A writer ultimately wants to see, no matter how rarified he may seem, a general well-being of mankind. That is a political attitude because something has to be done physically to make it happen. If you work in a kind of negativism that does not recognize the threat that art is, that is worse than having a government say, "Look, we want artists but you have to write like this." In that case you can tell them, "Fuck-off; I'm not doing that." Now, eventually any writer like me brought up under a democratic system of government will object, but I would prefer to see a party in power have a policy that says everything you write has to praise my government. That party is saying, for the general well-being of the country, this is what we believe. If it says there must be no art, then you get into a lot of trouble, and you know it. What *is* the horror is to be in a society that needs the art where the government pretends that it is *not* needed.

You echo the sentiment of actors and actresses whose greatest fear is not a bad press, but being ignored.
Yes, "Did they spell my name right?"

What about the status of criticism in the West Indies, the level and proliferation of it?

There is a whole new set of young critics who are examining what has been done. I think Gordon Rohlehr, Kenneth Ramchand, and people of that kind are doing a lot of good work. The good thing about them is they are not writing from outside positions; they are inside the society and are creating criticism that is as relevant as the writing. In fact, in many cases the criticism is better than the writing. A lot of Gordon's perceptions are superior to the work he reviews. What I'm not too happy about is, there is a general underlying tone of divisiveness—it's not purely racial—it's an emphasis on divisions. It lessens the general meaning of the criticism because then it is becoming so sociological and so particular that it cannot apply universally. Someone reading West Indian criticism is sometimes looking at little household quarrels. In terms of the larger perceptions drawn out of the body of West Indian literature so far, I don't think anything has yet been formulated by a critic, like a Coleridgean or a Wilsonian critic, who says what is deficient here is some sort of vision.

How does the foreign critic fit into the picture?

It is almost essential for a person to experience the society first. I think it may sound absurd to anyone writing West Indian criticism—by which I mean criticism of West Indian writing. The society as you get into it is far more complex than it looks. I think Vidia Naipaul, for instance, does not present it as a complex society. He simplifies the society. That is my viewpoint. Certain perceptions are made and certain conclusions are drawn, certain indications are shown. You have to understand in the case of Naipaul, the humiliation of what the Indians have undergone here. He is on an inferior platform, sociologically, when he's talking. Historically, the attitude of the Black toward the Indian has always been one of tolerated contempt, in a sense. The Indian to the Black has always been that these people don't work; they are just lying around. Without just making the thing racial, a critic may quickly say about a terrific writer like Naipaul that his conclusions are right, or his cynicism is justified. Another critic may say about a visionary writer like Wilson Harris, a very polemical writer like Lamming, that these people are overblowing the promise or the reality of a society. But in each case—Naipaul, Lamming,

Wilson Harris or whoever—you've got to understand what historical and racial kind of experience these people are writing out of. Although they have common experiences of sunlight, decay, poverty, those simplifications are there. It is harder for one to understand the beginnings of West Indian literature than it would be to try to understand the emergence of American literature; whether Melville or Hawthorne . . . , at least they had one common racial experience. They were on solid ground with no broken islands.

Yet there are similar problems for the artist in any nation emerging from colonial status. America in the early 1800's and Ireland in the late 1800's had internal crises, had to establish an authentic identity, had to settle linguistic and theological differences.

Yes, but what they have there, Bob, is an ideal called America and an ideal called Ireland. I'm not saying those conflicts were not there, religious or otherwise. But one had a metaphor called Ireland and a metaphor called America.

Are there no ideals or myths to provide adequate cohesiveness for West Indians?

It would be mythical if we had certain legends like the Irish legends. The only historical legends that one individual writer would have are ethnic legends of sorts. Each one of them is separate because the Indian would have India, the African would have Africa. But the point is that all of these have been erased from the memory or experience of the writer. So, what has not yet been created or is actually being created by its absence, by the chaos, by the necessity for it to be created—is a West Indies, a West Indian literature. Now that is being made out of the very knowledge that there is not one.

This raises the prospect of a writer losing his perspective in the void. Might the writer not lose himself in a role that he is forced to play?

Yes, definitely, because what one feels that is very dangerous is that people keep breathing down your back, and I'm talking about West Indian critics, I think that even if I wrote a bad poem—not that I've never written a bad poem—but if I intentionally wrote a bad poem, some attention would be paid to it. More attention would be paid to it because of the absence of any bulk of poetry, mainly

because I am a figure of literature in the West Indies. In the book I'm
working on now [*Sea Grapes*], I have had agony in taking out certain
poems about which some critic is justifiably going to say, "Here is
Walcott describing some such thing as an experience." It isn't that
that experience is not true, but one can get into the condition of habit
where he just puts the mask back on in a sense, and acquires a
reputation by following a certain role. I think for a long time Frost
played a role like that. I think occasionally Robert Lowell puts on the
anguished mask and so on. When you're in your forties, particularly
when you're getting a reputation and when you know the thing could
be exegeticized to death, it is harder to go and look for a poem that is
true to yourself. A whole body of critical work can spring out of one
bad piece of writing. I think a writer has to keep looking perpetually
for an anonymity. He has to keep forgetting his name and looking to
be anonymous again. There's a nice phrase from Dylan Thomas that
says something like how he used to long for the days when he was
lost, unknown and lost.

You have got to learn to please yourself.

A writer can get trapped in his own image: look what it did to
Hemingway. I think it destroyed him in the sense that he insisted that
he must keep that façade up. He was a tough guy and one not easily
broken; he was never afraid. Although if you read Hemingway deeply,
you know it's all about cowardice. It's in all of us—terror and cowardice.

*Hemingway wrote in American English, his native vernacular. Why
do you not write more poetry in the patois of your native St. Lucia?*

I have not only a dual racial personality but a dual linguistic
personality. My real language, and tonally my basic language, is
patois. Even though I do speak English, it may be that deep down
inside me the instinct that I have is to speak in that tongue. Well, I've
tried to write poems in patois and feel that later on, maybe in my
fifties, I will try to do something of that kind. On the other hand, it
sometimes seems to me to be an academic thing, and I would not like
to do anything consciously academic. I have a poem in . . . [*Sea
Grapes*] which is a translation of a St. Lucian song that feels very
fresh to me. Now I wouldn't mind getting a collection of those and
doing some more translations of them. But I don't think it's the actual

language that matters since I am workiing in English, and I am in an English situation.

As far as an audience goes, you just about have to prefer English.

Oh, but I want to. I'm just saying that underneath it all I think the whole thing is really a matter of tone. And the tone that I try to reach in a poem, the validity of a tone, takes you your lifetime or takes half your life anyway. So one can—although it seems ridiculous some-times—one can detect in the body of American poetry an American tone that is quite different from the tone of an English poem: that is in terms of its feeling.

Does the poem have its existence on the page ultimately, or in the poet's mind, or in the reader's mind?

I think it moves off the page and goes into the memory. It goes into the collective memory of the entire race. That's what I would say. Everybody may not use these old-fashioned phrases, but I think Robert Graves is absolutely correct in that there is an embodiment of something called a muse; there is an embodiment of the collective memory called poetry. The only poems that exist as *poems* are the ones that we remember the most of. That simplifies it to a point at which American poets or some contemporary English poets would reject it: poetry always is moving to a condition of song. That is definitely its impulse. For me there is absolutely no question about it. In terms of what the sound of the song is, one knows that it is not typography. It isn't how you lay it out on the page. What has happened is the denial on the part of metropolitan, city-oriented people that there is a totality of a song within a poem. So one gets phrases, fragmented phrases, ideas, quotes per line, per phrase. The whole concept of the entire poem as a totally remembered thing has died. Now, poetry dies in one area, and sometimes it dies when it seems to be flourishing most, when its bulk is impressive, and it flourishes in another area. I think in certain parts of what one calls the Third World, for instance, where (no matter how romantic that sounds) vocal music and imagination, or percussion, or dance is an active part of the society, then the poem's impulse is toward shaping itself within that context of a song. I didn't have much respect for Bob Dylan as a poet; but since I've been working in the theatre and listening over to some of his music and to his lyrics, I am getting quite a respect for him as a poet. I'm not happy about a lot of diffused, little cheating lines, second rate realism, that he sometimes offered. But in the same context, where the music is in a thriving rock culture, he's in that soft rock or whatever culture. Then he is a poet working within the same conditions that a Third World poet is working in because he is close to music and he's closer to the beat of the thing.

He is close to the people?

Right. There is a kind of mechanical output of thousands of books of verse coming out of the States of very, very talented poets which miss just one element—and that is not just a lyric: the element of the whole song. I think the typewriter has done a lot of damage to poetry. For me, where the poem comes, inevitably, is where I'm making contact between my hand and the paper, or between the mind and the paper. Writing is almost automatic. Holley Stevens, Wallace Stevens' daughter, told me that her father used to compose these long poems walking. She said he would go for long walks, talk to himself, and compose these things, then come back and write them down. Now, the pace of strolling is iambic pentameter, Right? So you see how you could keep going like that.

I believe Robert Frost said there are only two meters. The strict iambic and the loose iambic.

Is that what he says? He is absolutely right. Two poets who have written very little about the creation of poetry have been Graves and Frost, and they resemble each other a great deal. One of the truest things, to me, is Graves's statement that the root of a poem, the thing that comes out of it, always is a line and a half: that part, the second half of the pentameter and then another line. He has some kind of crazy theory about why that shape happens. All it means to me in a sense is that you can detect a frame which is ridged and not tilted or broken. I've been lecturing and reading in colleges: I think it's amazing to have had young poets asking, "I notice you use rhyme!" It's like saying, "By the way, your piano has eighty-eight keys!" Ezra Pound was a pretty regular poet you know. The Pound line which has got a loose feminine ending is consistent throughout everything. It's broken, but it's there. I think that William Carlos Williams lacks the language. It is like O'Neill's language, falling short of greatness. You feel O'Neill would have been, would be, up there in the company of

the greats. He is a great American dramatist, but taking him as a
universal playwright. . . . I mean the moment can be shattering;
characterization can be annihilating. What does not happen in terms
of language, what is said at the moment, is that illumination that
comes out of great tragic speech. And, to me, what is missing in
Williams is that illuminated moment. I think the person who did the
most for free verse in America is Hemingway. In terms of the
language, I think that one should pay more attention to the influence
of American prose on the poets in the twentieth century than the
poetry itself. It's stable; it came out of Stein, and you can take the
succession of things—through Stein, through Hemingway, through
Williams—you can see an American language. Maybe it needs an
extra dose of Joyce's term for illumination that Lorca had, that Joyce
had, that Hemingway had, where that moment is made radiant,
epiphany happens. For instance, it's not there in Robinson Jeffers.
Here is a man just short of the stature of those massive stones
he describes.

*Perhaps too much credit has been given and too much is allowed
for the sake of experimentation.*
I think that's a very bad thing about American poets. Young poets
should have no individuality. They should be total apprentices, if they
want to be masters. If you get a chance to paint a knuckle on a
painting by Leonardo, then you say, "Thank God!" and you just
paint a knuckle as well as you can. If you're told as a young poet,
"You go ahead and do what you want, and that's O.K. because you're
expert in your field," then you are not going to wind up anywhere as
a poet because you are going to be yearning for something that
is missing.

It is popular to break with tradition.
For a lot of people in colleges, the tradition begins at a broken
point, at the point where they say let us break up the pentameter and
see what happens. But if you don't know what you have broken, then
you cannot know what you are doing.

*As Eliot points out in "Tradition and the Individual Talent," the
tradition and the individual shape each other.*
Actually, I think the whole point of tradition in that respect is that

all English verse makes an agonized effort to return to the pentameter. It may take a devious route but its basic nostalgia and homesickness are for that language, that beat.

You mentioned to me that on his deathbed any poet might say there are three or four poems that he has written that he is not ashamed of. Up to this time what would you select from your work?

Well, I guess I'd have to be on my deathbed to say. Absolutely, finally, it may be up to another person to say. But as long as you can hear your own voice, you can never fully enjoy it. Poets enjoy other poet's work rather than their own.

Reflections Before and After Carnival: An Interview with Derek Walcott

Sharon Ciccarelli / 1977

From *Chant of Saints: A Gathering of Afro-American Literature, Art, and Scholarship,* edited by Michael S. Harper and Robert S. Stepto (Urbana: University of Illinois Press, 1979), 296–309. Reprinted by permission of Sharon Ciccarelli.

This interview was conducted in January and March 1977. The first session occurred in Port of Spain, Trinidad; the second, in New Haven, Connecticut. The interviewer is Sharon L. Ciccarelli.

[**Sharon Ciccarelli**]: Mr. Walcott, critics have stated that the traditional conception of poetry as primary dramatic narrative is nearly defunct. Your work, especially the drama, seems to challenge this statement. Does the folk content of your plays necessitate the various devices you employ—chorus, masks, chants, drumming—or are such devices a deliberate attempt to re-create an older form of dramatic narrative?

[**Derek Walcott**]: The rapid development of the novel has reduced the necessity of poetry as narrative, although a great deal of narrative poetry was written during earlier periods (for example, during the Victorian age) of the novel's development. Poetry has been backed against a wall by the existence of numerous narratives in the media, on film, television, etc. The concept of leisure has affected the concept of the poem as story-telling, since so many narrative forms are either immediately or ultimately visual. The only recent narrative poets who come to mind are Frost and Edwin Robinson. It has to do with the decline of the epic and the deterioration of tribal sense because of industrialization.

The point I am coming to is this: a lot of novelists who begin as poets think that the novel, because of its simultaneity, can serve them just as well as an epic poem. The greatest example of this is Joyce's

Ulysses. It seems that a lot of modern poets ultimately turn to narrative forms, principally the novel, and sometimes theatre.

The modern reader is an individual. The whole custom of reading to the family (which continued until the Victorian period), whether from a poem or from a novel, has been replaced by television and the cinema. Today, the visual narrative entails an individual spectator who is not *read to*. No one is told a story by a living voice.

The narrator as performer does not exist any more except in primal societies. And by primal society I mean any tight, familial, tribal society in which the reader or poet has a function. This society could be the society of Homer or the society of a Swahili tribesman.

Literature developed from the ear first, then the eye. That is, from an oral to a written tradition. So the society that existed before printing was invented, e.g., Homer's society, and the one that still exists without printed literature become the same in terms of oral narrative. West Indian society is within an oral tradition. This is a question of literacy rather than intelligence, and the reasons for such a society are many: poverty, poor access to written materials, isolation . . .

Story-telling, singing, and other forms of tribal entertainment continue with such phenomena as the calypso tents. That tradition is also African. The union of voice and drum, the drum being the most natural accompaniment of the human voice, is still very strong, and is the basis of our music.

If one begins to develop a theatre in which the drum provides the basic sound, other things will develop around it, such as the use of choral responses and dance. If we add to this the fact that the storyteller dominates all of these, then one is getting nearer to the origins of possibly oral theatre, but certainly African theatre. Oral theatre may be Greek, or Japanese, or West Indian, depending upon the shape percussion takes.

I don't think that in any of my plays there is innovation or discovery in terms of theatre. Rather, I attempt to use all the still viable, vital elements in a play.

The mask, for instance, is not, as it is in metropolitan theatre, a device: it is a totem. In my own experience, I have always been aware of the power of the mask, or mask-like make-up. In contemporary Carnival, masks have been forbidden, but they used to be an essential part of Carnival. The words "play masks" really mean "to play with a mask." It is a pity that the mask has been removed from Carnival, as it affects the power of the costume. If the face is bare, the rest is only rigid and artificial design. When one puts on the mask, one is creating theatre.

Modern playwrights who use masks (Genet and Brecht, for example) are not avant-garde, but are returning to the primal formalities of Chinese, Japanese, and African theatre.

[C]: In *Ti-Jean and His Brothers* the events of the tale occur over several days, yet the dramatic action emphasizes the compactness of time and event. In particular, the use of characters to recount action that has already occurred, or will occur, and the choral refrains that separate scenes concentrate the effect of the fable and heighten the anticipation of conflict between Ti-Jean and the Devil. What is your conscious manipulation of time as it relates to the narrated action of various characters, and how does this affect the way the plays are produced on stage?

[W]: Once you have a strong or accepted narrator, and once the audience gets into the rhythm of a piece, time ceases to be a problem. If the rhythm is strong, there is no need to show an interval as progressing chronologically.

In legend, a narrator manipulates his audience into the state of a child impatient with details of time. Such audiences are thus reduced to the credibility of children. The phrase about "suspension of disbelief" is applicable to this phenomenon, but is not always true of naturalistic fiction. To get back to *Ulysses,* which is the supreme work of naturalistic fiction, Joyce set himself twenty-four hours as a frame, not merely in order to retain any Aristotelian "unity," but because the accretion of detail and the creation of infinite sequences of epiphanies (making any object radiate its "whatness") could not extend beyond that time. The next day would demand another book of equal length.

I am strongly influenced by Japanese Noh theatre in which essentials are important, so that a piece of cloth becomes a stream, or a movement of the hand a fountain. In the final analysis, every play of that kind moves closer to a poem.

I attempted in *Dream* to let the action come out of successive detonations of images not dominated by a narrative logic, as occurs in the creative process of a poem, or in the integrity without logic of a dream.

When *Ti-Jean* was produced in the park, the lighting man said he would have problems with the many switches from day to night. Yet the play was written for conditions without technology, sets, or lighting. If the narrator is strong enough to say "it is now night"—it is night; there is no need for technology. This may be what Brecht is after: getting rid of the restraints, the chiaroscuro of metropolitan theatre.

The people in the forefront of twentieth-century theatre keep fighting technology. Brecht, Genet, Brook, they are all simply getting back to the true needs of theatre—to the human body alone, not gilded by equipment or effects. Too many plays (and I myself have been guilty of this) require the imitation of reality; whereas Aristotle's first principle still holds: drama depends not on the imitation of reality, but on the imitation of action. Real action in theatre doesn't require any furniture or machinery.

What the actor ultimately aims at is for his audience to contemplate his body as the only true instrument of theatre. The greater the actor, the less he needs around him.

The strongest theatre will always be the theatre of a primal society, one that goes directly to the elementals of art: ritualistic tragedy, satire, and comedy. Because the audience shares in, rather than being instructed by, the experience.

[C]: The tension between dream and reality in *Dream* becomes a vehicle that forces the ritualistic resolution. The relationship between dream, prophetic vision, and madness seems to be comparable to the relationship of image, metaphor, and symbol within the play. Was there a conscious linking of these psychological and literary terms? You refer to both Fanon and Sartre in epigraphs. Did your readings of their works influence the form of *Dream?*

[W]: I spent ten years, working on and off, creating this play. I worked on it in the same way I approach a poem, where the lines survive until the poem, ultimately, is finished. The impulse of creating scenes one out of another reflects the same process. It is essentially one metaphor with many components. Metaphor is basically a contradiction, though apparent, since two textures are fused. The comparison of a moon to a half-sucked sweet illustrates this; we know the contradiction inherent in this. But the moment of metaphor is not a moment of contradiction, even if the two elements are apparently opposite. My example is bad, because one can always ask ordinary questions. True, unshakable metaphor is one that causes the astonishment of truth. This process is not *shown* in poetry, but rather on stage where the metaphor cannot be simply heraldic. It becomes evident because theatre is action. Therefore the metaphor of a play is the full progression, even through contradiction of a final heraldic image. The great figures of theatre are metaphors, and in contemporary theatre, even if a figure lacks the support of legend, the greatest come closest to this.

In theatre we see this metaphor as a human being. The metaphor of *Dream* was, for me, an old man who looked like an ape, and above his shoulder, a round white full moon. And the journey of that moon which drew the man/ape through the cycle of one night multiplied (like all metaphors) into questions of human evolution, racial evolution, the search for self-respect and pride, and the reality which comes with the morning. Once a gong has been struck, the visible resonances of figure, sound, and image will all be concentric and will be subject to all kinds of true and perhaps contradictory interpretations. If one looks hard at any bright object it will multiply itself, will send out dimmer images around it. In *Dream*, the process of writing with that image in mind—the man, the moon, and the mountaintop—made the writing of the play equivalent to the poetic experience where the dominant metaphor creates others.

[C]: Do you feel that there is any connection between West Indian narrative forms and dionysian ritual?

[W]: The Greeks had so many gods they were godless in a way. In *Dream,* the frenzy comes out of a man's relationship to his dream. If this had been realized more heraldically, its power would have been akin to the power of Shango. Yet this might have been impossible, for if the play becomes that powerful, it becomes the ceremony it is imitating. The play is probably a little overwritten.

But to get back to your question . . . Carnival, which happens throughout the Caribbean, is a godless festival. Based on a Catholic conception of the last days before Lent, it is also related to crop-over (the burning of the cane). It is very African except for the fact that there is no god. It is interesting that *bacchanal* is the Trinidadian word for Carnival. The total surrender to the senses is what Carnival is about. But in Shango, one surrenders to the god. Carnival became more decorative as faith diminished, and now there is no one figure that represents the festival. And in dionysian ritual, the surrender to the senses is a means of surrendering to the god Dionysus. Yet in Carnival, we have a ritualistic mass form in which the high priest is the poet, the calypsonian, but there is no god. Or perhaps the only deity existing in Carnival is art, because in all of the song, orchestration, and costumes there is competition for recognition as an artist. Art substitutes for the god. There is nothing wrong in this, no inherent blasphemy, and when Carnival is over, the deification will not continue; there is no use trying to interest a Trinidadian in Carnival after the fact.

I suppose this is all a long way of saying "no," the West Indian narrative is not a dionysian ritual. All over the Caribbean one discovers repressed creativity: the steel bands, wire sculpture, the huge body of music produced within the folk culture. This is a society whose highest ritual is art, and that is pretty good.

[C]: In your essay "Twilight" you wrote: "In that simple schizophrenic boyhood one could lead two lives: the interior life of poetry, the outward life of action and dialect." Could you elaborate on this with regard to the development of a dramatic style? How does involvement with a particular acting company affect your writing?

[W]: The longer one remains in the Caribbean, the more certain things become evident. One cannot make a living as an artist, yet one is aware of a vitality that comes from living in certain root areas. Since a man does not choose to reduce himself to poverty, the exile of the West Indian artist has become a reality.

This society is still patterned on the stratification between rich and poor black. He who has acquired education finds himself on the thin line of the split in society. The artist instinctively moves towards his people on that root level, and yet, at the same time, he must survive. This split is equivalent to a state of schizophrenia.

Much deeper is the historic racial split resulting in two kinds of bloods, almost two kinds of people. Language and the experience of illiteracy among the poor is a profound problem that divides the West Indian writer. The more sophisticated he becomes, the more alienated is his mental state. It is not his business to lower his standards to insult the poor. When one is confronted with this problem of language, two situations occur: wanting to reach one's people; and realizing the harsh realities of the society, the depression and the economic exploitation. At the same time that one's intellect becomes refined, and one learns more about the society, there is a movement away from that society.

[C]: Black writers in the sixties formed a literal conception of language, approaching the essay; Ted Joans, for instance, influenced by this kind of writing, talks about "hand grenade poems." Do you think this was a necessary if futile theoretical exercise?

[W]: I think that, in the pressure of the physical revolution that was taking place, the poetry and the anger were synonymous. There are certain periods where a poet may consider the language of revolution more important than the poem itself. And if the poet knows that what he is doing is using the form of poetry as a weapon, without concerning himself too much with the poem, then I don't consider it to be futile. In a way, it *is* necessary, because any group of men marching or going in a common direction moves to a rhythm, whether it is an army in step or whether it is a bunch of people who are united by a song, or a slogan, or a shout. At that point a poet can provide the equivalent of a slogan, or a shout through his poems, as if he were at once a drummer and a poet, someone beating the rhythm. The poem's development would depend, I think, on the urgency with which the poem is surrounded, on the pressure of events surrounding the revolt. Now I have never been close to such a situation, but I would imagine that, like any other poet, one could articulate in a poem the expression of a common group in a rhythmic, defiant sort of sense. The only thing I would say here is that one may be convinced of the right in something that may be consciously ephemeral—just as a revolution between one goal and the next is a moment, however long that moment lasts—and it may then become expedient to write that kind of poem. I haven't had this kind of experience, but I can understand why, I can understand the necessity, in fact, of poets expressing the feelings or beliefs of a revolution in their poetry. All great revolutionary movements have had hymns and poems which united them in their beliefs.

I couldn't have been influenced by their poetry because I wasn't in the presence of that revolution, but I can understand Ted Joans's use of the phrase "hand grenade poems." If a poem is thrown at an enemy, it detonates some response on the part of the people who are afraid, or who understand that there is a likelihood of intense violence. I *understand* the use of the phrase, as I said, but (however conservative this may seem) there is another conception of poetry—a kind of universal reasoning—that may be more effective than abrupt, abusive, or hostile poems. Somebody, Auden I think, said that poetry makes nothing happen. Poetry itself may not make anything happen, but it has incited people to make things happen. The danger for a poet—for there is excitement in the passion of what he is believing—is to confuse what he thinks a poem can do with poetry itself. One must choose a language, or a tone. There is a tendency to oversimplify and also, of course, to take sides; and in one sense it is a kind of reduced poetry. But, as I said earlier, I think that if the poet knows that this is poetry used for a particular perhaps didactic function, and that it may not last beyond this time, he can justify this kind of writing.

[C]: What is the role of the artist in a political struggle?

[W]: If the struggle is intense, the role of an artist is to pick up a gun like everyone else. It depends on how physical the struggle is. One can write poems *and* carry guns, you know. So I think that if there is an active struggle, the role of the artist is to involve himself physically in the struggle.

[C]: T. S. Eliot postulated that all works of Western art, starting with Homer and extending in what he called an "unbroken arc" to the present, comprise a simultaneous existence and order. Do you think that the black arts comprise a similar, or the same, unbroken arc? And could this concept be expanded into a Pan-African movement? Or do political, cultural, and economic differences between Africa and Afro-America preclude such a notion?

[W]: I don't know. . . . You've got to think a long, long time about that thing from Eliot. . . . I suppose what Eliot is saying is that you can see Western civilization as a whole, as one immense sensibility starting with Greek moral and aesthetic traditions, that includes anyone who considers himself within the tradition of Western civilization. But I don't think that this general statement would necessarily be true of every Western culture; I can't say that this applies to the Americas. The whole of Western civilization *does not* share one

sensibility. If one postulates that, then one would have to overlook
racial or religious differences that exist in the very context of Western
civilization. The statement is, for me, too general, and would bear a
heavy amount of particular examination. It is contradictory, in a
sense. Take Spain, for example. One has to talk about the Moorish
influence and how this compares with Homeric ideals. Or take the
Afro-American situation: is it contained within an unbroken arc,
reaching from Africa to the Americas? What we have, obviously, is a
broken arc; we only know half the arc, and anything beyond that half
arc has been torn from our memory. I don't think that there is
anything "pure" on this side of the world; the whole feel of it is
multitudinous, several races with various ancestral ties. Does not
America—and I mean the land from Greenland right down to Tierra
del Fuego—argue against this unbroken arc, particularly in light of
the African experience, in light of the conditions in which he was
brought to the New World? The more time accelerates, the less we
remember—collectively—and it becomes impossible, artificial even,
to try to find this unbroken arc. When one considers the education of
the black in the Western world, and his being taught ideas such as
Eliot was talking about, the image of one unbroken arc seems even
ironic. A sensibility that has been broken and re-created is, I think, a
more accurate description of our present situation.

[C]: Earlier you mentioned that the folk form is a major part of your
mythic system. Do you think that the power of the folk idiom is
effectively portrayed in your drama?

[W]: No, I would say that a lot of it has had to be diluted theatri-
cally, for clarification. For instance, I can't create in pure Creole,
French, or English, for all sorts of reasons. You might be in a situation
where accents differ within a small area, among people who all speak
French Creole. The same applies to English Creole in the Caribbean.
It is very difficult, in one sense, for a Trinidadian to understand a
Jamaican, or for a Jamaican to understand a Barbadian, but since one
considers the Caribbean—the English-speaking Caribbean—as a
whole, as sharing one language with various contributory sources,
one must try to find, using syntaxes from various dialects if necessary,
one form that would be comprehensible not only to all the people in
the region that speak in that tone of voice, but to people everywhere.
It is like making an amalgam, a fusion, of all the dialects into

something that will work on stage. For instance, I've done a play, a
Rasta play, that was not written in pure Jamaican; it was conceived
and performed in Trinidad, it was played by Trinidadian actors, and I
had forgotten a lot of the complexities of Jamaican construction. If I
do it in Jamaica, I'll allow rephrasing of the wording, but I believe
that the tone itself is accurate. Even if, for instance, it is spoken with
a Trinidadian accent. In one of the best productions of my work I
have seen—a production of *Dream*—the actors settled on a common
accent for the entire company. The play thus had a harmony that
grew out of their decision to speak in the same way. You have such a
number of dialects in the West Indies, you have to decide that you are
going to use a general sound, even if you draw from more than
one dialect.

[C]: What about the Calypso play you just finished: Do you think
that it successfully rendered the folk accent?

[W]: Well, another thing about dialect is that since it is the jargon
of the people, of the street, it changes rapidly. You may have written
something two years ago, and now find a phrase already outdated.
The same is true, I think, of American black speech. But if the sound
of the work is right, usually all that is needed is to change an
expression or two, within what is being said.

[C]: Your characters are often highly typed, sometimes mythical;
their names and roles are not only symbolic of biblical or African
traditional figures, but it seems that, at times, they are even allegori-
cal. What relation does this kind of characterization have to the
reduction of the play's elements to an essential form, the kind of
process you mentioned earlier? Were the characters in *Dream* conceived as archetypes?

[W]: No, I think that the strength of the characterization does not
come from me, it comes from the imagination of my people. When,
like in a fable, a character is given an animal's name, like Tigre, or
Souris, or Makak, he becomes akin to the mythical figure. An animal
becomes a man, a man becomes an animal. So that what I am doing
is broadening, or clarifying, the kind of common folk imagination that
ascribes an animal's characteristics to a person. That happens in all
cultures, of course. In terms of reducing the play, I think it gives the
play a kind of form, the form of a fable. As soon as you do that, then
you are utilizing a very hierarchical, ritualistic, accepted form of

story-telling; the narrator says "once upon a time there was . . ." and the "once upon a time" acts upon the structure of the play, making it into a fable structure with a beginning, a middle, and an end. Whatever happens within the play must support the cycle. To me that kind of conception is more powerful than the individual attempt of avant-garde writers to restructure the idea of theatre. I think it is inescapable that once you open your mouth, you'll want to tell a story. If you don't open your mouth, if you work your device around the direct narration, there still remains an elemental progression from action to action. A man walks across the stage, you *know* something is going to happen; everything on stage is done for a reason, everything contributes to the general outline of the play. There is just no time for superfluities in drama. Think of how the ancients were weighed line for line . . .

What appears to be the most old-fashioned aspect of Third World writing, or to West Indian writing in particular, is really its most powerful aspect: the tribe is being told a story that comes from the memory of that tribe. I have had one volume of plays published, and those plays are all set in elemental situations. The elemental is the background, and people move within that element. These elements are as much forces within the plays as are the characters themselves; at times they are more important to the play's development than the characters that exist inside them. The sea is the major force in *Sea at Dauphin;* the forest—with its superstitions, its religion—dominates *Ti Jean;* the rain is the cleansing force in *Malcochon,* etc. But I have written a lot of other plays which are set within an urban or a naturalistic situation, and where a man moves through a non-elemental setting. *Sea at Dauphin* was an attempt to do the same kind of thing that Synge did. I made the figure of Afa larger than the average fisherman, and he may even be archetypical. I guess you could say my plays are like the flip sides of a coin; the one side naturalistic, the other ritualistic or elemental. And I do find that a lot of my principal characters are heightened by the fact that they come out of the depth of a folk consciousness.

[C]: How would you relate this to the idea of myth? Does the folk consciousness have a mythic structure?

[W]: I don't think one starts out consciously to create myth. The poet encounters many dangers when his work evolves from myth. He might just relate the story in a very one-dimensional manner. Most story-telling exists on this level; it is all incident, really, without any development of character. Or he might lean too heavily on the figures given in the fable, figures that have no psychology. These kinds of figures cannot be successfully played by actors. But in the Greek theatre, for instance, there is a psychology that motivates the characters. It is not only ritualistic; it is psychological as well. Oedipus and Creon are men, but the structure and mode of the play are ritualistic. This is a delicate point for Third World or West Indian theatre, which is only beginning to absorb the concept of psychology, of creating a character within a myth and of making the figure a man. But the very fact that these societies remain close to the mythical origins of story-telling can be turned into a creative advantage. Because we live in a society in which myth, superstition, and the folk memory are very strong, where ritual celebration abounds, there is the possibility that the character may become more than just a psychological figure. This character, because of the vitality of the story-telling tradition, may move towards the largeness of the mythical figure and still retain the essential quality of manhood.

[C]: Do you think that black writers should write in the language of their ex-colonizers; for instance, Césaire writing in French, or Soyinka writing in English? Should they attempt to master a traditional language—Swahili, Yoruba? Or should they work towards a fusion, say the way McKay used the Jamaican *patois* in his first volume of poetry, *Songs of Jamaica?*

[W]: I think the writer writing in English or in Spanish is lucky in the sense that he can master the original language, or the language of the master himself, and yet have it fertilized by the language of dialect. Someone who knows what he is doing, a good poet, recognizes the language's essential duality. The excitement is in joining the two parts. I don't think that one should attempt to destroy the syntax of one's own conversation. A Marquez or a Fuentes should follow the syntactical progression of someone speaking in Spanish. He may know the dialects of the country people, or of the ghetto people of his own country, and if so, he should capture their tone. It is like having two hands; one hand knows the language of the master, the other hand knows the language of dialect, and a fusion of both limbs takes place in the expression that you write down. I think it is a futile, stupid and political exercise to insist on "creating" language. One works within a language. Look at Ishmael Reed, who to me is one of the most exciting writers in the States, much more so than a lot of the celebrated Jewish novelists, for instance. To the extent that one can judge a writer and what he invents, the exercise must reflect the excitement one gets in reading him. And every time I re-read Reed, his work is as fresh to me, and as exhilarating and as funny as it was at the first reading. There is a delight in it—the same kind of delight I get when I read Joyce. I'm not comparing them in stature, but to me Reed's is a most fertile kind of writing.

What we should do, and there is so much to do, as African, or as African-sourced people, is not just learn Swahili—I don't have the time to go and learn Swahili, it would be more useful for me to learn Spanish—but one should be completely aware of the epic origins of one's literature, and of one's own race. If there is a great Swahili epic poem, then I should find it, and enjoy it, and I would perhaps find things there that would relate to me, to my writing. The fantastic thing about Trinidad—and it has been ignored to an amazing extent—is the diversity of culture: Chinese, Hindu, African. All of these races have their epics, and there is a kind of Hindu epic drama still performed on the island. If there could be even the most concentrated or minimal means of access to all of this racial knowledge, to the collective memory, one could enrich one's writing to a great extent. If I am a West Indian living in Trinidad, and if the Chinese, and the Indians, and the Africans all live there, and if I share my life with them, then, ideally, I should know the origins of all and yet still be *of* my race. That, I think, would be complete fulfillment for a West Indian. I'm not speaking about genealogy, I don't need so much to know *who* was my great-great-grandfather, but *what* was my great-great-grandfather, how did he live? One would know not Chinese, but the Chinese . . .

[C]: Could you elaborate a little on your comment about how learning Spanish would be useful to you?

[W]: Well, I live in a part of the world where a dominant culture influence is Spanish, Spanish-sourced anyway. I have found more of an affinity in Spanish-American poets than I have found in poets writing in England, or in America. We have a similar historical origin, similar problems of self-resolution, and I can recognize a sensibility as being very close to mine. So not only is there a possibility for

geographical or political exchange, there is the possibility of real
cultural and creative exchange. Yet I cannot really know how an
African thinks; I don't think in the African mode. And I'm not saying
that knowing Swahili would make me an African. The person over on
this part of the world is an American, whether he be a Latin American,
an Afro-American, or a West Indian American. Even the white
American had the same problem of identification. In fact, I think
this—identity—has been the obsession of any race in this part of the
world. Americans themselves have been made to feel inferior to
England in terms of literature, painting, etc. They used to be considered an inferior culture in general when compared to the richness of
European culture. White, black, any color, it has been a problem for
the American in this part of the world. So that if I understand Spanish,
if I can read Marquez in *his* language, then I understand him through
my immediate inquiry: what do we have in common? Whereas I know
that (and I say this without any desire to give offense) I have a way of
thinking that may be totally alien to the African. I probably am a total
stranger to the African, whereas I am not a stranger to Marquez, or
Fuentes, or Paz.

[C]: Who do you read?

[W]: Well, mostly I have been reading the poetry, and I have read a
couple of the novels in translation. The usual people. . . . But I
haven't had access to enough Spanish-American novels, and of those
I have read, I find some too long, too unwieldy; they are often poorly
modeled on the European epic, and frankly I find many boring. I'm
more interested in writers like Marquez who have an instinctive way
of handling the natural and the legendary in close proximity. This is
very understandable to me in my part of the world; something not
quite fantasy, and so much more compelling than the stilted natural-
ism of much metropolitan literature. He creates more than a mere
replica of what happened during the day, more than a record of who
said what.

[C]: Do you think it is a mistake for black writers to turn to
white writers?

[W]: I don't think there is any such thing as a black writer or a
white writer. Ultimately, there is someone whom one reads. Yet there
is no man that can, or should wish to escape his race; he should
accept and then begin to worry about being a good writer. If you think

of the greatest prose innovator of our time, Joyce, you might ask: who is Joyce? You know that Joyce is an Irishman, that he has written about Ireland, very particularly about Ireland; but is that Joyce? An Irish novelist? One can't approach literature that way. And this has been said many times before. Say a black man comes along and writes a *Ulysses,* something of that stature. You know that it is *by* a black man, that it might be *about* his own race; but ultimately one must go beyond these simple statements. If a writer learns from anyone he must learn from a great writer. What black writer can I learn from? I can't think of a black writer who I would call a master very simply because black writers have really evolved at the same time as I have—they are my contemporaries. And that writer I choose as a master would have to be someone of enormous and proven stature within the language, within the imagination of blackness, for me to learn from him. Generally, one learns from the great dead. Do you think of Shakespeare as a white writer? Or Tolstoy? Or Aeschylus? I would not like to be called a black writer, I would not like to be told that a white writer or a white reader would not read me because I am black. It doesn't make any sense.

[C]: What about Soyinka as a master?

[W]: I'm not saying that there aren't emerging black writers who could not be great, that there are not masterpieces among the emerging literature. I consider *The Road* a masterpiece. But the man is a contemporary of mine; we have gone through the same evolution in terms of writing in countries where, previously, there had not been a large body of recorded literature. So this masterpiece, any masterpiece created by a contemporary, is *his*. There is no one among my contemporaries whom I wish to apprentice myself to. If I were aware of some epic, some ancestral masterpiece, then I would perhaps regard that as a masterwork. But the fact remains, the masterpieces of the language in which I work are from a white literary history. That must not prevent me from mastering the language; it is not a matter of subservience, it is a matter of dominating. One becomes a master, one doesn't become a slave.

[C]: Do you see any valid place for "relevance" or political commitment in black aesthetic and critical values, or do you think that the way a poet uses language should be the critic's foremost concern?

[W]: I don't think you can separate the two things. A man, for

instance, might say: "All this fuss the niggers are making (to make
the statement crude and succinct) is a pain, and I'm withdrawing from
it, and that's my attitude, and I'm going to live in my black ivory
tower and not involve myself in any revolution." All right, that's his
stance. As a matter of fact there is a terrific West Indian writer, V. S.
Naipaul, who is very cynical of Caribbean political and racial endeavors. That has been his consistent position, and yet one is able to
admire him as a writer, and to respect his stance because he *writes*
out of it, and even to admit that he is a very good writer. I don't think
any critic can point out to him that his argument, that his cynicism, is
wrong and thus ignore his achievements as a writer. Reed speaks to
this problem. Every year a new bunch of people tell you to join this
group, to do this and that, they point out the people who are more
politically involved than you are, more revolutionary. A writer could
go crazy trying to keep up with the changes. . . . He's got to find his
own pivot, his own stance—to know what he believes in—and this
has to be, for him, a respectable truth. This is what enables him to
write, and that is the important thing. It is not the business of any
critic to tell any writer what his position should be, certainly not from
the point of view of criticism. From the politician's point of view,
possibly. But it is not the critic's duty to say, "You write terrific
poetry, but you should be more relevant."

An Interview with Derek Walcott
Edward Hirsch / 1977

From *Contemporary Literature*, Vol. 20, No. 3 (Summer 1979), 279–92. Reprinted by permission of The University of Wisconsin Press.

Derek Walcott is the most important poet and playwright writing in English in the West Indies today. For the past thirty years he has been engaged in a complex struggle to render in words his native Caribbean culture, the New World, first successor to Eden. From his first book of poems (*Twenty-Five Poems,* 1948) to his most recent book of plays (*The Joker of Seville* and *O Babylon!,* 1978) his work is characterized by an insistent naming of things, a resolute determination to capture the tensions and ambiguities of West Indian life without descending into the merely local or provincial. It has been his particular achievement to remain attentive to the diversity and reality of the West Indies without surrendering its symbolic resonances and possibilities.

Throughout his work Walcott has explored the paradoxes and enigmas of life as a West Indian artist. While titles like *The Gulf* and *The Castaway* reflect the burdens of artistic isolation, "the beauty of certain degradations," "the precocious resignation to fate" involved in life on a small island, his work is energized by an exhilarating sense of privilege and opportunity. For the Caribbean writers of Walcott's generation the experience of Adam naming things in the Garden is very real: there is a belief in the propitiousness of the hour. Aimé Césaire, the great French Caribbean poet, sings of this feeling in "Return to My Native Land": "Storm, I would say. River, I would command. Hurricane, I would say. I would utter 'leaf.' Tree. I would be drenched in all the rains, soaked in all the dews." Walcott's collected works—poems, plays, and essays—continually engage that crucial hour of naming.

Derek Walcott was born on the island of St. Lucia in 1930. He was educated at St. Mary's College of St. Lucia and at the University of the West Indies in Jamaica. He eventually settled in Trinidad, where he still lives, and in 1959 founded the Trinidad Theatre Workshop. His first two books of poems, *Twenty-Five Poems* and *Poems* (1953), are primarily apprentice works. His mature work begins with *In a Green Night: Poems 1948–1960* (1962), followed by *Selected Poems* (1964), *The Castaway and Other Poems* (1965), *The Gulf* (1970), an autobiographical book-length poem entitled *Another Life* (1973), and *Sea Grapes*

(1976). A new book of poems to be called *The Star-Apple Kingdom* is scheduled for publication in 1979. Walcott has also published two books of plays in America. Four of his most important earlier plays—*The Sea at Dauphin* (1954), *Ti-Jean and His Brothers* (1958), *Malcohon, or The Six in the Rain* (1959), and *Dream on Monkey Mountain* (1970)—have been collected in *Dream on Monkey Mountain and Other Plays* (1970). In addition, *O Babylon!* and *The Joker of Seville* have recently been published in one volume.

I went to meet Derek Walcott in his room at the Chelsea Hotel in New York City. He had just finished a semester teaching at the Yale Drama School and was on his way back to Trinidad. The interview that follows was recorded at the Chelsea on the day before Thanksgiving, 1977. For a true sense of what transpired one must imagine two voices—one American, one distinctly West Indian—punctuated by the endless sounds of traffic on West Twenty-Third Street. And then there is the texture and timbre of Walcott's voice, at once precise, articulate, and musical. He has the unique ability to be able to respond in remarkably full and complex sentences to the most diverse kinds of questions.

Q: In both historical and racial terms, the society of the West Indies seems particularly complex and diverse. Do you think it is possible to speak of a West Indian literature?

A: In terms of the English-speaking Caribbean, what has happened is that there has been a fragmentation of the whole area into nations. Absurdly, we now have a nationalist literature in small places like Jamaica and Trinidad. If we go by the political definitions of these places as units, as islands or nations, the term West Indian literature doesn't exist. But just as there is a West Indian cricket team, I suppose we can generally describe our literature written in English as West Indian.

I think that you can also trace through the entire archipelago a sort of circle of experience which can be called the "Caribbean Experience." This would include Cuba, Puerto Rico, the French islands, down to the edge of the Caribbean basin, and maybe even curving up and around the Gulf of Mexico. For instance, I just finished reading for the third time Marquez' *The Autumn of the Patriarch* and I think it is probably the most powerful Caribbean novel that I've read, even though it comes out of South America—the whole historical and, to a degree, racial experience is a totality in the Caribbean. I wouldn't confine West Indian literature to literature written in English.

Q: Most of the professional writers of your generation have emigrated to Europe or America. But you have, for the most part, stayed in the West Indies. Why?

A: Yes, I remained in the Caribbean. I have always been involved in the theater and, naturally, if you're working in the theater as a playwright and forming a theater group, the only place where you can do so is in your indigenous location. But even if I had moved from St. Lucia, the idea of trying to evolve and develop a West Indian theater meant my remaining in the West Indies. In terms of my poetry I felt it would be a very, very long time before I could feel secure enough as a West Indian to see or to experience the culture that England and Europe represented. I still have a subliminal fear of Europe; I think I would feel dislocated, alienated, or uprooted if I had some of the traditional great experiences like seeing the Colosseum or Chartres. I didn't want to be in Europe and write poems agbout magnificent monuments. I just felt that you had to find not magnificence, but the reality of the beauty of your immediate surroundings. Of course, this also involved the whole process of becoming a poet. It takes a long time for a West Indian to be able to say who he is. So I suppose that however heroic it looks, it really was a kind of fear, a kind of determination to make sure I was valid in the place where I was born.

Q: And yet several of your early poems seem to reflect the English literary tradition. Does that matter?

A: It was the way I began. I lived on a very small island [St. Lucia] with a good library and with some fantastic teachers who made world literature accessible to me from a very early age, and who treated me with remarkable familiarity. They were never condescending or avuncular in any way; they always treated me as someone who could talk to them. The availability of books and intelligent conversation gave me enough confidence to be who I was.

The other thing is that in small societies the young poet is anthology-influenced. But that's good, because what influences him are selections, essences that have been chosen by editors or anthologists, so that what he sees is not a bewildering volume of minor writers but the selection of masterpieces, or even excerpts of masterpieces. I think it would be the same if someone on a desert island had a copy

of Palgrave's *Golden Treasury*. I also felt that it was a privilege to
grow up as an English colonial child because politically and culturally
the British heritage was supposed to be mine. It was no problem for
me to feel that since I was writing in English, I was in tune with the
growth of the language. I was a contemporary of anyone writing in
English anywhere in the world. What is more important, however—
and I'm still working on this—was to find a voice that was not inflected
by influences. One didn't develop an English accent in speech; one
kept as close as possible to an inflection that was West Indian. The
aim was that a West Indian or an Englishman could read a single
poem, each with his own accent, without either one feeling that it was
written in dialect. You know that you just ravage and cannibalize
anything as a young poet; you have a very voracious appetite for
literature. The whole course of imitations and adaptations is simply a
method of apprenticeship. I knew I was copying and imitating and
learning, and when I was criticized for writing like Dylan Thomas, it
didn't bother me at all because I knew what I was doing. I knew I had
to absorb everything in order to be able to discover what I was
eventually trying to sound like.

Q: What English and American writers first influenced you?

A: The most exciting thing was to be able to pick up a book that
was current. I had a friend who had Rodman's anthologies and actual
volumes of Eliot and Spender. Just the physical pleasure of seeing the
living poem in print created an excitement and an interest in modern
poetry. The influences were the same as those on any poet writing in
England or the United States: Eliot, Thomas, Auden.

Q: Were there any West Indian writers?

A: No. I think that one of the things that I took upon myself—and
perhaps I am still suffering from this—was a kind of responsibility
that was almost schoolmasterish. The bulk of West Indian poetry was
very bad. There were so many easy references to bright blue seas, so
many colorful depictions of peasant life; it was postcard poetry. West
Indian verse seemed to have more of the flavor of a library than the
most metropolitan verse not at all related to the Caribbean experience;
and naturally I went in the direction in which the language was most
vigorous and alive. I had to impose on myself the severe discipline of
making sure that what I was doing was difficult; it was not willful
obscurity. There weren't any West Indian poets to influence me. The

one person whose book I remember getting elated over was the
Jamaican poet George Campbell. I was struck by it, not because it
had anything particularly new to offer in terms of its structural
devices, but just because the man was a poet and he was mentioning
things I knew. I'm forty-seven now, and I can still remember the
tremendous elation I had at eighteen just standing on a little hill
somewhere and looking around at the sea and the sky and the town,
knowing that nobody had really written about this. It was exhilarating
to know that I was privileged to be the first one to put down the name
of a certain town, or fisherman, or road—a privilege very few writers
ever have.

Q: Throughout your work you refer to the New World as a kind of
Eden. How literally should we take the comparison?

A: I think it remains valid. I've just come back from Jamaica, which
is in a terrible state. The violence is incredible and terrifying. The
country is in great despair; it is very divided. On this trip we left
Kingston and went just a little way up into the mountains. There is a
dramatic contrast between the problems of Kingston, which are
known, residual problems of the Third World, and the beauty of the
surrounding countryside. Looking across the mountains isn't simply
seeing one of those "views"; it isn't panoramic, it is a spiritual thing.
In Jamaica you can have this spiritual experience standing on a
mountain looking across and seeing the light on the hills; or else you
may be on a very small island in the Caribbean, looking out at the
sea, at an empty beach. The fact is, the beauty is overwhelming, it
really is. It's not a used beauty, there are no houses there; it's not a
known beauty, and so the privilege of just looking at these places and
seeing their totally uncorrupted existence remains an Adamic experience. Looking across at the mountains, or walking on a beach that is
really deserted on an early morning, you can't avoid the feeling that
this is a new world.

Q: You talk about "the ancient war between obsession and responsibility." Is that involved in your decision not to leave the West Indies?

A: A title I've used, "The Castaway," is representative of my
stance: the person who has to work out his destiny on an island. It
may be a very blatant Methodist morality that I have, but it's very
difficult for me to justify desertion in terms of the people that I'm
from. I think I would suffer a great deal from that kind of escape. So

even if I get very bitter and despondent about the politics, the changes
in the Caribbean—the fact that there has been a profound political
betrayal of a people—I always go back. I try to return not with a
sense of desolation, but with a sense of participating in something
collective. The only possible realization in the West Indies is art. I see
no possibility of the country becoming unified and having its own
strengths except in its art. Because there is no economic power, there
is no political power. Art is lasting. It will outlast these things.

Q: In the "Overture" to *Dream on Monkey Mountain* you talk
about the sacred urge of actors everywhere to record the anguish of
their race. Do you see that as the central function of the theater?

A: Sometimes when I read the prologue to that book it sounds so, I
don't know, "spiritualistic" that I find it difficult to imagine that
people outside the Caribbean believe it. It sounds pontifical and
pietistic. But an actor working in Trinidad is fighting a despair that is
the reality of knowing that he can't make a living from his work, that
he can't get a certain kind of recognition. Therefore, he's simply
doing what actors have been doing from the very beginning, and that
is to be making himself voluble, not for himself alone, but for the
entire community around him. And it's for that reason that a lot of
actors in the Caribbean finally give up, because it means a dissolution
of the ego; it means saying, either I stay in this country or I go to
New York or London where at least I can make a living, at least I can
be recognized and rewarded. I hate the fact that every generation has
a large number of people emerging who are not offered even the
simplest future in terms of realizing their art. In its attitudes, its
politics, the Caribbean has been criminally neglectful. Even the simple
things have been neglected; like having a theater, organizing a company of dancers, creating a music school. It's beginning, but it's very,
very minor. And yet the actors want to broaden and develop their
work: that's the duty that the actor can't avoid if he's an artist. It's
the same for a poet or a sculptor or anyone else.

Q: At one point in the poem "Names," you speak of a "mind
halved by a horizon." The poem refers to the goldsmith from Benares,
the stonecutter from Canton, the bronzesmith from Benin. I'm also
thinking of "A Far Cry from Africa," which closes with "How can I
turn from Africa and live?" And yet at another juncture you speak of
the African revival as a kind of simplification, although a glamorous

one, for the Caribbean writer. Do you want to talk about the Caribbean writer's special relationship to Africa?

A: West Indians are always being seduced by opportunities to be re-imperialized. And unless we recognize this very clearly we will always be putting ourselves under another yoke. Within my own experience, I have been British; I have been a citizen of the Caribbean federation; now I'm supposed to be either a Trinidadian or a St. Lucian but with a British passport. I find that I am able to make a living in America (and I owe America a great deal for its recognition and the fact that I can work here); and there is the same danger, the same seduction in saying that I really am African and should be in Africa, or that my whole experience is African. This can be simply another longing, even a slave longing, for another master. There is no West Indian who is black, or even one who is not black, who is not aware of the existence of Africa in all of us. I was writing against the African influence during a period when the political nostalgia seemed to be a deceit because it meant that if one was lifting up a spade or fork, all one had to do was to throw it down and turn and look toward Africa and say, well, I shouldn't be digging up the ground in St. Lucia, or I shouldn't be doing whatever job I am doing in any one of the islands. I should really be in some sort of pastoral idealized place where I won't have to work, or where I may be working for Mother Africa. The fact is that every West Indian has been severed from a continent, whether he is Indian, Chinese, Portuguese, or black. To have the population induced into a mass nostalgia to be somewhere else seemed to me to be about as ennobling as wishing that the whole population was in Brooklyn, or Brickston. What I think was especially irritating to me was the fact that this idea was continually being dramatized in poems being offered to the masses—mainly the urban masses—as an escape. It would be equally abhorrent to me to say "I wish we were English again" as to say "I wish we were African again." The reality is that one has to build in the West Indies. But that is not to say one doesn't know who one is: our music, our speech—all the things that are organic in the way we live—are African.

Q: In your plays, and more recently in your poems, you rely on charms, jokes, folksongs, fables, and folktales. How important is oral literature to your work, and how much do you rely on its forms and structures?

A: I have always locked in on the fact that there is a living tradition around me, a tradition of chanting, of oral theater in terms of storytelling and the enjoyment of rhetoric. I was lucky to be born as a poet in a tradition that uses poetry as demonstration, as theater. That is why I don't feel like an outcast, or like someone trying something avantgarde, just because my plays are in verse. I don't feel I'm Christopher Fry trying to revive Elizabethan and Jacobean theater, nor am I Eliot trying to do contemporary ritualistic theater, nor am I Maxwell Anderson—I am someone who is simply coming out of a tradition and trying to formalize that tradition in terms of the necessity for structure in theater. There is something in Calypso which is active and responded to by thousands of people who, publicly, judge the poet. It is the simple eloquence and delight in polysyllables that you can get in knocking rhetoric, like the robber in Carnival tradition, or in people making speeches, or in the sort of extravagant care that the West Indian takes in cursing someone else, in looking for new metaphors. Graves has written something about the decline of swearing in metropolitan situations. People swear very simply here in New York; they are in a hurry and they just use a short, casual expletive. But in other places, the pastoral or semideveloped situations, the backyard and the street where people are alive and in contact with each other, the care required to curse a man thoroughly is a poetic form of expression. The storyteller tradition is still very prevalent in the Caribbean. The chant, the response, and the dance are immediate things to me; they are not anachronistic or literary.

Q: There is a very moving moment in the poem "St. Lucia" when you say, "Come back to me my language, come back," and the poem seems to move on three or four linguistic levels. Would you talk about your linguistic heritage?

A: Every island in the Caribbean has its own syntactical structure: a Trinidadian is not going to understand a Jamaican the first time off. On every island there is a dialect, a patois, which can become a world of fascination for someone who may want to write, or use, or absorb it into the whole West Indian idea of language. Most West Indians speak two languages, if you want to call a dialect a language. They speak Creole English, which one would call Trinidadian or Jamaican, and they speak standard English with an inflection of a kind, a native inflection. Sometimes you can even hear a West Indian, if he's going

to speak English, go up socially in his attack on the language for
clarity or for communication or depending on the social situation.

I have a three language background: French Creole, English Creole,
and English. With three languages, one oral, and access to, say,
English literature. . . . Well, having all of those things inside me was a
privilege. Once I knew that the richness of Creole was as whole
uncharted territory for a writer, I became excited. I also knew that it
couldn't be separated from the landscape, because the things I saw
around me were being named by people in a new language, even if
that language was being called Creole, or vulgar, or patois, or a
dialect, or whatever. The metaphors that one heard from peasants
describing a tree, a flower, an insect, anything, were not like the Latin
names for those things. The word "beetle" must have some metaphorical root, but who knows what it is now? Let's say you're looking up
at a bird in the sky over St. Lucia and somebody says "ciseau la
mer." Now "ciseau la mer" means "scissor of the sea," and that's
much more startling, much more exciting than saying "martin" or
"tern." The metaphor is almost calligraphic: when it is pronounced
you can almost see it. It is a little extravagant naming. Throughout
my whole youth that was happening. It was the experience of a whole
race renaming something that had been named by someone else and
giving that object its own metaphoric power. That was a privilege of
being born in what is usually called an underprivileged, backward,
underdeveloped society. It was a primal situation.

Q: It seems that your plays lean a lot more heavily on Creole than
your poems do. Is that true, and why?

A: In plays, you base characters on real people talking; you don't
want to make them sound falsely articulate. But since my own
education, my own development, has been academically privileged in
a sense, I couldn't pretend that my voice was the voice of the St.
Lucia peasant or fisherman. So for the poetry to be true, it had to be
accurate, quietly accurate in terms of the sound of my own voice. In
the plays I have tried to articulate the rude speech of the people I was
writing about. There are many passages in the plays that move away
from what could possibly be said by a St. Lucian fisherman or
charcoal burner. But what I have tried to do—and I think it is the
same sort of thing that lots of Third World writers have been trying to

do—is to combine my own individual poetic sensibility with the strength of the root, the mass racial sensibility of expression.

Q: Do you feel any problem of allegiance between your work as a poet and your commitment to theater?

A: No. In the West Indies the immediacy of the poet's address to an audience, particularly in Calypso, makes him a performer. The idea of the poet as performer, a public performer, is not very prevalent in the States. I suppose it is not prevalent in the Caribbean either, because we poets down there don't come out in front of an audience and sing, though this is what should be happening. In a sense, my plays are large poems that are performed before an audience. I hope to have the same immediacy, the same roar of response or roar of disapproval that the Calypsonian receives.

Q: I know that *The Sea at Dauphin* is modeled closely on Synge's *Riders to the Sea*. I'm interested in the influence of Synge and Yeats on your dramatic work and the parallels between the Irish Renaissance and the situation in the West Indies.

A: The whole Irish influence was for me a very intimate one. When the Irish brothers came to teach at the college in St. Lucia, I had been reading a lot of Irish literature: I read Joyce, naturally I knew Yeats, and so on. I've always felt some kind of intimacy with the Irish poets because one realized that they were also colonials with the same kind of problems that existed in the Caribbean. They were the niggers of Britain. Now, with all of that, to have those astounding achievements of genius, whether by Joyce or Yeats or Beckett, illustrated that one could come out of a depressed, deprived, oppressed situation and be defiant and creative at the same time. As a Methodist in a Catholic country, I also sympathized with the most rebellious aspect of Irish literature, priest-hating and such. After all, I had seen the overwhelming surrender to superstition—not the church's superstition, but the power of French provincial priests in our island.

And then the whole question of dialect began to interest me. When I read Synge's *Riders to the Sea* I realized what he had attempted to do with the language of the Irish. He had taken a fishing-port kind of language and gotten beauty out of it, a beat, something lyrical. Now that was inspiring, and the obvious model for *The Sea at Dauphin*. I guess I knew then that the more you imitate when you're young, the more original you become. If you know very clearly that you are imitating such and such a work, it isn't that you're adopting another man's genius; it is that he has done an experiment that has worked and will be useful to all writers afterwards. When I tried to translate the speech of the St. Lucian fisherman into an English Creole, all I was doing was taking that kind of speech and translating it, or retranslating it, into an English-inflected Creole, and that was a totally new experience for me, even if it did come out of Synge.

Q: Would you say that Synge gave you a model that wasn't available in West Indian literature?

A: No. I wouldn't have done this if there hadn't been people around who were aware of the poetic power of dialect. I think all of us, Naipaul, Hearne, all of my contemporaries had this tremendous sense of elation from really being the owners of a people—I mean aesthetically, creatively. Having an entire history, an entire country given to you is a tremendous gift for anyone. Whatever tools you used to capture the experience were legitimate.

Q: Yeats not only considered himself a maker of Irish literature but also saw his role as setting standards for the literary revival. Do you think of yourself in a similar way, or as having a similar function in the West Indies?

A: Well, to quote Joyce, "Where there's a reconciliation, there must first have been a sundering." Where there's a revival, there must have been a thing before. My work wasn't a revival; it was total originality.

Q: But you did say there was a kind of postcard verse.

A: That was generally abhorrent in terms of its laziness, its self-conscious association with a certain tradition. There was nothing that one could use, certainly not in the poetry. One felt more of an heir to the language, but if you picked up your pen to write, the person who preceded you as a poet may have been Keats, may have been anyone else, but he was *not* a West Indian. There simply wasn't any poet in the Caribbean that one could attach oneself to as a disciple. I think if the development of West Indian literature continues, my generation of writers will be known as people who had to go through a very anguished kind of identity crisis. And if we've set down West Indian roots, if we've used the language we heard around us and described the things we saw and the experiences we went through as a people, it has been to lay the foundation for whatever masterpieces would later come out of that part of the world.

Q: Many of the poems in *Sea Grapes* are less metrically formal than in your earlier books, more open, somehow both fiercer and quieter. I'm thinking of a moment in "Winding Up" when you say "Now I require nothing from poetry but true feeling, no pity, no pain, no healing." Is this a new departure for you? And would you call it a deliberate aesthetic stance?

A: I thought after finishing the book that it was going to be too bland, too downbeat, and I really didn't care very much about the reception either in the Caribbean or elsewhere. I guess I've also been a little surprised that many of the poems seem so even in terms of the interior tone: I began to hear the interior quiet that probably is the way I am. When we come, as poets, to a certain age, we may be a little disappointed in the fact that the voice, the tone of our ambition, seems to be less rhetorical than we thought it might have been. I find it difficult to read much Yeats now, except when I am in a heightened mood of aggressiveness and gesturing, whereas I can read a lot of Hardy. I think that's what I mean by finding at a certain age that one's tone is much more resigned, and less fussy, and probably humbler, than one imagines one would have been twenty or thirty years ago.

Q: I'm interested in the influence of American poets on your work. There are poems in *Sea Grapes* dedicated to James Wright and Frank O'Hara. The poem "Over Colorado" enters into a kind of dialogue with Whitman, and I know you and Robert Lowell were friends. Do you feel any special affinity with American poetry?

A: I think that part of my sense of isolation in the Caribbean comes out of the fact that a lot of poetry is so bad, so undisciplined, so casual, so aggressive that I feel perhaps a closer affinity to what is being done anywhere else in the world with English poetry. It isn't that I identify myself as an American poet, but if structural advances are made, experiments are made, if there is a search by all poets everywhere to find a more immediate idiom, then naturally they are going to be influential. When I look at work which I have influenced in the Caribbean, I find myself horrified that people choose to glorify my worst vices. There is an excess of metaphor, a diffuse but gnarled kind of poem which people imitate. If that is the sound I'm supposed to make, then it's distressing. I think that is one of the reasons that I have tried to move more and more away from what people believe I sound like, or maybe what I really do sound like. In that sense, the casual, colloquial force of American poetry has appealed to me. And yet, behind it all, I have a strong sense of structure, which is an English thing, because I live with a structured, formal public kind of expression in Calypso. I can't eradicate song from my own air: I'm surrounded by it in the Caribbean. Rhyme is a natural thing to me. People have asked me, "do you still use rhyme, do you still use pentameter?" The Calypso is pentametric in composition, and rhyme is essential. While it may seem old-fashioned or archaic to an American poet, we're talking about a living, vital tradition that I come out of.

I think the primary impulse of poetry is to ascend into song. And when you read a poem on a platform, you are asking an audience to make an effort of memory, no matter how difficult the poem is. I think this has been lost in Western poetry: memory is not a part of it anymore, and if that is denied, you're not going to get any real poetry. Whitman's instinct was toward song, toward recitation. The function of poetry is to recite.

Q: So poetry has a bardic function.

A: Well, I don't think poetry has any other function, as poetry. Because we have the typewriter, because we have the literary magazine, the poet separates himself from the poem and gives it away. Poets should have the same instincts as singers. If that happened I think there would be less difficult, complicated, attractive modern verse, and more poetry.

Q: Does living abroad affect your writing? I know New York City has given you fine poems like "A Village Life" and "Chelsea."

A: I'm working on a long prose book now to be called *American without America*. The influence of this country is not basically aggressive. Even if there is negative evidence politically, the America the people love and believe in is an America that is fairly well realized in terms of the individual. Now this is not to be blind to the realities of ghettos, racial prejudice, anti-semitism, rich or monolithic capitalism. I'm talking about a place where there is a sense of equality. Anybody who comes to America begins with an anonymity that is first of all very crushing: it doesn't matter a damn who the person next to you in the subway is. Of course I'm only talking about New York. Now, after you get over the frightening anonymity, you're bound to be influenced psychologically into becoming some kind of American. The more you go back and forth between the countries, the more you see things here that you wish were true where you come from. I'll give you a simple example: a lot of our islands criticize American imperialism and interference, even though repression of self-expression in these islands cannot be compared to the freedom of expression in the States. Each island is getting closer and closer to a kind of very cautious tyranny that is visible to people who look hard. One would like to see our society function with a similar openness to speech and, well, to a kind of life.

Q: What kind of book is *American without America?* Essays or fiction?

A: It's an extension of *Another Life* in prose. Broadly speaking, it is autobiographical, but it is also about our current West Indian dilemma, our fear of being absorbed into American culture. We're trying to retain an identity.

Q: You often make reference to masterpieces that seem to be close to your own work: I'm thinking of *Robinson Crusoe.*

A: The Crusoe thing is inevitable because of his two conditions. One is the elation of being "the monarch of all he surveys." We are Crusoes: as poets, as novelists, as playwrights, we survey islands, and we feel they belong to us—not in a bad, godlike manner, but with that sense of exhilaration, of creative possession. The other side is the despair of Crusoe, the despair of always being alone. That is our true condition as writers.

Interview

Ned Thomas / 1980

From *Kunapipi* (India), Vol. 3, No. 2 (1981), 42–47. Reprinted by permission of *Kunapipi*.

In the autumn of 1980 Derek Walcott toured Wales as the recipient of the Welsh Arts Council's International Writer's Prize. This interview was conducted during that visit.

Can I start by asking you where you are now living and working?

What I've been doing recently is getting invitations to be at various American universities for one semester at a time—I've been at Yale, in the department of Afro-American studies, and also in the drama department with young playwrights; and I've been at Columbia, this is now my second time there, and I'm also doing a class at New York University with Joseph Brodsky. The two of us share a class—I've never done this before—and I find it quite exciting. Next year I'm going to be at Harvard doing the same thing as Seamus Heaney did. So most of my working life is spent in the States—it's a bit of a wrench, because ideally I would like to teach in the Caribbean in the University, and also work in the theatre there, because the theatre itself is very much a part of my being in the Caribbean.

Does this mean you've had to stop directing, except occasionally?

Well, there is some plan for me to be able to do things in the summer, with a company in the Caribbean, so I hope I shall be able to do theatre work between April and September.

How do you organize time for your writing?

Because I write plays as well as poems, and recently have been working on a prose book as well, I always have something to do in the mornings whether it is re-writing a scene from a play or whatever—I mean I don't get up in the morning saying 'I am going to write poems', but you can always work *on* them. My ritual is still, even if I live in a temperate country, to get up very early in the morning, have a cup of coffee, watch the sunrise come up, smoking like hell unfortunately and drinking too much coffee. So my working day, if I've had a good night's sleep, and I try to sleep as much as I can, starts at about 6 a.m. I get tired of work at about half-past ten to eleven in the mornings, and I never work in the afternoons except when I'm lying down scribbling, and never at night, absolutely not at night. It's a terrific kind of life when you're on an island, a small island like Tobago, where you can get up early in the morning—it's cool and it's quiet and beautiful—you work and then go for a swim; that's really a millionaire's paradise, but you don't have to be rich to do it though.

Is the Caribbean getting a harder place to live these days?
In many ways, yes.

The Star-Apple Kingdom *seemed to me a rather anguished poem.*
We are going in a very frightening direction. I think part of it is the result of panic. I think the kind of socialism we are embracing—the kind of Marxism if you wish—is on a very superficial level in terms of any effect, any presence it can have in terms of world power. What the leaders in the Caribbean refuse to admit to themselves is that we are powerless. We are powerless people. Or I would say that the real power we have is in our people, in the artists and so on. This may sound very visionary and silly and adolescent, but once the Caribbean accepts the fact that this is where its power lies, then it is possible that what I thought would happen might again begin to be discerned; if we see that the richness we have is in the cultural diversity, the mixture, the fact that we *do* live together very well, only disturbed by politicians. Anyone can exploit, with the proper techniques, the Afro-Indian division, but the day-to-day life in Trinidad of African and Indian is visibly normal. Guyana was of course the example—*that* was provoked.
It is a bitter thing for me to see people manipulated. It becomes more and more infuriating. When you are younger and you don't know who are in power you are in awe. When the people who are in power are in some cases your own age, or younger, then you see them, you see right through them, and that infuriates you.

It's the same everywhere. But presumably underlying those divisions that can be exploited, there is the basic economic problem.
But the economic problem is again exploited—by the old leaning-

on-slavery attitude, which is very convenient; or leaning-on-capital-
ism, or leaning on American interference, or anything you want to
lean on but the reality of the fact that you are poor. We still do not
tell people that they are poor. The Caribbean politicians describe
problems to their own people as if they, the politicians, were spokes-
men at the big tables of the world, as if someone from Trinidad or
Jamaica really counts for Kissinger or Kosygin.

But I'm saying that one needn't become a satellite because one
accepts that one is on a lower level of economic life. If only one could
be addressed simply and directly by the politicians, saying 'Look, we
are poor, this is where we begin'. If the mass says 'Yes, we are poor',
then you can say 'What are we going to do about it?' and begin from
there. But what is said is something about Russia, or 'America is
giving us a hard time', or 'The Arabs are giving us a hard time'—it's
a whole system of blaming. I'm not saying the problems aren't there,
but instead of turning around and confronting them—which metropolitan countries do because their problems are close to them—we don't
do it, we pretend to be metropolitan countries with problems which
can be settled around the conference tables of the world. The politicians have a misconception of what the Caribbean people will accept.
We have come out of slavery in something close to living memory,
and people who have endured that should not be encouraged to think
in terms of becoming rich overnight, nor do they believe that it is
possible. But if you delude them into thinking either that a completely
Socialist economy is going to do that, or that the diametric opposite
is going to cure things, then you're doing a very dangerous thing. The
violence that has come is a consequence of that lie. We are paying for
telling people that if they get rid of X, then it will all be theirs. You
give them a sense of inheritance and right which generates a violence.
These people put themselves in a position where they themselves will
be annihilated by the very people they incite.

*I read somewhere (though it doesn't entirely square with my own
reading) that in* The Star-Apple Kingdom *you are writing in the
person of Michael Manley.*

It is obviously Jamaica. I am—I was—very close to Michael Manley, but it isn't him entirely, and of course the poem is modelled very
closely on Marquez's *Autumn of a Patriarch*. The *persona* is a leader

who is in Jamaica, but his background is not Manley's background, there's a great house fiction. So the character does become fictional, but I think what I was concerned about was that Michael does have a profound love of his country, Jamaica, and he's a fighter, and I wanted to catch the poise of anguish that comes from wishing for a kind of order that can only perhaps be imposed by a kind of discipline, 'heavy manners' if you want. The poem is poised at that point and I've been criticised by radicals who say 'It doesn't get you anywhere, it's the usual middle-of-the-road balance thing'. But that's the poise of the poem. My private opinion about what should or should not happen has nothing to do with it. I have always been very careful—that's the balance of the poet—not to move into propaganda, on either side. Rigidity comes in when the poet is tempted in a totalitarian regime to appear to be non-conformist, or in a democratic regime to make sure he is radical enough.

I understand you are bringing out a new volume of poems in the Spring. What direction will that take? You seem recently to have been writing longer poems, a number of them in a persona *which allows you to develop if not dialect, then an accented version of standard English.*

In the new book I have a long poem called 'The Spoiler's Return' which is based on a Calypsonian—I won't go into that, but that's the one dialect poem in there. You see I no longer think in terms of a tool—either dialect or standard English—I think, if it works, it works, for the one or the other.

Perhaps it's the situation in the Caribbean, perhaps it's becoming older and getting a deepening sense of history, but I find myself very drawn, not so much to the style but to the *idea* of the Roman poets. I have this feeling of being on the outskirts, in a colony or provinces that have changed empires, from British to American, and economically I cannot see us avoiding, not a fate but the reality that the world is divided between America, Russia, China. That is what has been happening. I've felt parallel with some of the Latin poets, coming from my archipelago on the fringe towards the capital. I'm interested in that balance. I also think that very often the capital can become numb, because its preoccupation is with power, with the function of power, and somehow the poetry goes out of it. If you want to put it this way you can say that where there's concrete, there the power is, and the further you go from the concrete the more you come to the vegetation, nature and so on.

And the correlative of that is that at the fringes there is *no power.*

Yet you're drawn to it, you're looking in that direction. I think also that there can be long periods, long, long centuries, in which a civilization can be very powerful and not produce a culture, and we forget that. When we're within a dying system we don't know it is dying. Maybe Europe, for all its economic vigour—I'm not *saying* it is a dying culture—but maybe it is not the center of the spirit. The centre of poetry need not be in London—it may be in Wales, it may be anywhere else but in that concrete and steel thing.

I think it's very exciting to be *outside* English literature, English literature in a hierarchic sense. Now if I wrote well as an Englishman, in any sizeable history of English literature I would at least have a footnote. If I worked hard enough I'd achieve a footnote. There's this hierarchic thing, your name would be there somewhere between A and Z. Now most poets in a tradition have that kind of listlessness that if they work mildly enough something is going to happen, and certainly if they live long enough they will become part of some kind of club. Now we don't have that in the Caribbean luckily. The danger which we *do* have, of course, is that if you're virtually the only writer in some area you become over-important. But finally your responsibility and your own critical assessment of yourself is freer. You don't really think of yourself as being part of a tradition, nor do you think of yourself as some fantastic pioneer. You simply are in a position where you can judge yourself by what your own estimate of your work is. In that way I'm completely free. I'm not part of the establishment. I'm not part of the gang. I'm not part of the club.

If I've worked out the dates right, you're now fifty, and you've already projected yourself in poems as senex, *the oak, and so on. Do you think of life as stages? Do you think of what you have to write now as being different?*

In terms of the poetry I think that for a long time I didn't realise that I was being paid any attention to, and that kept me clear-headed. Now I'm a little disconcerted that there are a lot of things being published about my work—a lot of praising things are being said—and

I'd like to shake off any responsibility that one might feel about becoming 'important'. I think it's possible to do it because I can always go back to the Caribbean and be just someone else, you know.

And probably to be discovered younger is more dangerous to one's self-judgement than later.

I think that's what attracts me to the Roman poets. I think there's something about age in them that I find understandable—the Horatian farm, that kind of thing, the retreat, not from fame but into a craft. At fifty I feel secure, I think for the first time in my life. Certainly I feel sure about who I am and what I want to do. Towards this period of my life I would like to write just much better, much clearer, much simpler and much more honestly. Not that I was dishonest, but around fifty you come to a kind of honesty in which the awkward can be accepted, and what you're good at can also be accepted. There's a kind of equanimity that comes.

This Country Is a Very Small Place

Anthony Milne / 1982

From *Sunday Express* (Trinidad), 14 March 1982, 18–19. Reprinted by permission of the *Express*.

Derek Walcott was in Trinidad last week. While here he gave a reading at the Royal Victoria Institute, and met with members of the Trinidad Theatre Workshop who are to produce his play, *The Joker of Seville,* later this year.

Walcott was staying, as is his wont, at the Hotel Normandie, and when EXPRESS feature writer Anthony Milne went to see him he was lounging by the pool. The interview was conducted beneath a poolside umbrella until the wind and the rain made this impossible. The rest of the interview took place in Walcott's hotel room, in between interviews with members of the Theatre Workshop.

Express: What is it like living in the United States, and what are you doing there?

Walcott: I used to teach in a university there one term, or semester, at a time. I was making my living that way. Of course, the money was rapidly consumed; whatever I saved went very quickly while I was in Trinidad. I was living in hotels while I was here. I decided last year, having got an offer from Boston University, that I would take a permanent job there because it would involve the reality that my children would get a free university education.

Just to try to create a kind of continuity I thought I would take the job for a period of time and test it and see how long I wanted to remain there. Then I got the MacArthur award, which is a good amount of money, and one has to live in a place that is one's own, so I got a place in Boston quite near to the university.

But I genuinely consider that I have a kind of even balance, geographically and even mentally now between the United States and Trinidad, or the Caribbean, because another place I like to go to in summer, I do a workshop up there, is St. Thomas in the Virgin

70

Islands. I run a playwrights' workshop there, and I'm going to go back there this summer with my daughters, to do a combined work-vacation type of thing.

Then, of course, I'm here in Trinidad during the vacations, and the summer vacation is, of course, quite long, beginning at the end of May and continuing till the first week in September. I am very active. There are a lot of things I plan to do here, with the theatre particularly.

Since I have got this grant from the MacArthur Foundation, and since the grant included $36,000 annually to be used by any institution I associate myself with, that sum will go, on alternate years, to Boston University and to the Trinidad Theatre Workshop.

So I think I have achieved a kind of balance which I have sought for a long time. I'm not doing enough, and one needs a hell of a lot more money, but this whole question of exchanging talent, which I am continuing with, is not just for my sake; it's something that needs to be done. The actors here need to have fresh professional actors come down to work with them. And the actors who come down from New York, or wherever, will also benefit from the experience of coming to the Caribbean.

Express: Who now constitute the Theatre Workshop?

Walcott: Just recently Albert La Veau was appointed to be a new director of the workshop, and there is evidently going to be a new board. I created the workshop, but I'm not in it, I'm outside of it, so that's where the interest lies. There is also an executive board, and also a board of trustees which has to be there before the grant can be administered.

But what I want to do in a broader sense, if it's possible (and this is where one can test whether there is any guided philanthropy in Trinidad), if that $36,000 goes to the workshop, which is quite likely, then what will be necessary, to ensure there is enough money for a solid programme, are matching grants either from the government or from business people. Because generally the situation has always been that you go and beg and so on, and there have been instances of people endorsing things, and signs that they will do so again. But if you have that initial sum, from the grant, you can go to people and ask whether they will match the amount, and that way you can find out if people are really interested in developing the theatre here: the arts on the whole.

I'm not saying that there has been no funding in the past, but at times the funding is minimal (it certainly has been sporadic), and sometimes it has been overblown. In other words there has been immense investment in things that are basically ephemeral. Over the next five years during which that grant is administered, I want to get people to come down here.

I have spoken to some very important actors and directors in America who say they will come down. Lloyd Richards, who is the artistic director and Dean of the Yale Drama School, will be coming down in the summer to do a ten-day master-class in acting. I've spoken to another American director who did a play of mine; and I've also spoken to a world-renowned actress, a terrific actress, I won't tell you her name now, because the thing is still being negotiated, and there are a couple other people who will come down to help create this widening, mutual area of experience.

It is about time the experience of the theatre here be expanded, and certainly it shouldn't contract itself racially. That is a danger here as well. You can see that there is almost beginning to be a division in terms of colour in the theatre. People may say I'm talking nonsense, but I'm watching it and I think that the more nationalistic you get, because of the nature of the bulk of the population here, the more the thinking may tend to be only in black or in Indian, and that is not what the West Indies is supposed to mean, or Trinidad certainly.

So I'm talking about white actors too. I'm not interested in making a black theatre in the Caribbean, absolutely not, because that would exclude everybody, apart from the black.

Express: Do you know about the controversy over the role of the Little Carib Theatre?

Walcott: Yes, that is a complicated question. I suppose I'm skirting the question, but let me say that I think that one of the problems is that this country is a very small place, and the biggest danger here is for people to self-inflate their reputations, tend to become disproportionately blind about what is really valuable. I find that increasingly frightening and distressing. It's all around. Very inexperienced people who may have zeal (which in itself is all right) but whose zeal gets transformed into very large egos, can do a lot of damage in terms of restraining or misdirecting certain things.

This is a place where if you just get something published a couple of times you are automatically a poet; if you write a play you are a playwright; if you go on the stage you are an actor. Because of nationalism, because of this greed to have an identity that is purely Trinidadian, with the loss of the sense of patience and building that is necessary in any craft, people have overblown reputations, and tend after a while to believe in their own reflections.

I think it's all around now. I have come back here and seen people's names billed as stars, and I'm talking about totally inexperienced young actors. I've seen directors' names put above the names of authors; so that playwrights established worldwide get second billing. It's insanity, and it looks foolish, because I have had friends down here, professional theatre people, and it makes us look damn silly, that's all I'm saying. There's some sanity required to get back into a modesty of discipline and direction that has been derailed by this inflation of egos here.

I go through a hell of a lot in terms of this kind of thing. I've just had two plays done in America that have got very bad reviews and these are sobering experiences. Down here my reputation is big, but when I'm in America I'm among other people who can be sliced in a review the next day, so I always have that chastening experience of knowing I'm not finished working. A lot of people here have the feeling that in six months' time they can become actors or directors or producers. I think that's the worst aspect of things here now.

Express: There was an article about Vidia Naipaul in last Sunday's *Express which was perhaps evidence of the kind of thing you are* *talking about. The writer joined in the criticism of both Naipaul and* *yourself, apparently because you don't always say the things a certain* *kind of person likes to hear. It seems as though that type of person* *feels he must revile those who, by international standards, are the* *finest literary products of the region.*

Walcott: I don't think that is of any importance whatsoever, because no matter what is said in terms of being criticised locally, it is expected. You have a village mentality, and if you walk down a village street dressed differently you get people heckling you at a street corner. So when you encounter a village mentality you ignore it, otherwise you would never work. And a village mentality can exist on an official level, on very responsible levels. It still remains a village mentality.

Certainly anyone can say what they want about Naipaul, in terms of his philosophy or his attitude to Trinidad, but it is impossible to degrade him as an artist, because the work is there. So that is only village jeering and is of absolutely no consequence; that is just standpipe criticism.

Express: Would you say that this kind of thing, this attitude, and the danger of assuming an inflated ego makes it difficult for a person who is trying to become a serious writer or artist in Trinidad?

Walcott: In days gone by, and this may seem like nostalgia because I am 52, a different kind of thing happened. There were values in the colonial system of education, and the colonial system of hierarchy that were over-turned with independence, but people revert to them. One of the obvious symptoms of hierarchy is the hierarchy of language.

If you live in a society in which bad language (and by bad I don't mean immoral, but ill-expressed language) is acceptable not only as a norm but as an expression of Patriotism (so that if you don't speak badly you become an enemy of the people, because the people don't talk that way) you get a deterioration of syntax. A deterioration of syntax is related to the threat of deterioration in a society. Because the next thing that happens is that anyone with any talent or with any ambition is called a showoff, because there is an attempt to force that person to become democratic.

But art is not democratic, art is hierarchical, and all artists know that. They know that it takes all your life to achieve some level where you can be among your peers. But if immediately your peers are made to be illiterate, or the people who feel education is restricted entirely to self-expression without craft, then the society is in danger. It is in more danger than it is from terrorists or revolutionaries.

But I think the standard of education here, just from speaking to my daughters, is high, it remains high. That is one good aspect of the colonial heritage. We mustn't look on colonialism simply as oppression, there are certain things in it that, however irascible they make some people, form the basis of the kind of democratic society that exists here. It is not a matter of race. It is a matter of racelessness, really.

For us to teach art as race, which is typical independence type of thinking, that will go away. Because I don't think anyone is going to prevent the artist from having a universal type of mind. But I will say again that I think the standard of education here remains high, because it depends on the severe discipline of studying, which I think is good.

Express: It seems that what you are saying is that there is sometimes a confusion between colonial standards and standards which are universal; that people reject a certain standard, saying that it is colonial, when it is important to maintain that standard.

Walcott: Yes, or they make the silly mistake of confusing race with culture. Now I'm not saying that colonial culture is the only culture. I am saying that the exclusion of good speech, the exclusion of books, of art, or whatever, as a sort of historical revenge, as a revenge on history, is very short-sighted, and is fatal.

The question of emphasizing an African or Indian identity is irrelevant, because you are African or you are Indian and no one can take that away in terms of identity. To exclude yourself, like some other Third World countries would do, to think that everything there is tainted and poisoned, is immature.

Express: The same way that the primitive Britons benefited from Roman Colonialism?

Walcott: Exactly. The whole process of civilization is cyclical. The good civilization absorbs a certain amount, like the Greeks. Empires are smart enough to steal from the people they conquer. They steal the best things. And the people who have been conquered should have enough sense to steal back.

Express: But is there a difference between Roman-British colonialism and British-West African colonialism because of greater racial differences in the latter?

Walcott: Colonialism is often based on race. You are going out there to subdue heathen races, and so on. But it isn't always based on race, it isn't always that you are subduing the heathen, although you have to think of people as heathen. It depends on how much power exists at the moment, in the empire. For example, when Britain invaded India it was invading a civilization older than its own.

All of what is called the Third World is now confronted by this crisis of restoration. The Moslem thing that Naipaul talks about in his recent book, though it is not a very profound book, but one of the things it talks about is the extreme and frenzied rejection of everything Christian in Islamic countries; that's not what you want.

To be told by politicians, or by critics, or by anyone at all, or by Naipaul himself (this is where he contradicts himself), that you are imitating is odd. On the one hand you say embrace, and on the other you say don't imitate. But you cannot embrace without imitation. The trouble with it is that when the empire does it, it is known as acquisition and when it is done by colonials it is known as imitation. The amorality of that is absurd.

My main concern is not with any political refutation of the past, but with the reality of the day-to-day experience of language and literature, and so on. I think that the situation here is almost obscene in the fact that there isn't a good library still, and other things. All those things that should be there.

These things are not false. It isn't that you are putting up the structure and hoping to fill it. The point is that you have the personnel, you have the people, you have the enthusiasm, the drive, you have the reality of people's becoming; but what you don't have is those moulds to contain and shape that expression. What you do have, unfortunately, is a government, which has been re-elected, that is not going to suddenly get a new vision of the situation.

It may be that their vision will broaden and they will see the obvious need for certain things which one has been crying out for a quarter of a century. I am not cynical any more. I am just resigned to the fact that I don't expect anything to be done. But that does not mean that I don't have the faith that another generation of people will insist on their right to have civic buildings where they can express themselves: museums, theatres, and so on. Another generation is going to make damn sure they get these things.

Express: With regard to what you were saying about language and its deterioration, does that have to do with the way in which language and thought are connected, in that subtley of thought needs subtlety of language?

Walcott: It is hard to measure that, but I don't think you can say that a thought is more subtle in an imperial language than it is in a colonial dialect. I know a feeling cannot be. I think that artists have acute, more accentuated, more mercurial feelings, because they train their minds towards this daily. They become over-sensitive and more receptive.

But the average person in one culture is not more sensitive than the average person in another culture, because the same experiences go through each culture, whether it is death or fear, just to take the large ones. In terms of subtleties of feeling no man is different from another man.

The acuteness of the artist in terms of representing or experiencing those feelings is a difference, definitely. But you cannot be an artist without the discipline of thought, and that discipline of thought must be within a structure of language. That structure of language may begin in dialect, originate in dialect.

I don't think we have as yet managed to express fully the subtleties that are possible in dialect. They have been expressed, but as a generic thing, as a large thing. You have the kind of dialect writing that is humorous or satirical, which pretends to be nationalistic, but which is really poking fun at itself. You also have, as with Naipaul or Selvon, artists working in the language and making some masterful little variations in the language. So that it is there.

But to say that when someone is writing a dialect story that person is thinking in the imperial language, I don't know if that's true. I think that the confidence you have in the language is that you are saying that one is no better than the other. It's like Dante writing "The Divine Comedy" in the vulgar tongue, or Chaucer, or Joyce, or Synge.

Express: But what about the other functions of language, in philosophy, for example?

Walcott: Well, the language in art is the language that is used in schools, and if we look very carefully, we realize, for instance, that the diction of teachers in schools cannot be tolerated purely as being nationalistic diction. In other words, to mispronounce words, to say "de" instead of "the," is not a nationalistic thing.

It is crippling and limiting the width of a child's mind if, at an early age, he's not taught what is correct speech (and there is no question about what is correct speech, correct speech is agreed upon by what grammar is)—and we're talking about the schools principally. And if the subtlety of a philosophical thought contradicts itself in dialect then you have no confidence in the dialect and you have more confidence in the imperial language, the source of the language.

So that whole problem is centered in education, because every artist either is self-educated to the same degree that he was his own teacher, very rigidly, or he had a formal education in which he was trained by teachers who had enough confidence to be what they were.

Express: Do you think that syntactical breakdown is part of a process by which something new may be formed?

Walcott: Certainly, because that happens with the artist; but what I'm saying is that the artist has the duality of confidence in either language. If Naipaul wants to write a dialect story, like "Tell Me Who To Kill," which is a little masterpiece, he does that; then he does another kind of story, in English. He can choose either tool he likes. But when you have someone else who is not a writer, or an artist, patriotically affirming that this is our language, then just purely as an academic exercise, for the sake of an examination, or for the sake of getting a job, beginning to treat English as some kind of device by which one can advance oneself, purely for that reason, then you are limiting what I still think is the range of the West Indian experience. Which is world-wide range. It's like teaching bad Hindu, or Hebrew, or Swahili.

Express: In spite of all the attendant problems, how do you feel about living and working in Trinidad again.

Walcott: My whole thing about Trinidad is that it is more enriching, however embittering or degrading or frustrating sometimes. It is a richer experience for me to be in Trinidad than it is to be in America. The challenge of the experience of what it means to be at the beginning of a society is more exciting than to be in one that is too large to influence, to help direct. As I explained, I think I have achieved a balance between being in the United States and Trinidad.

An Interview with Derek Walcott

Leif Sjöberg / 1983

From *Artes* (Sweden), No. 1 (1983), 23–27. Reprinted by permission of *Artes* and Leif Sjöberg.

Leif Sjöberg: You have been criticized on some occasions in your native Caribbean home region, for not being patriotic enough or nationalistic enough, not radical enough, not sufficiently oriented towards Africa but rather towards Britain and the United States. What do you say to such charges?

Derek Walcott: My answer to these accusations or criticisms is that the Caribbean is both a new and an old society. Old in history, new in the experiment of multi-national concentration in small spaces. To look backwards is to think linearly, the fate of any concept of progress. Linear thinking is not inevitable. The African experience is historically remote, but spiritually ineradicable. Nothing has really been lost. Heredity does not need explication. What is radical in history is ephemeral. What is radical in art is eternal. Truths exist in all societies, no one race has that privilege. What we owe the past as human beings we owe completely. That is the intellectual exhilaration in the Caribbean experience.

LS: Your former compatriot Naipaul stated that the Caribbeans "lived in a society which denied itself heroes." You have quoted this in your book-length autobiographical poem, *Another Life*. Now, usually we think of a "hero" as the one who gets our sympathies, while the villain gets our scorn or our hate, but judging from the cast of *Dream on Monkey Mountain,* you clearly have another type of heroic concept in mind: there are poor fishermen, derelicts, eccentric persons, saxophonists, alcoholics, transvestites, workers, common people. There is also a remarkable grocer who dreams of returning to Africa and leading the exodus to the new Jerusalem. There are peasants, charcoal-burners, coal-carrying women, carpenters, cripples, felons, paupers, priests.

DW: But also dancers, singers, musicians, dreamers, philosophers, artists.

LS: These people speak in their own voice, such as it is. Even if they are failures in many ways and have all kinds of problems and difficulties, they are, generally, presented with sympathy and a certain warmth; it is "la condition humaine" in a sense. Now, if in 1973 you agreed with Naipaul by quoting him, do you also want to prove him wrong by attempting to create "heroes," but of a "mixed" type, perhaps with traits of the villain as well as the authentic tragic hero; of both holy and unholy, spiritual and depraved, complicated and simple, all in one person?

DW: No, no! I do not believe in heroes. I do not believe in human progress, that is, that man gets better. How can one, after Auschwitz, My Lai, Beirut, or whatever.

The search for heroes in history is a Mosaic anachronism. See Brecht. Pity the society that needs heroes.

The people I honor and glorify from simplicity, not from a Marxist or political viewpoint, rather say from a Whitmanesque one, are my heroes. Fisherman. Working men, isolated artists. Not political figures: That develops fascism!

Makak (the main character in *Dream on Monkey Mountain*) is a man who is tempted into being such a hero. When he awakens from his dream, his wisdom is that he has refused the opportunity. He is himself, not what others would make of him.

LS: You moved from Saint Lucia to Trinidad in 1959 and have lived there ever since, except for the semesters when you have taught at Columbia, Yale, Harvard, and Boston University. Now, Naipaul is from Trinidad, but he abandoned the island, apparently very pessimistic about the opportunities there, and settled in London. It seems almost as if he is ashamed of his poor, underprivileged background, if one may judge from the *Mimic Men*. Sven Birkerts has juxtaposed a number of quotations from Naipaul with statements from you and the differences are striking. Let me hasten to add that Naipaul appears to be one of the most intelligent authors around today, and I admire his *A House for Mr. Biswas,* but something deplorable has happened to him; following his successful novel *Guerillas* (1975), I have had no interest in his books or, at any rate, any existing interest has cooled off considerably. With *A Bend in the River* (1979) it ceased. His cynicism and pessimism require a greater reader input than I am willing to commit. That his is an incredible intelligence is obvious, but

I leave undiscussed the question whether he is the kind of writer we need nowadays.

But here we get to your attitude towards Naipaul. It seems to have been rather vacillating. As Birkerts has pointed out, you have on the one hand dedicated a poem, "Laventille," to Naipaul in your collection, *Castaway* (1965). On the other hand, you have called his novel, *A Bend in the River* (1979), "a racist joke," indicating serious differences with him.

There are obvious parallels between you two, of course, and the most basic is, I suppose, what has been described as "deep conflicts and a certain degree of ambivalence" vis-a-vis the Caribbean and its future. You both appear shocked by today's "progress," but your attitudes, in general, seem quite different.

Now, I notice that in your latest collection of poetry, *The Fortunate Traveller,* you call him "V. S. Nightfall" in the poem "Spoiler's Return." What is it that you now protest against in Naipaul which, previously, you apparently were undecided about?

DW: Naipaul's contempt and self-contempt, in my view, have now reached a state of psychic disorder controlled, almost at the edge of hysteria, by a style. Because he himself is now in mid-passage, because he has great integrity and is honest (honest even about his contempts), if he emerges into the warmth he began with, if he can be blessed again with a breadth or tenderness, he will become a great writer. No one is content with being a superb stylist. Dostoevsky has no style. Minor writers think style is all. Naipaul is better than that.

LS: White in soul, black in body is an expression that appears in *Dauphin,* I believe. What does this mean to you? In other poems you talk of your white grandfather and your reader senses a profound division. It is as if you were saying, Oh yes, black, but not black enough; white, but to no advantage. What loyalties are at stake? What difficulties have you encountered, and what "solutions" have you come up with in your writings?

DW: The quotation is wrong. Race, despite what critics think, has meant nothing to me past early manhood. Race is ridiculous. Even racial war is, at base, humorous. Different colored ants fighting. I have no loyalties to one race more than to another.

LS: You simply feel loyalty to the human race?

DW: The conduct of a race is its own fault, not mine! Black or white!

LS: You have mastered the language of the masters, yet you employ *patois* in some works. Reason?

DW: I do not consider English to be the language of my masters. I consider language to be my birthright. I happen to have been born in an English and a Creole place, and love both languages. It is the passion, futility and industry of critics to perpetuate this ambiguity. It is their profession. It is mine to do what other poets before me did, Dante, Chaucer, Villon, Burns, which is to fuse the noble and the common language, the streets and the law courts, in a tone that is true to my own voice, in which both accents are heard naturally.

LS: The question of language is very important to you, obviously, and is touched upon repeatedly in your poetry. Sometimes the poems tend to be declamatory and elevated to a point where they become inflated; at other times you go the opposite way and deflate language. In which of these categories do you have the greatest hopes to achieve poems that ring true?

DW: Inflating language? My society loves rhetoric, performance, panache, melodrama, carnival, dressing up, playing roles. Thank God I was born in it, which made me love life and artificial theater. Even pomposity can be charming. I'd rather be pompous than dull, rather go for the big swipe than the timid, decent drawing-room gesture. I am an open-air person, hence the loud pitch of my voice.

LS: For someone who has ambitions to be truthful, you employ a great number of allusions, quotations, literary devices. What do you want to achieve with those techniques? (with that "learned" language?)

DW: I do not recognize literary devices. I cannot name metres. I am not interested in the nomenclature of Latin scansions. I count on my fingers. Everything else is by accident, and I hope divine.

LS: In the manner of the nineteenth century you quote quite liberally, especially preceding a poem or a play, and all of these quotes, whether from Sartre, Fanon, Euripides, Sophocles, Malraux, Alejo Carpenter, César Vallejo, Saint-John Perse, or others, are well chosen. But in addition you employ another method with quotations in the actual poems. In those cases you do not indicate the source, often not even the fact that it is a matter of a "loan," and appropriation, but like Eliot, proceed as if they were your own property.

Do you not sometimes hesitate when incorporating the felicitous, or, perhaps, the less felicitous expressions of others into your work, without giving any credit-line? Of course, if the quotations are famous and from long dead poets or classics, I guess the hermetic/modernistic tradition allows you to do as you please—but what if they are more recent? Do you not recognize a risk that, on occasion, you go too far and imitate? That your own voice is not heard so well?

DW: I have always believed in fierce, devoted apprenticeship. I have learned that from drawing. You copy Dürer; you copy the great draftsmen because they themselves did. I have always tried to keep my mind Gothic in its devotions to the concept of master and apprentice. The old masters made new masters by the discipline of severity. One's own voice is an anthology of all the sounds one has heard. As it is with children, so with poets.

Originality is the obsession of ambitious talent. Contemptible from early on and insufferable in the young. I will never lay claim to hearing my own voice in my work. If I knew what that was, what infinite boredom and repetition would lie ahead, I would fall asleep at its sound. What keeps me awake is tribute—to the dead, who to me are not dead, but are at my elbow. All I ask is an approving nod from them, as Verrocchio may have nodded at Leonardo, his assistant, or was it vice versa?

LS: Hayden Carruth believes that in your poetry and in your cultural activities you manage to maintain a connection with the whole community. This is hard to prove, and it is not clear to me exactly what he refers to. Do you think it is your total contribution—i.e., your art, poetry, your founding the theater in Trinidad, your public readings, your articles, etc.—that he has in mind?

DW: My community, that of any twentieth century artist, is the world. I turn on the TV. A child is dead in Beirut. A child is dead in El Salvador. A woman lies sprawled in rubble, killed by men. Men, I would hope, have had it, as rulers. That is my 'whole community.'

LS: What do you think you have achieved in your drama? And in directing especially your own dramas? And what would you like to achieve with your dramatic production?

DW: I don't think I have achieved in my drama much more than a large and unsatisfying body of work. I have written about two dozen plays, many lost, many luckily forgotten, not one a big commercial hit, thank God; though I think I could endure it now. To list the successes apart from the failures would be to judge them on the wrong basis. At fifty-three I am still breaking my behind to write plays. And one gets no nearer; one only knows what didn't work last time. An estimate of my success in the theater would be based on reviews, and when were reviewers ever a judge of permanence?

LS: God does not play a very large part in your poetry, but I do recall some phrases, among them one in which you say, ''God put beast and spirit in all of us.''

DW: God must not play 'a very large part' in poetry because it is not for God to perform for the good of the poet. I am a believer, and my gratitude is to be honest by his gift. Poetry, in a way, is a quarrel with God, one which I imagine God understands.

The concept of evil is impenetrable, even to Milton, even to Blake. One surrenders to His will, as Dante has taught.

LS: Do you go so far as to claim that poetry is a divine gift?

DW: Yes, I do, however foolish this may sound. We lose religion, and we lose poetry. But how can religion ever be lost? Haven't the Communists learned that yet?

LS: You use satire and irony in places. How can one know that you do not get misunderstood? Does that happen? What are your views on satire and irony, please.

DW: I make no distinctions between satire and irony. I keep my vulgarity healthy by living in a 'backward' but hearty place, the Caribbean. There laughter is loud and ringing, weeping is wailing, everything is at the pitch it must have been with the early Greeks. Primal, even provincial tragedy, bawdy, vulgar, even cliché humor. Suppose Aristophanes had had good taste?

LS: Especially in *Another Life,* but also in other places, you employ Greek and Roman myths or allude to them, or to mythological names. Do you wish to elevate/upgrade the fictional environment by means of classical allusions, or simply to draw parallels, in addition to creating anonymity? Or are you perhaps attempting something entirely different?

DW: Many assume that we live in a world of myths which constantly are replaced with new myths.

LS: Which myths would you then want to do away with? And which ones do you endeavor to create?

DW: I believe myths are unkillable. Either man is a myth or a piece of dirt. I prefer the former view. Whatever happened before me is mine, the guilt is mine, the grandeur and the horror were mine. Roman, Greek, African, all mine, veined in me, more alive than marble, bleeding and drying up. Literature reopens wounds more deeply than history does. It also releases the force of joy.

My calling as a poet is votive, sacred, out-dated, if you will, but it was a cherished vow taken in my young dead father's name, and my life is to honor that vow. I believe this through all adversities. I have been blessed. I am lucky to have been born in the Caribbean at such a time.

An Interview with Nancy Schoenberger

Nancy Schoenberger / 1983

From *Threepenny Review,* Fall 1983, 16–17. Reprinted by permission of Nancy Schoenberger.

Derek Walcott was born in St. Lucia, West Indies, in 1930. He is the author of twelve books of poetry and several collections of plays, including *Dream on Monkey Mountain,* which won the Obie Award for Drama in 1971. His newest collection of poems, *Midsummer,* is due out this fall from Farrar, Straus & Giroux. The following interview took place in Boston shortly after the publication of *The Fortunate Traveller.*

Schoenberger: I want to ask you about the title of your collection of poems, *The Fortunate Traveller.* Earlier in your career you wrote, "The inevitable problem of the island artist is the choice of home or exile, self-realization or spiritual betrayal of one's country. Travel widens this breach." In light of that, is the title of your new book ironic, or is there a resolution involved in moving, as you do, from North to South and back to North?

Walcott: Well, the title of the book was really going to be *The Unfortunate Traveller.*

Schoenberger: That's quite a switch.

Walcott: Right. It's a title from Thomas Nashe about the plague. The irony is in the character in the title poem, in the sense that what he sees in his travels is misfortune. What he sees is plague and hunger and so on. He's fortunate in the sense that he can get out of it.

Schoenberger: But he carries that misfortune within—that global sorrow, that sense of responsibility and failure.

Walcott: Yes, but he can get out. There are a lot of people who have sympathy for Bangladesh and for famine, but they can leave. The people who are doomed are the people who are in the famine. But what I was really trying to do was to write a thriller in a few pages. Any writer from the colonies or the provinces or the outskirts of an

empire—if he is cut off, severed from his roots, politically or culturally, well, that's a pain I don't know because I don't have that
situation. I'm not a political exile. And "exile" is a good word, but
we use the word in a very romantic sense. By exile we only mean a
very extended vacation, in a sense.

Schoenberger: But what is meant is that inability to return home;
your homeland is denied you.

Walcott: But then there is the Wordsworthian sense that you don't
return to what you once were, so even if you are home, you are not
back to what you were.

Schoenberger: You're a stranger in your own land.

Walcott: No, it's just that you have grown up, or the land has grown
up differently, so you don't really connect. If one is leaving a society
like Russia or Poland where the regime is definable or the background
against which you stand is delineated—the background stays the
same. In the Caribbean you are a part of the growth of that background—for me, anyway, and for V. S. Naipaul, though Naipaul
makes a career out of his severance: "O, I am severed from my
roots!"

Schoenberger: But he is not a true exile . . .

Walcott: He can go back. Joyce uses the word "exile" too. But in a
sense Joyce is not really an exile. He is an exile from Ireland in a
mental sense. He found Ireland too provincial, too tiring, too Catholic,
too hidebound. In that sense he is an exile, and that may be a deep
sense. But the political reality of an Irishman living in Paris or Trieste
or Zurich—well, there's a difference. I know I need to go back to
Trinidad, not purely for my family (my children are here now), but I
still feel I have to go back to Trinidad regularly. There are certain
things that are inexplicable in terms of the strength and pull of longing,
and these become simpler as you get older: one of these is the taste
of food, cooking, the taste of a particular dish, a fruit—

Schoenberger: I know what you mean. Certain scents, smells, can
overwhelmingly remind you of your childhood—

Walcott: Yes, and other simple things, like, for me, the sea. For
other people, something equally simple. When I was young I used to
read poems about exile or poems about dislocation. The word "exile"
used to mean to me the political definition of being separated from
your country. I didn't understand the profundity of the punishment

because I did not understand at that time—being too young—that what they were writing about was what they were missing. It's like love. When somebody you love leaves you, there's the absence of that person, and that is heartbreaking, but when you finally cry it's because you've touched something—some object—that immediately detonates all this flooding of feeling—simply by the touch of an object. It's like Proust's Madeleine. To go back is to renourish that.

Schoenberger: In an autobiographical essay in *Antaeus* you talk about the opposite feeling: the youthful desire to leave home, to leave the country, to escape, in fact.

Walcott: I have to quote Joyce again, because there can only be a reconciliation when there has been a sundering. The mood to sunder is just a process of growth. One has to sever oneself from the authority of one's parents. In the same way a writer has to do this, to delineate himself from his background, so he can be *in* it distinctly, so he can be outlined within that background.

Still, there remains a separation—he's not blended into that background, and that may be merely in terms of psychic resolution. It's like a Greek tragedy in which there are three things: the beginning, which is the threat and the sin is committed; the middle, which is the torment; and the third, which is the reconciliation. Think of Oedipus. The incomplete writer does not do the third act. He does not come back. I think that's what happened to Hemingway. There are two acts, really, and had he returned spiritually to America he would have been a greater writer—he is a great writer, but he would have been even greater had he come back to make the final link in the circle.

Now this can be done without the physical presence. This is what Pasternak did: it's the reaffirmation. It's stronger and stronger in Joseph Brodsky's poetry, and it's not just nostalgia. It's that final segment of the circle that makes the thing complete.

Schoenberger: Could that return be a recreation of the homeland in the interior landscape?

Walcott: Yes, because it's a spiritual return. What is achieved when a writer reaches that stage is, first, a bleakness beyond nostalgia, and then a radiant serenity. It's a superior feeling. I think of Dante and Sophocles, or Shakespeare's *The Tempest:* at the end of it there's a kind of quiet light, a kind of powerful radiance, very serene and very clear, which is the completion of a return, and not the senility of a return to a second childhood.

Schoenberger: You're talking about an acceptance of loss—

Walcott: It's what Oedipus achieves at the end of *Oedipus at Colonus:* a resignation that is not surrender, a resignation that has radiance in it.

Schoenberger: In much of your work you try to reconcile your devotion to literature and your awareness of political and social realities. For example, in "The Fortunate Traveller" (the title poem) you juxtapose your love of Jacobean drama with an image of children fighting with rats for green meat.

Walcott: First, it's very hard for people to understand my love of the Jacobean—it's not from a distance. If you hear a guy from Barbados, or Jamaica, speaking English, and you listen to that speech, you hear seventeenth-century constructions. I once heard in *Henry V* a soldier speaking in a Yorkshire dialect and it sounded like pure Barbadian speech. If I heard this in Kansas, I would say this guy is speaking Shakespearean. I am in Trinidad; I say this guy is speaking Barbadian. So, my relationship to what's called Jacobean by critics is not nostalgia. I have known the simplest people and have heard them talk and I'm certain the constructions are the same. I am writing with a specific sound of speech that is not extravagant but just as eccentric in its composition, but it isn't eccentric to me.

Schoenberger: But going back to the initial charge of poetry being removed from the harsher realities of life. For example, Amiri Baraka (LeRoi Jones) was teaching at Columbia the same time that you were. I think of him as a writer who puts his politics before his love of language. I think you do the opposite—

Walcott: You're making a distinction I don't accept. I mean, for the first thing, for a poet, literature is stronger than life. Life is less than literature. Otherwise, you would not work for the immortality of the poem. There is no less an end than that. And by the immortality of the poem that is simply what depends on the memory of one's race—and then maybe if it's good enough it enters the memory of the race of the whole language and then the memory of the world. Everybody knows Homer regardless of what language one speaks. One attempts to remember Dante, even in the original language. Modesty keeps us from talking about this!

Schoenberger: The Argentinian poet Jorge Luis Borges says the same thing: he doesn't care if his name disappears after his death, if only something he has written—a fable, a phrase even—enters the language and lives on after him.

Walcott: Exactly. But to go back. The separation of life and literature. Are you talking about literature as an alternative? Or literature as immortality, which is stronger than life?

Schoenberger: In your play *Remembrance,* Jordan has a great love of British culture, but the sense of betrayal comes in when he looks back with nostalgia on British rule of Trinidad—

Walcott: That's not nostalgia. That's the point. It's belief. If a Catholic living in a communist country celebrates the Mass, he doesn't celebrate out of nostalgia. He's enacting what he believes in.

Schoenberger: But Jordan opens himself up to the charges of being a traitor to free Trinidad—

Walcott: Certainly. And the Catholic priest in a totalitarian country lays himself open to those charges.

Schoenberger: So when you write about these subjects, it's clear what side you're on.

Walcott: This is the question, really: I write a poem, and people come up to me and say, "I can't understand your poetry." Fine. What I'm interested in is whether or not another poet believes what I'm saying. For one to understand poetry completely, one has to become a poet. But that requires an effort so intense and demands so wide an education that people abandon it. It's taking on too much! But that's all right, too. You know, the comprehension of poetry is not *limited* to poets because there *is* a wide audience for poetry—I believe there is.

Schoenberger: So you became a poet more out of commitment to language than because there were burning issues you wanted to write about.

Walcott: People ask, how can you—or V. S. Naipaul—or a lot of other writers I know—come from such a backward country? It's related to the idea of language as sophistication and culture. The reality of it is that it's not possible to produce a good writer out of the blue. Writers come out of the intelligence of the country.

Schoenberger: You mean there already has to be an existing tradition.

Walcott: There are predecessors—there's nothing without a predecessor in literature, no matter how minimal. Naipaul may have become a writer because his father was a writer. My father also wrote, and so forth. It's ancestral in the best sense. There is also the *aural* experience of the writer: if the speech were not interesting—if the convolutions, the dictions, the novelty and the sounds were not alive, it would not produce writers.

Schoenberger: And it is very much alive. In a recent *Paris Review* interview, Carlos Fuentes talks about the culture of the Caribbean, which includes Faulkner, Carpentier, García Márquez, Aimée Cesaire, and Derek Walcott—"a trilingual culture in and around the whirlpool of the Baroque, which is the Caribbean, the Gulf of Mexico. Think of Jean Rhys's *Wide Sargasso Sea*."

Walcott: The company is very flattering. I think what Fuentes means by the Baroque is not in the decadent sense that one uses in art history, "baroque" as "excess," but in the best sense of the Baroque.

Schoenberger: He talks about the literature as being self-allusive, using cyclical rather than linear time—

Walcott: In a sense, the Caribbean has a stagnancy about it. Well, that stagnancy is very fertilizing. You can look at stagnancy and say, well, this is a pool or a pond or what you can see is a whole succession of detonating organisms that are quite surprising—the fertility of that apparently stagnant pool. Now, the point is that if this pond doesn't have an outlet, it stinks. But there are outlets. If you look at the Caribbean, there are outlets: the Panama Canal on the Atlantic, for example. That pond is moving water. But the stillness of it is within the Caribbean basin. In that basin, genuinely—without any ghetto romanticizing about mixed cultures—there is a breeding of cultural organisms going on at a rapid pace.

Schoenberger: So "derivative" becomes the critical remark—

Walcott: And everything in nature is derivative.

Schoenberger: I'm curious about Faulkner being included in that group.

Walcott: It's like Mississippi soil: it's thick and rich and things grow in it very fast. The shape of what grows out of it is convoluted, like the plants of the Caribbean. They're Baroque plants. I mean, the landscape has been criticized by writers coming down to the Carib-

bean and feeling it out of control, excessive . . . it's Nature itself
saying, well, you've done pretty well up North but here you've gotten
a little extravagant. It's an aesthetic based on vegetation.

Schoenberger: You've often referred to V. S. Naipaul's remark that
Trinidad is "a country that has denied itself heroes." Do you think of
yourself as a writer who has set out to provide the heroes, the myths,
etc., of the West Indies?

Walcott: That would be impossible to do. You cannot create a
mythology, and there's no culture that doesn't have a mythology—
that's taking away the vital organs of a country. What he means by
that—what I hope he means—is that these things are not being
recorded in terms of a literature. There are a number of mythologies
that survive in the Caribbean from the Chinese, the Lebanese, the
Indian, the African, and so on. If he means that there is a kind of
chemical deficiency in the society and I'm artificially pumping that
kind of adrenalin into the society—well, that is not the case.

Schoenberger: Some of your poems have epic proportions, such as
"The Schooner Flight."

Walcott: The only epical thing in "The Schooner Flight" is the
width of the sea, for which I'm not responsible. It's not my intention
to have a hero who takes on battles, who becomes an emblematic
figure. The fact is, critics are looking for a repetition of the past; one
wants a sort of *Iliad* in blackface. Writers won't do that. What's new
about a classic is that it stays new. You have your debts to your
predecessors; your acknowledgment is a votive acknowledgment.
Seamus Heaney recognized in a review that "The Schooner Flight"
opens like *Piers Plowman*. You put that there deliberately: "as this
reminded me of that, so let it remind you also."

Schoenberger: You're a successful playwright as well as a poet.
There are not many writers today who are doing both, though you are
a part of a long tradition of poet/playwrights: Eliot, Brecht, Dryden,
Marlow, Shakespeare. Is there a cross-fertilization that takes place?

Walcott: I have a belief that a poet is instinctively closer to the
theater than a novelist or fiction writer because, structurally, the feel
of the poem is the feel of a play, or the feel of a play is like a very
large poem . . . they both have the same kind of chording. It's a little
amazing to me that more poets aren't attracted to the theater. As you

know, I tried doing some of that when I was teaching in the Writing Program at Columbia.

Schoenberger: Was that a successful experiment?

Walcott: What was happening there was astonishing to the poets because they had to get down to something that had colloquial power, that was casual and true and speakable. It works both ways: the lyric impulse generally needs to be fortified by dramatic experience, and the reverse should be true.

Schoenberger: When an actor speaks your lines, you have to edit out whatever sounds unnatural—

Walcott: Not only that. Chekhov is natural and Shakespeare is unnatural, in the sound of the lines. It isn't purely the naturalistic manner—it's the choice of the tone. American diction in poetry has acquired the casual force of exchange—sometimes in most poems it really is dramatized speech, stage diction, that comes out of a soliloquy or biography. I'm saying that *that* colloquial power is ready to be used in theater.

Schoenberger: The disturbing thing about poetry today is that it has become a very insular activity—a poet writes in a garret-like situation and then hopes to publish in that vast land of the small press magazines that you can disappear into forever . . . and he teaches, and often those are the only professional experiences the poet seems to have, which doesn't do poetry or poets any good at all.

Walcott: It's not that poetry is an all-consuming thing. You can work hard at it but you can't produce a poem every day. There are other aspects of a poet's life that also require fulfillment. There's this division that happens in American literature, but I think there are very few people with only one talent. Shakespeare was an actor, Molière was an actor, Brecht was a director. In this country, people do a certain job and get very good at that job and get categorized as being only able to do that. And if you cross over and do more than one thing, people are astonished.

Not only that, but a poem here is treated as if it were something that was really private and done in a garret—the garret equivalent being, well, chap-books or something—and the very modesty of the poem tends to make a lot of contemporary American poetry very mousy and reserved. The public access is there—I give a lot of readings across the country and the audiences are there—but it has to do with recitation as an idea; it has to do with memory and meter.

Schoenberger: Obviously it's different in Russia, where the recitation of poetry is a public event.

Walcott: One has it here, the public side, but that kind of attitude within poetry itself—that minimal withdrawing, taciturn kind of composition—begins to wither memory. In a sense, when one reads a poem out loud, one is, first of all, presenting a poem to an audience, and secondly, one is also asking them to memorize it.

Schoenberger: So the contemporary poem is no longer memorizable. Donald Justice said that most contemporary poetry is occasional poetry from which the occasion has been removed. The reader is not aware of what that occasion is—it remains private.

Walcott: Yes.

Schoenberger: What poets do you read of your contemporaries? Whom do you read for ideas or inspiration?

Walcott: I read for benign jealousy. The person I read most for benign jealousy—and who I'm very close to—is Joseph Brodsky. The people I enjoy, and enjoyment is—

Schoenberger: Different from benign jealousy? I'd hate to think you didn't *enjoy* reading Brodsky . . .

Walcott: *(laughter)* Oh no. Let's see, I read Seamus Heaney. One poet in English who gives me a steady delight is Philip Larkin. I go back to him again and again. Sadly, the American voice is dominated by careerism. It's too belligerent, too "shove it, man, I'm the big guy around here." To put it pretentiously, it's offensive to the Muse, to any Muse.

The Art of Poetry XXXVII: Derek Walcott

Edward Hirsch / 1985

From *The Paris Review,* 101 (Winter 1986), 196–230. Reprinted by permission of *The Paris Review.*

I went to visit Derek Walcott on his home island of St. Lucia in mid-June, 1985. St. Lucia is one of the four Windward Islands in the eastern Caribbean, a small mountainous island which faces the Atlantic Ocean on one side and the Caribbean Sea on the other. For a week Walcott and I stayed in adjacent bungalows, called "Hunt's Beach Cottages," just a few miles from the harbor city of Castries where he was born and raised. Outside of our large, mildly ramshackle cottages, a few stone tables and chairs were cemented into a strip of grass; beyond was a row of coconut trees and then, just a few yards away, what Walcott has called "the theater of the sea," the Caribbean. One is always aware of the sea in St. Lucia—an inescapable natural presence which has deeply affected Walcott's sense of being an islander, a new world poet.

Derek Walcott was born in 1930. He was educated at St. Mary's College in St. Lucia and at the University of the West Indies in Jamaica. For many years he lived in Trinidad—he still spends most of his summers there—where from 1959 to 1976 he directed the Trinidad Theatre Workshop. Since then he has spent much of his time in the United States, living first in New York City and more recently in Boston. Currently, he holds a MacArthur Fellowship and teaches at Boston University. Walcott's first three booklets—*25 Poems* (1948), *Epitaph for the Young* (1949), and *Poems* (1951)—were privately printed in the West Indies. His mature work begins with *In a Green Night: Poems 1948–1960* (1962) and *Selected Poems* (1964). Since then he has published seven individual poetry books: *The Castaway* (1965), *The Gulf* (1969), the book-length autobiographical poem *Another Life* (1973), *Sea Grapes* (1976), *The Star-Apple Kingdom* (1979), *The Fortunate Traveller* (1981) and *Midsummer* (1984). At the time of this interview Walcott was looking forward to the publication of his *Collected Poems*—which appeared in the winter of 1986. Considering himself equally a poet and a playwright, Walcott has also published three books of plays in America: *Dream on Monkey Mountain and Other Plays* (1970), *The Joker of Seville and O Babylon!* (1978), and *Remembrance and Pantomime: Two Plays* (1980).

To live next door to Walcott, even for a week, is to understand how he has managed to be so productive over the years. A prodigious worker, he often starts at about 4:30 in the morning and continues until he has done a four or five hour stint—by the time most people are getting up for the day. On a small easel next to a small blue portable typewriter, he had recently done a pencil drawing of his wife, Norline, and a couple of new watercolors to serve as storyboards for a film version of *Pantomime* (he is doing the film script); he had also just finished the draft of an original screenplay about a steel band, as well as an extended essay about the Grenada invasion (to be called "Good Old Heart of Darkness"), and a new manuscript of poems, *The Arkansas Testament* (Spring, 1987). At the time of this interview the cuttings for two more films were all but complete: a film version of his play, *Haitian Earth* (which he had produced in St. Lucia the previous year), and a documentary film about Hart Crane for public television. At times one gets the impression that the poetry for which he is primarily known has had to be squeezed between all his other projects.

And yet while I was in St. Lucia, most of Walcott's other activities were suspended as he worked on a new poem, "The Light of the World." It is a homecoming poem, a narrative lyric about returning to Castries. The poem is set on a transport—what we would call a mini-bus—and characterizes the poet's sense of feeling both separated from, and connected to, the life of the people around him. Once more he is struck by the grace as well as the difficult poverty of his people; he reexperiences the beauty of St. Lucian women and feels the weight of their daily lives. "The Light of the World" is a large poem of guilt and expiation, and it gives a good sense of Walcott's inner feelings during the time of our interview.

Our conversation took place over three days—beginning in the late afternoon or early evening and continuing until dark. We talked at the table and chairs outside our cottages where we could hear the wind in the coconut trees and the waves breaking on the shore. A compact man in his mid-fifties, Walcott was still dressed from his afternoon on the beach—barefoot, a pair of brown beach trunks and a thin cotton shirt. Often he kept a striped beach towel draped around his shoulders, a white flour-sack beach hat pushed forward jauntily on his head. He seemed always to be either smoking or about to start.

Interviewer: I'd like to begin by asking you to talk about your family background. In many ways it was atypical for St. Lucia. For example, you were raised as a Methodist on a primarily Catholic island. Your family also seems to have been unusually oriented toward the arts.

Derek Walcott: My family background really only consists of my mother. She was a widow. My father died quite young; he must have been thirty-one. Then there was my twin brother and my sister. We had two aunts as well, my father's sisters. But the immediate family consisted of my mother, my brother, my sister, and me. I remember from very early childhood my mother, who was a teacher, reciting a lot around the house. I remember coming across drawings that my father had done, poems that he had written, watercolors that were hanging in our living room—his original watercolors—and a terrific series of books: a lot of Dickens, Scott, quite a lot of poetry. There was also an old victrola with a lot of classical records. And so my family always had this interest in the arts. Coming from a Methodist minority in a French Catholic island, we also felt a little beleaguered. The Catholicism propounded by the French provincial priests in St. Lucia was a very hide-bound, prejudiced, medieval, almost hounding kind of Catholicism. The doctrine that was taught assigned all Protestants to limbo. So we felt defensive about our position. This never came to a head, but we did feel we had to stay close together. It was good for me too, to be able to ask questions as a Protestant, to question large authority. Nobody in my generation at my age would dare question the complete and absolute authority of the church. Even into sixth form, my school friends and I used to have some terrific arguments about religious doctrine. It was a good thing. I think young writers ought to be heretical.

Interviewer: In an essay called "Leaving School" you suggest that the artifacts of your father's twin avocations, poetry and painting, made your own sense of vocation seem inevitable. Would you describe his creative work and how it affected you?

Walcott: My mother, who is nearly ninety now, still talks continually about my father. All my life I've been aware of her grief about his absence and her strong pride in his conduct. He was very young when he died of mastoiditis, which is an ear infection. Medicine in St. Lucia in those days was crude or very minimal; I know he had to go to Barbados for operations. I don't remember the death or anything like that, but I always felt his presence because of the paintings that he did. He had a self-portrait in watercolor in an oval frame next to a portrait of my mother, an oil that was very good for an amateur painter. I remember once coming across a backcloth of a very ordi-

nary kind of moonlight scene that he had painted for some number
that was going to be done by a group of people who did concerts and
recitations and stuff like that. So that was always there. Now that
didn't make me a morose, morbid child. Rather, in a sense, it gave
me a kind of impetus and a strong sense of continuity. I felt that what
had been cut off in him somehow was an extension that I was continuing.

Interviewer: When did you first discover his poems?

Walcott: The poems I'm talking about are not a collection. I remember a couple of funny lyrics that were done in a southern American
dialect for some show he was probably presenting. They were witty
little satirical things. I can't remember any poems of a serious nature.
I remember more of his art work. I remember a fine watercolor copy
of Millet's "The Gleaners" which we had in the living room. The
original is an oil painting and even now I am aware of the delicacy of
that copy. He had a delicate sense of watercolor. Later on I discovered that my friend Harold Simmons, who was a professional painter,
evidently was encouraged by my father to be a painter. So there's
always this continuity in my association with people who knew him
and people who were very proud to be his friend. My mother would
tell us that, and that's what I felt.

Interviewer: Your book-length autobiographical poem, *Another
Life*, makes it clear that two painters were crucial to your development: your mentor Harold Simmons, called Harry in the poem, and
your friend Dunstan St. Omer, renamed Gregorias. Would you talk
about their importance to you?

Walcott: Harry taught us. He had paints, he had music in his studio,
and he was evidently a good friend of my father's. When he found out
that we liked painting, he invited about four or five of us to come up
to his studio and sit out on his veranda. He gave us equipment and
told us to draw. Now that may seem very ordinary in a city, in another
place, but in a very small, poor country like St. Lucia it was extraordinary. He encouraged us to spend our Saturday afternoons painting;
he surrounded us with examples of his own painting. Just to let us be
there and to have the ambience of his books, his music, his own
supervision and the stillness and dedication that his life meant in that
studio was a terrific example. The influence was not so much technical. Of course, I picked up a few things from him in terms of

technique: how to do a good sky, how to water the paper, how to circle it, how to draw properly and concentrate on it, and all of that. But there were other things apart from the drawing. Mostly, it was the model of the man as a professional artist that was the example. After a while, the younger guys dropped out of the drawing thing and Dunstan St. Omer and I were left. We used to go out and paint together. We discovered it at the same time.

Interviewer: Did you have a favorite painter then?

Walcott: The painter I really thought I could learn from was Cézanne—some sort of resemblance to oranges and greens and browns of the dry season in St. Lucia. I used to look across from the roof towards Vigie—the barracks were there and I'd see the pale orange roofs and the brickwork and the screen of trees and the cliff and the very flat blue and think a lot of Cézanne. Maybe because of the rigidity of the cubes and the verticals and so on. It's as if he knew the St. Lucian landscape—you could see his painting happening there. There were other painters of course, like Giorgione, but I think it gave me a lot of strength to think of Cézanne when I was painting.

Interviewer: What would you say about the epiphanic experience described in *Another Life,* which seems to have confirmed your destiny as a poet and sealed a bond to your native island?

Walcott: There are some things people avoid saying in interviews because they sound pompous or sentimental or too mystical. I have never separated the writing of poetry from prayer. I have grown up believing it is a vocation, a religious vocation. What I described in *Another Life*—about being on the hill and feeling the sort of dissolution that happened—is a frequent experience in a younger writer. I felt this sweetness of melancholy, of a sense of mortality, or rather of immortality, a sense of gratitude both for what you feel is a gift and for the beauty of the earth, the beauty of life around us. When that's forceful in a young writer, it can make you cry. It's just clear tears; it's not grimacing or being contorted, it's just a flow that happens. The body feels it is melting into what it has seen. This continues in the poet. It may be repressed in some way, but I think we continue in all our lives to have that sense of melting, of the "I" not being important. That is the ecstasy. It doesn't happen as much when you get older. There's that wonderful passage in Traherne where he talks about seeing the children as moving jewels until they learn the dirty devices of the world. It's not *that* mystic. Ultimately, it's what Yeats says: "Such a sweetness flows into the breast that we laugh at everything and everything we look upon is blessed." That's always there. It's a benediction, a transference. It's gratitude, really. The more of that a poet keeps, the more genuine his nature. I've always felt that sense of gratitude. I've never felt equal to it in terms of my writing, but I've never felt that I was ever less than that. And so in that particular passage in *Another Life* I was recording a particular moment.

Interviewer: How do you write? In regard to your equation of poetry and prayer, is the writing ritualized in any way?

Walcott: I don't know how many writers are willing to confess to their private preparatory rituals before they get down to putting something on paper. But I imagine that all artists and all writers in that moment before they begin their working day or working night have that area between beginning and preparation, and however brief it is, there is something about it votive and humble and in a sense ritualistic. Individual writers have different postures, different stances, even different physical attitudes as they stand or sit over their blank paper, and in a sense, without doing it, they are crossing themselves; I mean, it's like the habit of Catholics going into water: you cross yourself before you go in. Any serious attempt to try to do something worthwhile *is* ritualistic. I haven't noticed what my own devices are. But I do know that if one thinks a poem is coming on—in spite of the noise of the typewriter, or the traffic outside the window, or whatever—you do make a retreat, a withdrawal into some kind of silence that cuts out everything around you. What you're taking on is really not a renewal of your identity but actually a renewal of your *anonymity* so that what's in front of you becomes more important than what you are. Equally—and it may be a little pretentious-sounding to say it—sometimes if I feel that I have done good work I do pray, I do say thanks. It isn't often, of course. I don't do it every day. I'm not a monk, but if something does happen I say thanks because I feel that it is really a piece of luck, a kind of fleeting grace that has happened to one. Between the beginning and the ending and the actual composition that goes on, there is a kind of trance that you hope to enter where every aspect of your intellect is functioning simultaneously for the progress of the composition. But there is no way you can induce that trance.

Lately, I find myself getting up earlier, which may be a sign of late middle-age. It worries me a bit. I guess this is part of the ritual: I go and make a cup of coffee, put on the kettle, and have a cigarette. By now I'm not too sure if out of habit I'm getting up for the coffee rather than to write. I may be getting up that early to smoke, not really to write.

Interviewer: What time is this?

Walcott: It can vary. Sometimes it's as early as half-past three, which is, you know, not too nice. The average time would be about five. It depends on how well I'm sleeping. But that hour, that whole time of day, is wonderful in the Caribbean. I love the cool darkness and the joy and splendor of the sunrise coming up. I guess I would say, especially in the location of where I am, the early dark and the sunrise, and being up with the coffee and with whatever you're working on, is a very ritualistic thing. I'd even go further and say it's a religious thing. It has its instruments and its surroundings. And you can feel your own spirit waking.

Interviewer: Recently, I heard you say that you were deeply formed by Methodism. How?

Walcott: In a private way, I think I still have a very simple, straightforward foursquare Methodism in me. I admire the quiet, pragmatic reason that is there in a faith like Methodism, which is a very practical thing of conduct. I'm not talking about a fanatical fundamentalism. I suppose the best word for it is "decency." Decency and understanding are what I've learned from being a Methodist. Always, one was responsible to God for one's inner conduct and not to any immense hierarchy of angels and saints. In a way I think I tried to say that in some earlier poems. There's also a very strong sense of carpentry in Protestantism, in making things simply and in a utilitarian way. At this period of my life and work, I think of myself in a way as a carpenter, as one making frames, simply and well. I'm working a lot in quatrains, or I have been, and I feel that there is something in that that *is* very ordinary, you know, without any mystique. I'm trying to get rid of the mystique as much as possible. And so I find myself wanting to write very simply cut, very contracted, very speakable and very challenging quatrains in rhymes.

Any other shape seems ornate, an elaboration on that essential cube that really is the poem. So we can then say the craft is as ritualistic as that of a carpenter putting down his plane and measuring his stanzas and setting them squarely. And the frame becomes more important than the carpenter.

Interviewer: *Another Life* suggests that eventually you gave up painting as a vocation and decided to concentrate on poetry. Recently, though, you seem to be at work on your watercolors again. What happened?

Walcott: What I tried to say in *Another Life* is that the act of painting is not an intellectual act dictated by reason. It is an act that is swept very physically by the sensuality of the brushstroke. I've always felt that some kind of intellect, some kind of preordering, some kind of criticism of the thing before it is done, has always interfered with my ability to do a painting. I am in fairly continual practice. I think I'm getting adept at watercolor. I'm less mucky. I think I could do a reasonable oil painting. I could probably, if I really set out, be a fairly good painter. I can approach the sensuality. I know how it feels, but for me there is just no completion. I'm content to be a moderately good watercolorist. But I'm not content to be a moderately good poet. That's a very different thing.

Interviewer: Am I correct that you published your first poem, "The Voice of St. Lucia," at the precocious age of fourteen? I've read that the poem stirred up a considerable local controversy.

Walcott: I wrote a poem talking about learning about God through nature and not through the church. The poem was Miltonic and posed nature as a way to learn. I sent it to the local papers and it was printed. Of course, to see your work in print for any younger writer is a great kick. And then the paper printed a letter in which a priest replied (in verse!) stating that what I was saying was blasphemous and that the proper place to find God was in church. For a young boy to get that sort of response from a mature older man, a priest who was an Englishman, and to be accused of blasphemy was a shock. What was a more chastising thing was that the response was in verse. The point of course was to show me that he was also capable of writing verse. He did his in couplets and mine was in blank verse. I would imagine if I looked at both now that mine was better.

Interviewer: Most American and English readers think of *In a Green*

Night as your first book. Before you published abroad, however, you had already printed three booklets at your own expense in the West Indies. How did you come to publish the first one, *25 Poems*?

Walcott: I used to write every day in an exercise book, and when I first wrote I wrote with great originality. I just wrote as hard and as well as I felt. I remember the great elation and release I felt, a sort of hooking on to a thing, when I read Auden, Eliot, and everyone. One day I would write like Spender, another day I would write like Dylan Thomas. When I felt I had enough poems that I liked, I wanted to see them in print. We had no publishing house in St. Lucia or in the Caribbean. There was a Faber collection of books that had come out with poets like Eliot and Auden, and I liked the type-face and how the books looked. I thought, "I want to have a book like that." So I selected a collection of twenty-five of them and thought, "Well, these will look good because they'll look like they came from abroad; they'll look like a published book." I went to my mother and said, "I'd like to publish a book of poems, and I think it's going to cost me two hundred dollars." She was just a seamstress and a schoolteacher, and I remember her being very upset because she wanted to do it. Somehow she got it;—a lot of money for a woman to have found on her salary. She gave it to me, and I sent off to Trinidad and had the book printed. When the books came back I would sell them to friends. I made the money back. In terms of seeing a book in print, the only way I could have done it was to publish it myself.

Interviewer: Frank Collymore wrote a very appreciative essay about your early poetry. That must have been a heady experience for a nineteen year-old. After all, he was the editor of the groundbreaking Caribbean literary magazine, *Bim,* a man that Edward Braithwaite once called "the greatest of West Indian literary godfathers."

Walcott: Frank Collymore was an absolute saint. I got to know him through Harry Simmons. I have never met a more benign, gentle, considerate, selfless person. I'll never forget the whole experience of going over to Barbados and meeting him. To be treated at that age by a much older man with such care and love and so on was wonderful. He treated George Lamming the same way. There are people like that, people who love other people, love them for their work and what it is. He was not by any means a patronizing man. He never treated you as if he were a schoolmaster doing you good. I had great fortune when I was young in being treated like that by people, by people much older than I was who treated me, who treated my mind, as if I were equal to them. He was the best example of that.

Interviewer: You once described yourself at nineteen as "an elated, exuberant poet madly in love with English" and said that as a young writer you viewed yourself as legitimately prolonging "the mighty line" of Marlowe and Milton. Will you talk about that sense of yourself?

Walcott: I come from a place that likes grandeur; it likes large gestures; it is not inhibited by flourish; it is a rhetorical society; it is a society of physical performance; it is a society of style. The highest achievement of style is rhetoric, as it is in speech and performance. It isn't a modest society. A performer in the Caribbean has to perform with the right flourish. A Calypsonian performer is equivalent to a bullfighter in the ring. He has to come over. He can write the wittiest Calypso, but if he's going to deliver it, he has to deliver it well, and he has to hit the audience with whatever technique he has. Modesty is not possible in performance in the Caribbean, and that's wonderful. It's better to be large and to make huge gestures than to be modest and do tiptoeing types of presentations of oneself. Even if it's a private platform, it is a platform. The voice does go up in a poem. It is an address, even if it is to oneself. And the greatest address is in the rhetoric. I grew up in a place in which if you learned poetry, you shouted it out. Boys would scream it out and perform it and do it and flourish it. If you wanted to approximate that thunder or that power of speech, it couldn't be done by a little modest voice in which you muttered something to someone else. I came out of that society of the huge gesture. And literature is like that, I mean *theatrical* literature is like that, whether it's Greek or whatever. The recitation element in poetry is one I hope I never lose because it's an essential part of the voice being asked to perform. If we have poets we're really asking them, "Okay, tell me a poem." Generally the implication is, "Mutter me a poem." I'm not in that group.

Interviewer: There is a confident, fiery sense of privilege in your early work. In a recent poem, *Midsummer,* you write "Forty years gone, in my island childhood, I felt that/the gift of poetry had made me one of the chosen,/that all experience was kindling to the fire of the Muse."

Walcott: I never thought of my gift—I have to say "my gift" because I believe it is a gift—as anything that I did completely on my own. I have felt from my boyhood that I had one function and that was somehow to articulate, not my own experience, but what I saw around me. From the time I was a child I knew it was beautiful. If you go to a peak anywhere in St. Lucia, you feel a simultaneous newness and sense of timelessness at the same time—the presence of where you are. It's a primal thing and it has always been that way. At the same time I knew that the poor people around me were not beautiful in the romantic sense of being colorful people to paint or to write about. I lived, I have seen them and I have seen things that I don't need to go far to see. I felt that that was what I would write about. That's what I felt my job was. It's something that other writers have said in their own way, even if it sounds arrogant. Yeats has said it; Joyce has said it. It's amazing Joyce could say that he wants to write for his race, meaning the Irish. You'd think that Joyce would have a larger, more continental kind of mind, but Joyce continued insisting on his provinciality at the same time he had the most universal mind since Shakespeare. What we can do as poets in terms of our honesty is simply to write within the immediate perimeter of not more than twenty miles really.

Interviewer: How does your sense of discovery of new subject matter integrate with the formal elements in your work?

Walcott: One of the things that people have to look at in West Indian literature is this: that what we were deprived of was also our privilege. There was a great joy in making a world which so far, up to then, had been undefined. And yet the imagination wants its limits and delights in its limits. It finds its freedom in the definition of those limits. In a sense, you want to give more symmetry to lives that have been undefined. My generation of West Indian writers has felt such a powerful elation at having the privilege of writing about places and people for the first time and, simultaneously, having behind them the tradition of knowing how well it can be done—by a Defoe, a Dickens, a Richardson. Our world made us yearn for structure as opposed to wishing to break away from it because there was no burden, no excess of literature in our heads. It was all new.

Interviewer: Well, then how do you see yourself in terms of the great tradition of poetry in the English language?

Walcott: I don't. I am primarily, absolutely a Caribbean writer. The English language is nobody's special property. It is the property of the imagination: it is the property of the language itself. I have never felt inhibited in trying to write as well as the greatest English poets. Now that has led to a lot of provincial criticism: the Caribbean critic may say, "You are trying to be English," and the English critic may say, "Welcome to the club." These are two provincial statements at either end of the spectrum. It's not a matter of trying to be English. I am obviously a Caribbean poet. I yearn for the company of better Caribbean poets, quite frankly. I feel a little lonely. I don't see what I thought might have happened—a stronger energy, a stronger discipline, and a stronger drive in Caribbean poetry. That may be because the Caribbean is more musical: every culture has its particular emphasis and obviously the Caribbean's poetry, talent, and genius is in its music. But then again the modern Caribbean is a very young thing. I consider myself at the beginning, rather than at the end, of a tradition.

Interviewer: Would you say that your relationship to English poetry has changed over the years? As your work has progressed you seem to have increasingly affiliated yourself with a line of New World poets from Whitman through St. John Perse to Aimé Césaire and Pablo Neruda.

Walcott: Carlos Fuentes talked in a *Paris Review* interview about the essential Central American experience, which includes the whole basin of the Caribbean—that it is already a place of tremendous fertility. The whole new world experience here is shared by Márquez as it is by Borges, as it is still by American writers. In fact, too many American poets don't take on the scale of America. Not because we should write epics but because it seems to be our place to try to understand. In places that are yet undefined the energy comes with the knowledge that this has not yet been described, this has not yet been painted. This means that I'm standing here like a pioneer. I'm the first person to look at this mountain and try to write about it. I'm the first person to see this lagoon, this piece of land. Here I am with this enormous privilege of just being someone who can take up a brush. My generation of West Indian writers, following after C. L. R. James, all felt the thrill of the absolute sense of discovery. That energy is concomitant with being where we are; it's part of the whole idea of America. And by America, I mean from Alaska right down to Curaçao.

Interviewer: How do you respond to V. S. Naipaul's repeated assertion—borrowed from Trollope—that "Nothing was created in the British West Indies"?

Walcott: Perhaps it should read that "Nothing was created *by the British* in the West Indies." Maybe that's the answer. The departure of the British required and still requires a great deal of endeavor, of repairing the psychological damage done by their laziness and by their indifference. The desolation of poverty that exists in the Caribbean can be very depressing. The only way that one can look at it and draw anything of value from it is to have a fantastic depth of strength and belief, not in the past but in the immediate future. And I think that whenever I come back here, however desolate and however despairing I see the conditions around me to be, I know that I have to draw on terrible reserves of conviction. To abandon that conviction is to betray your origins; it's to feel superior to your family, to your past. And I'm not capable of that.

Interviewer: Why is the figure of Robinson Crusoe so important to you?

Walcott: I wrote a poem called "The Castaway." I told my wife I was going to stay by myself for a weekend somewhere down in Trinidad. My wife agreed. I stayed in a beach house by myself and I wrote the poem there. I had an image of the West Indian artist as someone who was in a shipwrecked position. I'm not saying that's the origin of my Crusoe idea. But it's possible. The beaches around here are generally very empty—just you, the sea, and the vegetation around you, and you're very much by yourself. The poems I have written around the Crusoe theme vary. One of the more positive aspects of the Crusoe idea is that in a sense every race that has come to the Caribbean has been brought here under situations of servitude or rejection, and that is the metaphor of the shipwreck, I think. Then you look around you and you have to make your own tools. Whether that tool is a pen or a hammer, you are building in a situation that's Adamic; you are rebuilding not only from necessity but also with some idea that you will be here for a long time and with a sense of proprietorship as well. Very broadly that is what has interested me in it. There are other ironies, like the position of Friday as the one who is being civilized. Actually, the reverse happens. People who come out to the Caribbean from the cities and the continents go through a process of being recultured. What they encounter here, if they surrender to their seeing, has a lot to teach them, first of all the proven adaptability of races living next to each other, particularly in places like Trinidad and Jamaica. And then also in the erasure of the idea of history. To me there are always images of erasure in the Caribbean—in the surf which continually wipes the sand clean, in the fact that those huge clouds change so quickly. There is a continual sense of motion in the Caribbean—caused by the sea and the feeling that one is almost traveling through water and not stationary. The size of time is larger—a very different thing in the islands than in the cities. We don't live so much by the clock. If you have to be in a place where you create your own time, what you learn, I think, is a patience, a tolerance, how to make an artisan of yourself rather than being an artist.

Interviewer: Your recent play *Pantomime* explores the racial and economic side of the relationship between Crusoe and Friday. In the play, a white English hotel owner in Tobago proposes that he and his black handyman work up a satire on the Crusoe story for the entertainment of the guests. Is the play a parable about colonialism?

Walcott: The point of the play is very simple. There are two types. The prototypical Englishman is not supposed to show his grief publicly. He keeps a stiff upper lip. Emotion and passion are supposed to be things that a trueblood Englishman avoids. What the West Indian character does is to try to wear him down into confessing that he is capable of such emotion and there's nothing wrong in showing it. Some sort of catharsis is possible. That is the main point of the play. It's to take two types and put them together, put them in one arena and have that happen. I have never thought of it really as a play about racial conflict. When it's done in America, it becomes a very tense play because of the racial situation there. When it's done here, it doesn't have those deep historical overtones of real bitterness. I meant it to be basically a farce that might instruct. And the instruction is that we can't just contain our grief, that there's purgation in tears, that tears can renew. Of course, inside the play there's a point in which both characters have to confront the fact that one is white and one is black. They have to confront their history. But once that peak is passed, once the ritual of confrontation is over, then that's the beginning of the play. I've had people say they think the ending is corny, but generally that criticism has come when I'm in America. The idea of some reconciliation or some adaptability of being able to live together, that is sometimes rejected by people as being a facile solution. But I believe it's possible.

Interviewer: How would you differentiate your work of the middle and late sixties, *The Castaway* and *The Gulf,* from your previous writing?

Walcott: There's a vague period in any poet's life between thirty and forty that is crucial because you can either keep working in one direction, or you can look back on your earlier work as juvenilia, a nice thing to look at from a distance. You have to head toward being forty with a certain kind of mindset to try to recreate chaos so you can learn from it. Yet you also have the fear that your work really has been basically mediocre, a failure, predictable. You find yourself at a point at which you say, ah, so you have become exactly what you were afraid of becoming: this person, this writer, with a certain name and a certain thing expected of you, and you are fulfilling that mold. The later books attempt to work against the given identity. At this point I don't think they're deep enough in terms of their sense of sin. Their sense of guilt could be more profound. In a way a lot of these poems smooth over while seething underneath the surface. One can always put a sort of poster over the rough, you know. A smoothness of attitude over something that's basically quite null and chaotic and unsettling. A lot of the roughness is missing in these books, but then that dissatisfaction continues all one's life.

Interviewer: Would you talk about your experience in the Trinidad Theatre Workshop which you founded in 1959 and finally left in 1976? You once stated that you wanted to create a theater where someone could produce Shakespeare and sing Calypso with equal conviction. Did the idea succeed?

Walcott: Yes, I think I made that happen. The best West Indian actors are phenomenal. Most West Indian actors have gone to West Indian secondary schools. The classical training and reading they get there is pretty wide and impressive—a lot of Shakespeare, and all the great English writers. Once that happens people read much more widely than if they hadn't done the great poets. So most West Indian

actors have a familiarity with the classic theater of the English
language. They also have an accent, not an affected accent, but a
speech that is good diction. Some of the finest Shakespeare I have
ever heard was spoken by West Indian actors. The sound of Shakespeare is certainly not the sound we now hear in Shakespeare, that
androgynous BBC-type, high-tone thing. It's a coarse thing—a great
range between a wonderful vulgarity and a great refinement, and we
have that here. We have that vulgarity and we also have that refinement in terms of the diction. The West Indian actor has a great
rhetorical interest in language. In addition to that, the actor is like the
West Indian writer in that he is a new person: what he is articulating
has just begun to be defined. There's a sense of pioneering. For me
writing plays was even more exciting than working on poems because
it was a communal effort, people getting together and trying to find
things. When I won a fellowship to go to America in 1958, I wanted
to have, much as the Actors Studio did, a place where West Indian
actors, without belonging to any company, could just come together
and try and find out simple things such as how to talk like ourselves
without being affected or without being incoherent, how to treat
dialect as respectfully as if we were doing Shakespeare or Chekhov,
and what was our own inner psychology as individuals, in a people,
as part of a people. The first couple of years we had a very tough
time. Very few people would come. We didn't know what we were
doing; we just improvised and explored and tried things. I was
determined not to do a production until I thought we had some kind
of ensemble. I had no intention of forming a company. At that time,
all I wanted to do was to have the actors come and begin to work
together. It took a very long time. But eventually we did put on a play
and for about seventeen years I had a terrific company. It also began
to involve dancers and some great actors. I remember Terry Hands
came once (he is now one of the associate directors of the Royal
Shakespeare Company) for a performance of *The Joker of Seville* that
Margaret, my then wife, suggested we do. We had this little arena,
like a bullfight ring, or a cockfight ring, and we served sandwiches
and coffee and oranges and so on, and the crowd by that time had
begun to know the songs and they were singing along with the actors.
Terry said to me, "Derek, you're doing what Brecht tried to do."
Well, I felt terrific because I knew what he meant. Brecht's idea of

the participation of the audience, the whole idea of the boxing ring as a stage or the stage as an arena, had happened. But after several years of falling out and fighting and coming back together, eventually, for all sorts of reasons, the thing wore down. Although I still use actors from the company singly, I no longer run the company. But seventeen years is a long time to run a theater company.

Interviewer: You've written that you first began writing drama "in the faith that one was creating not merely a play, but a theater, and not merely a theater, but its environment." But by the time you came to write the prologue to *Dream on Monkey Mountain* in 1970, the feeling of pride was replaced mainly by exhaustion and the sense of innocence seems to have given way to despair. What happened?

Walcott: Well, right now I'm writing a play called *A Branch of the Blue Nile*—about actors, a small company of actors and how they fall apart. I don't know up to now—and I'll have to decide pretty quickly—if it's going to end badly. The epiphany of the whole thing, the end of it, is a question that remains.

Interviewer: Is the problem at all related to questions of whether the state should support the arts?

Walcott: I'm fifty-five now and all my life I've tried to fight and write and jeer and encourage the idea that the state owes its artists a lot. When I was young it looked like a romance; now that I'm older and I pay taxes, it is a fact. But not only do I want roads, I want pleasure, I want art. This is the terrible thing in the Caribbean. The middle class in the Caribbean is a venal, self-centered, indifferent, self-satisfied, smug society. It enjoys its philistinism. It pays very short lip-service to its own writers and artists. This is a reality every artist knows. The point is whether you say that and then turn your back on it and say to hell with it for life. I haven't done that and I don't think I'm capable of doing it. What's wrong is this: a legacy has been left by the British empire of amateurism. What we still have as an inheritance is that art is an amateur occupation. That attitude is combined with some of the worst aspects of bourgeois mercantilism, whether it is French, Danish, British, or Spanish bourgeois. The whole of the Caribbean that I can think of has this stubborn, clog-headed indifference to things around them. The philanthropy that exists in the Caribbean is negligible. Money is here—you just have to see the houses and the cars, and to look at the scale of living in any one of these islands—but nobody gives anything. If they do, I don't know what they give to, but that penny-pinching thing is typical of the petty-bourgeois merchant, the hoarder of money. Without any bitterness I can say that anything that I have gotten, whether earned or not, has been from America and not from the Caribbean.

Interviewer: What constitutes an artistic generation in the Caribbean?

Walcott: An artistic generation in this part of the world is about five years. Five years of endurance. After that, I think people give up. I see five years of humanity and boredom and futility. I keep looking at younger writers, and I begin to see the same kind of despair forming and the same wish to say the hell with it, I'm getting out of here. There's also a problem with government support. We have come to a kind of mechanistic thinking that says, a government concerns itself with housing, food, and whatever. There will always be priorities in terms of sewage and electricity. If only a government could form the idea that any sensible human being wants not only to have running water, but a book in hand and a picture on the wall. That is the kind of government I had envisaged in the Caribbean when I was eighteen or nineteen. At fifty-five, I have only seen an increase in venality, an increase in selfishness, and worse than that, a shallow kind of service paid to the arts. I'm very bitter about the philistinism of the Caribbean. It is tough to see a people who have only one strength and that is their culture. Trinidad is perhaps the most concentrated example of a culture that has produced so many thousands and thousands of artisans at Carnival. Now Carnival is supported by the government, but that's a seasonal kind of thinking. I'm talking about something more endemic, more rooted, more organic to the idea of the Caribbean. Because we have been colonies, we have inherited everything and the very thing we used to think was imperial has been repeated by our own stubbornness, stupidity, and blindness.

Interviewer: Your prologue to *Dream on Monkey Mountain* also blasts the crass, state-sponsored commercialization of folk culture. One of your subjects in both poetry and essays has been how negatively tourism has affected the West Indies. Would you discuss that?

Walcott: Once I saw tourism as a terrible danger to a culture. Now I don't, maybe because I come down here so often that perhaps literally I'm a tourist *myself* coming from America. But a culture is only in danger if it allows itself to be. Everybody has a right to come down in the winter and enjoy the sun. Nobody has a right to abuse anybody, and so I don't think that if I'm an American anybody should tell me, please don't come here because this beach is ours, or whatever. During the period I'm talking about, certainly, servility was a part of the whole deal—the waiters had to smile, and we had to do this and so forth. In tourism, it was just an extension really of master/servant. I don't think it's so anymore. Here we have a generation that has strengthened itself beyond that. As a matter of fact, it can go beyond a balance and there's sullenness and a hostility toward people who are your guests. It can swing too far as well. But again, it's not enough to put on steel bands and to have people in the hotels entertaining and maybe to have a little show somewhere to keep them what they think is light-minded and happy and indifferent and so on. If that's the opinion that the government or culture has of itself, then it deserves to be insulted. But if it were doing something more rooted in terms of the arts, in terms of its writers, its painters, and its performers, and if there were more pride in that and not the kind of thing you see of guys walking around town totally bored and hoping that something can happen. . . . I'm not one to say that you can't do things for yourself because certainly having spent all my life in the Caribbean theater and certainly seventeen very exacting years in the workshop, I do say, yes—get up and do it yourself and stop depending on the government. But there is a point where you have to turn to the state and say, "Look man, this is ridiculous. I pay my taxes. I'm a citizen. I don't have a museum. I don't have a good library. I don't have a place where I can perform. I don't have a place where I can dance." That's criminal. It's a carry-over of the same thing I said about the West Indies being seized and atrophied by a petty-bourgeois mentality from the metropolis that has been adopted by the Creole idea of life which is simply to have a damn good time and that's it, basically. I mean that's the worst aspect of West Indian life: have a good time, period.

Interviewer: What do you have against folklorists and anthropologists? Some people think of them as an intellectually respectable lot.

Walcott: I don't trust them. They either embarrass or elevate too much. They can do a good service if they are reticent and keep out of the way. But when they begin to tell people who they are and what they are, they are terrifying. I've gone to seminars in which people in the audience who are the people the folklorists are talking about, are totally baffled by their theories.

Interviewer: One of your most well-known early poems, "A Far Cry from Africa," ends with the question, "How can I turn from Africa and Live?" However, by 1970 you could write that "The African revival is escape to another dignity," and that "Once we have lost our wish to be white, we develop a longing to become black, and those two may be different, but are still careers." You also assert that the claim to be African is not an inheritance but a bequest, "a bill for the condition of our arrival as slaves." These are controversial statements. What is your current sense of the West Indian writer's relationship to Africa?

Walcott: There is a duty in every son to become his own man. The son severs himself from the father. The Caribbean very often refuses to cut that umbilical cord to confront its own stature. So a lot of people exploit an idea of Africa out of both the wrong kind of pride and the wrong kind of heroic idealism. At great cost and a lot of criticism, what I used to try to point out was that there is a great danger in historical sentimentality. We are most prone to this because of suffering, of slavery. There's a sense of skipping the part about slavery, and going straight back to a kind of Eden-like grandeur, hunting lions, that sort of thing. Whereas what I'm saying is to take in the fact of slavery, if you're capable of it, without bitterness, because bitterness is going to lead to the fatality of thinking in terms of revenge. A lot of the apathy in the Caribbean is based on this historical sullenness. It is based on the feeling of "Look what you did to me." Well, "Look what you did to me," is juvenile, right? And also, "Look what I'm going to do to you," is wrong. Think about illegitimacy in the Caribbean! Few people can claim to find their ancestry in the linear way. The whole situation in the Caribbean is an illegitimate situation. If we admit that from the beginning that there is no shame in that historical bastardy, then we can be men. But if we continue to sulk and say, "Look at what the slave-owner did," and so forth, we will never mature. While we sit moping or writing morose poems and novels that glorify a nonexistent past, then time passes us by. We continue in one mood, which is in too much of Caribbean writing: that sort of chafing and rubbing of an old sore. It is not because one wishes to forget; on the contrary, you accept it as much as anybody accepts a wound as being a part of his body. But this doesn't mean that you nurse it all your life.

Interviewer: *The Fortunate Traveller* is filled with poems set in a wide variety of places. The title poem itself elaborates the crisis of a fortunate traveller who goes from one underdeveloped country to another. And in "North and South" you write that "I accept my function/as a colonial upstart at the end of an empire,/a single, circling, homeless satellite." Has the Castaway given way to the Traveller? Do you still feel the old tugs between home and abroad?

Walcott: I've never felt that I belong anywhere else but in St. Lucia. The geographical and spiritual fixity is there. However, there's a reality here as well. This afternoon I asked myself if I would stay here for the rest of my life if I had the chance of leaving. The answer really is, I suppose, no. I don't know if I'm distressed by that. One is bound to feel the difference between these poor, dark, very small houses, the people in the streets, and yourself because you always have the chance of taking a plane out. Basically you are a fortunate traveller, a visitor; your luck is that you can always leave. And it's hard to imagine that there are people around you unable, incapable of leaving either because of money or because of any number of ties. And yet the more I come back here the less I feel that I'm a prodigal or a castaway returning. And it may be that as it deepens with age, you get more locked into what your life is and where you've come from and what you misunderstand and what you should have understood and what you're trying to reunderstand and so on. I'll continue to come back to see if what I write is not beyond the true experience of the person next to me on the bus—not in terms of talking down to that person, but of sharing that person's pain and strength necessary in those pathetically cruel circumstances in which people have found themselves following the devastations of colonialism.

Interviewer: What led you to assert, as you do in *Midsummer*, that "to curse your birthplace is the final evil"?

Walcott: I think it is. I think the earth that you come from is your mother and if you turn around and curse it, you've cursed your mother.

Interviewer: You've written a number of poems about New York

City, Boston, old New England, and the southern United States. I'm
thinking in particular of the first section of *The Fortunate Traveller*
where one of the poems is entitled "American Muse" and another
asserts "I'm falling in love with America." What are your feelings
about living in the United States? Do you think you've been Ameri-
canized in any way?

Walcott: If so, voluntarily. I don't think I've been brainwashed. I
don't think I have been seduced by all the prizes and rewards.
America has been extremely generous to me—not in a strictly philan-
thropical sense; I've earned that generosity. But it has given me a lot
of help. The real thing that counts is whether that line is true about
falling in love with America. That came about because I was travelling
on a bus from one place to another, on a long ride looking at the
American landscape. If you fall in love with the landscape of a place
the next thing that comes is the people, right? The average American
is not like the average Roman or British citizen. The average American
doesn't think that the world belongs to him or her; Americans don't
have imperialist designs in their heads. I find a gentleness and a
courtesy in them. And they have ideals. I've travelled widely across
America and I see things in America that I still believe in, that I like
a lot.

Interviewer: What are your feelings about Boston, which you have
called the "city of my exile"?

Walcott: I've always told myself that I've got to stop using the word
"exile." Real exile means a complete loss of the home. Joseph
Brodsky is an exile; I'm not really an exile. I have access to my home.
Given enough stress and longing I can always get enough money to
get back home and refresh myself with the sea, the sky, whatever. I
was very hostile about Boston in the beginning, perhaps because I
love New York. In jokes, I've always said that Boston should be the
capital of Canada. But it's a city that grows on you gradually. And
where I live is very comfortable. It's close to the university. I work
well there, and I very much enjoy teaching. I don't think of myself as
having two homes; I have one home, but two places.

Interviewer: Robert Lowell had a powerful influence on you. I'm
thinking of your memorial poem "RTSL" as well as the poem in
Midsummer where you assert that "Cal's bulk haunts my classes."
Would you discuss your relationship to Lowell?

Walcott: Lowell and Elizabeth Hardwick were on a tour going to Brazil and they stopped off in Trinidad. I remember meeting them at Queen's Park Hotel and being so flustered that I called Elizabeth Hardwick, Edna St. Vincent Millay. She said, "I'm not that old yet." I was just flabbergasted. And then we became very friendly. My wife Margaret and I took them up to the beach. Their daughter, Harriet, was there. I remember being up at this beach house with Lowell. His daughter and his wife, I think, must have gone to bed. We had gas lanterns. *Imitations* had just come out and I remember that he showed me his imitations of Hugo and Rilke and asked me what I thought about them. I asked him if two of the stanzas were from Rilke, and he said, "No, these are mine." It was a very flattering and warm feeling to have this fine man with this great reputation really asking me what I thought. He did that with a lot of people, very honestly, humbly, and directly. I cherish that memory a lot. When we went back to New York, Cal and Lizzy had a big party for us with a lot of people there, and we became very close. Cal was a big man in bulk but an extremely gentle, poignant person, and very funny. I don't think any of the biographies have caught the sort of gentle, amused, benign beauty of him when he was calm. He kept a picture of Peter, my son, and Harriet for a long time in his wallet, and he'd take it out and show it to me. He was sweetly impulsive. Once I went to visit him and he said, "Let's call up Allen Ginsberg and ask him to come over." That's so cherishable that it's a very hard thing for me to think of him as not being around. In a way, I can't separate my affection for Lowell from his influence on me. I think of his character and gentleness, the immediacy that was part of knowing him. I loved his openness to receive influences. He was not a poet who said, "I'm an American poet, I'm going to be peculiar, and I'm going to have my own voice which is going to be different from anybody's voice." He was a poet who said, "I'm going to take in everything." He had a kind of multifaceted imagination; he was not embarrassed to admit that he was influenced even in his middle-age by William Carlos Williams, or by François Villon, or by Boris Pasternak, all at the same time. That was wonderful.

Interviewer: What about specific poetic influence?

Walcott: One of the things he said to me was, "You must put more of yourself in your poems." Also he suggested that I drop the capital letters at the top of the line, use the lower-case. I did it and felt very refreshed; it made me relax. It was a simple suggestion, but it's one of those things that a great poet can tell you that can be phenomenal—a little opening. The influence of Lowell on everyone, I think, is in his brutal honesty, his trying to get into the poetry a fictional power that wasn't there before, as if your life was a section of a novel—not because you are the hero, but because some of the things that were not in poems, some of the very ordinary banal details, can be illumined. Lowell emphasized the banality. In a sense to keep the banality banal and still make it poetic is a great achievement. I think that's one of the greatest things that he did in terms of his directness, his confrontation of ordinariness.

Interviewer: Would you tell the story of your first poetry reading in the States? It must have been rewarding to hear Lowell's extravagant introduction.

Walcott: Well, I didn't know what he said because I was in back of the curtain, I think it was at the Guggenheim. I was staying at the Chelsea Hotel, and that day I felt I needed a haircut, so, foolishly, I went around the corner and sat down. The barber took the electric razor and gave me one of the wildest haircuts I think I've ever had. It infuriated me, but you can't put your hair back on. I even thought of wearing a hat. But I went on anyway, my head looked like hell. I had gotten some distance into the reading—I was reading "A Far Cry From Africa"—when suddenly there was the sound of applause from the auditorium. Now I had never heard applause at a poetry reading before. I don't think I'd ever given a formal poetry reading, and I thought for some reason that the applause was saying it was time to stop, that they thought it was over. So I walked off the stage. I felt in a state of shock. I actually walked off feeling the clapping was their way of saying, "Well, thank you, it's been nice." Someone in charge asked me to go back and finish the reading, but I said no. I must have sounded extremely arrogant, but I felt that if I went back out there it would have been conceited. I went back to Trinidad. Since I hadn't heard Lowell's introduction. I asked someone for it at the Federal Building, which had archives of radio tapes from the Voice of America. I said I would like to hear the Lowell tape, and the guy said, "I think we erased that." It was only years later that I really heard what Cal said, and it was very flattering.

Interviewer: How did you become friends with Joseph Brodsky?

Walcott: Well, ironically enough, I met Brodsky at Lowell's funeral. Roger Straus, Susan Sontag, and I went up to Boston for the funeral. We waited somewhere for Joseph, probably at the airport, but for some reason he was delayed. At the service I was in this pew when a man sat down next to me. I didn't know him. When I stood up as the service was being said, I looked at him and I thought, if this man is not going to cry then *I'm* not going to cry, either. I kept stealing glances at him to see if anything was happening, but he was very stern looking. That helped me to contain my own tears. Of course it was Brodsky. Later, we met. We went to Elizabeth Bishop's house, and I got to know him a little better. The affection that developed after that was very quick and, I think, permanent—to be specific about it is hard. I admire Joseph for his industry, his valor, and his intelligence. He's a terrific example of someone who is a complete poet, who doesn't treat poetry as anything else but a very hard job that he does as well as he can. Lowell worked very hard too, but you feel in Joseph that that is all he lives for. In a sense that's all any of us lives for or can hope to live for. Joseph's industry is an example that I cherish a great deal.

Interviewer: When did you first become friends with Seamus Heaney?

Walcott: There was a review by A. Alvarez of Seamus's book, a very upsetting review—to put it mildly—in which he was describing Heaney as a sort of blue-eyed boy. English literature always has a sort of blue-eyed boy. I got very angry over the review and sent Seamus a note via my editor with a little obscenity in it. Just for some encouragement. Later, in New York we had a drink at someone's house. From then on, the friendship has developed. I see him a lot when he is in Boston at Harvard. I just feel very lucky to have friends like Joseph and Seamus. The three of us are outside of the American experience. Seamus is Irish, Joseph is Russian, I'm West Indian. We don't get embroiled in the controversies about who's a soft poet, who's a hard poet, who's a free verse poet, who's not a poet, and all of that. It's good to be on the rim of that quarreling. We're on the perimeter of the American literary scene. We can float out here happily not really committed to any kind of particular school or body of enthusiasm or criticism.

Interviewer: Over the years your style seems to have gotten increasingly plainer and more direct, less gnarled, more casual, somehow both quieter and fiercer at the same time. Is that an accurate assessment of the poetic style of your middle age? I can't imagine a book like *Midsummer* from the young Derek Walcott.

Walcott: It varies, of course. When I finished *Another Life,* I felt like writing short poems, more essential, to the point, things that were contracted. They didn't have the scale of the large book and so on. It goes in that kind of swing, in that kind of pendulum. In the case of *Midsummer,* I felt that for the time being I didn't want to write any more poems, although that sounds arrogant. I just felt perhaps I was overworking myself. I was going to concentrate purely on trying to develop my painting. While painting, I would find lines coming into my head. I would almost self-destruct them; I'd say all right, I'll put them down . . . but with antipoetic vehemence. If they don't work, then I'll just forget it. What kept happening is that the lines would come anyway, perhaps out of that very irritation, and then I would make a very arbitrary collage of them and find they would take some sort of loose shape. Inevitably, of course, you try to join the seams. I was trying to do something, I think, that was against the imagination, that was not dictated in a sort of linear, lyrical, smooth, melodic—but rather something that was antimelodic. For a poem, if you give a poem personality, that's the most exciting thing—to feel that it is becoming antimelodic. The vocabulary becomes even more challenging, the meter more interesting, and so on. So what happened was that by the very wish not to write, or to write a poem that was against the idea of writing poems, it all became more fertile and more contradictory and more complex. Gradually a book began to emerge. Inevitably you can't leave things lying around with unjoined shapes, little fragments and so on. I began to weld everything together—to keep everything that I felt worthwhile. I thought, well, whether this is just an ordinary thing or not, it has as much a right to be considered as something a little more grandiose. That's what I think happened in *Midsummer.*

Interviewer: How do you feel about publishing your *Collected Poems*?

Walcott: You're aware of the fact that you have reached a certain stage in your life. You're also aware that you have failed your imagination to some degree, your ambitions. This is an amazingly difficult time for me. I'm absolutely terrified. It's not because I have a kind of J. D. Salinger thing about running away from publicity. It's really not wanting to see myself reflected in that way. I don't think that that's what the boy I knew—the boy who started to write poetry—wanted at all, not praise, not publicity. But it's troubling. I remember Dylan Thomas saying somewhere that he liked it better when he was not famous. All I can say is this: I do have another book about ready, and I hope it will be a compensation for all the deficiencies in the *Collected Poems,* something that will redeem the *Collected Poems.*

An Interview with Derek Walcott

Charles H. Rowell / 1987

From *Callaloo,* 34 (Winter 1988), 80–89. Reprinted by permission of *Callaloo* and Charles H. Rowell.

The text which follows is an excerpt from a three-hour interview conducted on September 19, 1987, at Derek Walcott's home in Boston, Massachusetts.

Rowell: I would like to begin this interview with your background and early poetry. Are we to read "Prelude" (1948), the opening selection in your *Collected Poems 1948–1984* (1986), as an "autobiographical" or a "confessional" poem? If so, what, then, are we to make of the following stanzas:

> And my life, too early of course for the profound cigarette,
> The turned doorhandle, the knife turning
> In the bowels of the hours, must not be made public
> Until I learnt to suffer
> In accurate iambics.
>
> ....
> Until from all I turn to think
> In the middle of the journey through my life,
> O how I came upon you, my
> Reluctant leopard of the slow eyes.

More specifically, what are we to think of "Until I have learnt to suffer / In accurate iambics" and "my / Reluctant leopard of the slow eyes"? Will you talk about your artistic background, your education, which is partly Caribbean and partly British.

Walcott: There's a widespread sense of division which I myself may have encouraged, perhaps too deeply or too repetitively in certain aspects of poetry, when I was a little older than the poem you are quoting. I think it became more defined, almost more historical or even melodramatic, as I grew older. The young person—the child or adolescent—generally has a stronger sense of the unity of being in a particular place than, say, those divisions that tend to come later, such as the relationship of family, history, or whatever. I think I wrote that poem ["Prelude"] when I was probably sixteen or seventeen, somewhere during that time when I was very excited about my discovery, through several older people, of the poetry of W. H. Auden, T. S. Eliot, and Dylan Thomas—physical books that I had, books whose print I liked. So the sense of separation, which very often people writing about my work define, is not that early. It comes a little later. In other words, by 1947 or 1948, when we were boys at college, we felt that we were part of the heritage of the British Empire—its language, its history, and so on. We were quite aware of the fact that the background of the Caribbean was a background of slavery. But my generation was not schizophrenic about the heritage of the Empire and the heritage of the Caribbean. It was a double rather than a split thing. In other words, we had an interior life, the life of education. So I think that a kind of examination came later; it came with the growth of looking at things. As for inheritance, one has to remember that—even if one calls it brain-washing or whatever definition one may make about feeling that one was British—it was quite a sincere and common feeling to generations of people in the colonies and dominions and the protectorates of the British Empire. Of course, this is post-war, but even the war unified the British Empire for a common cause that was being fought by New Zealand, by Canada, by India, and by other countries. People went to the war to fight for certain values that were challenged by Nazi Germany and by Japan and by Mussolini's Italy. So after the war there was a sense that the heritage was shared physically. Later on when things began to happen, then one became affected by the historical realities of certain experiences in a sharper sense of not so much separation really but as a problem of unifying. It was not like a cleavage so much as an urge to unify. In other words, we would leave school, be taught English history or be taught English poets, without feeling that we were afflicted with that kind of knowledge. For example, the context of the poetry we read was not political. It was a context that took aesthetic values in the delight of a recitation or the enjoyment of the poem. It really didn't divide one inside. Later on in *Another Life,* I wrote about the divided child. But I think that that division, the slow perception of that division, came with a gradual sense of a loss of innocence about history. So in those lines about being willing "to suffer in accurate iambics" are really an attempt to see in a very Audenesque way. I would like to be able to write a poem or verse that is true to the immediacy around me. The citation from Dante was a young man's reference, not a love affair, to a girl. It's not the leopard of Dante; it is a girl. So it's not a presumption to say that I am undertaking a *Divina Commedia*. I liked the word "reluctant" when I, at sixteen or seventeen, found it. I had found a word which contains the leisure and tension of the leopard as an image. That's the word in there that makes me feel that some little seizure, some little perception, was happening which made me feel that I was going on the right track. The relationship between the girl and the iambics is also sort of an introductory prayer to the hope that both the art and love could somehow be connected.

Rowell: To an American in the U.S.A., it is a bit surprising that you, at the age of sixteen or seventeen, had studied Dante and Auden.

Walcott: Well, I wouldn't have read all of Dante. . . .

Rowell: Or that you knew the reference and that, at your early age, it was really meaningful to you and that you could synthesize it. How did you come upon these texts or these writers?

Walcott: I am going to try and talk as carefully as possible. One of the easiest delusions has been the continued effort—for the sake of isolating writers like V. S. Naipaul, Edward Brathwaite, C. L. R. James, and myself, or any other West Indian writer—to think that we were remarkable as intellects because of the conditions of our background, our common West Indian background, and that in some way we escaped through will or through hard work or through this wish to get out of the Caribbean as quickly as possible. We were in some ways peculiar or singular. In reality no one still has written or defined— although I have tried to—what was the content of Caribbean education based on the English public school model. No one has really discussed how formidable it was and how exciting and how severe and, in a way, excitingly tough it was for generations of West Indian boys going to college. Obviously, when you look back, the gap between the college boy and the other boy in the street, who was not at college, is a social crime in a sense. Now it is considerably modified by the fact that there is free secondary education. But it was a pattern based on an elitism that was, of course, monetary as well. Who could afford to pay to go to college? It was extremely competitive, because, during my youth, there was only one island scholarship for two years, but only one boy or only one girl (girls came later) was allowed to win a scholarship to a top university in England or Canada. But to go back to the idea of thoroughness, or even the attractions of the directions, offered in terms of the secondary school education . . . you see in those days there was no science—science had not come into the curriculum. So what we had was a humanist kind of education on a secondary level, following the war and preceding the war, too. The science curriculum didn't exist. It never existed in Barbados. Some of my friends who went to school in Barbados were studying Greek and Latin, as well as other subjects. It meant that the model of one's education was that of someone being trained to enter Oxford or Cambridge as if the culmination of one's education were to be Cambridge or Oxford. In fact, the examinations we took were called the Oxford or Cambridge examinations. So the whole direction and competitiveness of the system could be rather cruel in many ways, and socially, in a sense, unjust in others. In the usual pattern of British colonialism, then, one made an elite of one's students . . . and that elitism continues still in the system of British education. It is, also, the pattern of British foreign service and the pattern of administration and the pattern of the Empire and the pattern of England still. It was what we went through. I don't think that we felt arrogant as college boys. That is, my familiarity with the texts—taught in some cases by very good teachers, some cases some haphazard ones—was not an individual thing. People in my class might not have been writers, but they were acquainted with Shakespeare and with hints of Catullus and hints of Virgil. We did Latin and we translated scenes, and so forth. A good secondary school education and the solidity of it in the Caribbean about that time is a fact. I know the dismal standards of semi-literacy that exist in the U.S.A. Very often the people in my class may make a reference to a new writer. People may have read it or may not. I don't want to elaborate on things or methods of education in America. But there are aspects to a democratic education in which the concept is strictly to please, accommodate, the most deprived, and socially deprived, young minds. That accommodation leads to a lot of conflict, because an aspect of a democratic culture is generally to thin out quality for the sake of spreading it even on a

level surface. And that has its conflicts. But not calling the group of
my generation intellectually elite, in a sense, is unfair. One earned
one's position by endeavor and by study. Very, very hard study.
There's a friend of mine who is now Governor General of St. Lucia
who came from an extremely deprived background, who had to study
without electric light. I just had lunch at the Governor General's
house the other day. He was my schoolmate. He is an extremely
sharp mind. Because writers get more attention paid to their minds,
because they are visible products of the intelligence in the form of
books, theater or whatever, they tend to be treated as a kind of
isolated phenomenon. But we cannot come out of such backgrounds
if there were not behind us a solid situation of our choosing to be
writers instead of doctors or instead of legislators or instead of
journalists or whatever. So brilliance or just academic endeavor is a
common background in the Caribbean experience. The fact that I may
be better known as a West Indian intellect than my friend who is
Governor General of St. Lucia now doesn't mean that I was better in
class in all these different subjects. He was brilliant in mathematics,
for instance; I was lousy in mathematics, and I don't know law. I
imagine that if his intellect continued in the way that it did in college,
he must be an extremely brilliant lawyer. Now if I am a good writer,
he may be a much more brilliant lawyer than I am a good writer. And
that's part of what I am saying in terms of the astonishment you may
feel for a West Indian for having had that kind of background. It is in
a way a debt to that very Empire.

Rowell: Well, do you think there is an aesthetic reconciliation or
synthesis of that British education and that Caribbean landscape?

Walcott: Are you saying how do you relate Wordsworth's poetry to
coconut trees?

Rowell: How do you write in those "accurate iambics" that you
spoke of in "Prelude"? You spoke of the difficulty of learning to write
in British English. You lived in the Caribbean.

Walcott: Oh, no, that's a misunderstood part. The misunderstood
part is not my learning English in terms of learning English poetry.
To grow up in those two languages [British English and Caribbean
English] is not to feel that there was, in any way, an internal conflict.
There was absolutely no problem in reciting a passage from *Henry V*
in class and going outside of class and relaxing; there was no tension

in the recitation of the passage from *Henry V* and going outside and making jokes in patois or relaxing in a kind of combination patois of English and French. So it was not that one was going through the experience of translating one's self into something else. It was a reality that there was an excitement that could be shared in both languages at the same time. I don't like to dismiss my early work as a young man's work. To say I "learnt to suffer in accurate iambics" means that, at some point in the future, my poetry would be dominated by the accuracy of art, of craft. But to feel as if it were someone going through kind of conversion into another language is inaccurate, because in St. Lucia we were not surrounded by people who did professional jobs and then changed and spoke another language entirely. I suppose in retrospect another generation might have called those people that I knew in my boyhood pompous or pretentious, but now I see that they were not so but that they were people of great delicacy in terms of the environment they were in. I am talking about people as I have written about them, who were amateur violinists, amateur actors . . . people who memorized the best in the language, people who had all these things as natural to them as any other aspiration. So it is not a matter of confronting the page at a certain age, sixteen or seventeen, and saying now I had better learn to speak English. I grew up in a household where my mother recited poems. She can still recite poems even though she's ninety now. There were books around our home. I only became aware of the distance later, I think. Later I might have been playing tapes of *Henry V* or something, and next door to me there were people who were very, very poor. But at an earlier age I didn't feel—until the challenge to articulate came—that there was really that much of a division.

Rowell: I was trying to get at the difference between the English or voice in the school and *Another Life* as opposed to the English in "The Schooner *Flight*." In "The Schooner *Flight*" there is a play with folk speech as opposed to the very refined and extended English in *Another Life*. The English of the latter is closer—for my ear—to Shakespeare.

Walcott: This is a subtle question, and it has led to a lot of division, dramatic divisions, polar placing of Edward Brathwaite and myself, for instance.

Rowell: No, that's not my intention.

Walcott: I understand that. But it develops into a split among
Caribbean writers which I think is very corny and very much exagger-
ated. It's not a matter of the language; it's a matter of the accent, it's
a matter of the tone. In other words, if one felt affected reciting a
passage from Shakespeare, or one was also singing a calypso, or
reciting a poem from any Caribbean writer. . . . What is the question?
The question is does the reader or the reciter sociologically heighten
his voice to a level where he is not at home, where he is elevating his
mind socially, if he is doing Shakespeare. Right? And whether he is
therefore more natural, more relaxed, if he is supposed to be doing
the full accent. I think the example I can give is to make it actual. I
have just come back from St. Lucia. I have a very good friend there
who is a good poet who should write more. Satirically, he calls himself
a dilettante. He has published his own poetry privately. I encouraged
him to do it, and he did it. He published his own little book of poems
which he called *First and Last Poems*. Now this man—his name is
Hunter Francois, and I don't want to make anything mythological out
of the simple experience—is the Ombudsman in St. Lucia. He is a
lawyer, and he's been in politics. He's been the Minister of Education.
He is also from St. Mary's College. He lives on his own bay on a
beautiful cove in St. Lucia. One afternoon I was out there with some
friends. He loves to play the piano, and he quoted, which he knew by
heart, about two or three pages of Thomas Macaulay. Remember this
is a passage of prose from Macaulay. Now what was he doing? If he
had in the slightest manner affected an accent in doing that, he would
have been an affected man who was displaced in the society that he
was in. He would have been even displaced in the cove where he was
living. The accent was consistent. The accent of conversation, talking
to me, and the accent in reciting the Macaulay or the accent in the
making of a joke—none of that altered. So it's not a matter of the
language that is used, but it is a matter of how true is the tone of the
voice that one is speaking in. If you are doing the Macaulay by heart,
what tends to sound like affectation is that the syntax appears to
create an affectation in the voice. Because of the tone and resonance
in Macaulay, it would appear to be the same thing for an Englishman
reciting him by heart. The syntactical elevation, the rhetoricism
speaking, the historical address in the Macaulay turns the voice into
the oratorical, elevates anyone onto another platform that is above

the normal pitch of the human voice—or subdued or elevated, for that matter. It doesn't really matter whether you take it down or you take it low. I think it is a division that is spurious, because those divisions are not real. It is equally true that one can affect to be a dialect poet. There are many people who do not have the background of the roots experience. They've never hustled in the streets; they don't know the street language; and they've never been in situations in which they were really desperate. Therefore, the language of desperation used by the real people out in the streets hustling is not an artifice: it is real talk. That's how the people feel. As a matter of fact, it is even more threatening, I think, now in the Caribbean—the language and the aesthetic, the truth, of those people who are not middle class. College boys trying to get "rootsie" are no more artificial than the other person who is saying, "Oh, well, you talk like Shakespeare." But you see that whole thing has been so beautifully resolved in this astonishingly quiet and beautiful book, *Beyond the Boundary,* by C. L. R. James. I thought that by now that argument would have been annihilated or hermetically sealed by what James has written in that book. I was telling my daughter the other day that I went to a lecture by James on Heidegger or Hegel—I don't remember which philosopher. I sat in the audience, and for an hour, easily—and this without any exaggeration—I was transposing the oral language onto the page. The syntactical balance, and the directness without any sort of "ahs" and "ums" and whatever could have been immediately translated onto the page. This was not remembering a lecture by heart; this was just unadorned quality and direct brilliance, done in an accent by a man who has spent a half a century or more in England—a man who still had an accent whose melody remained Caribbean. The accuracy of the melody is the thing. And it is very easy to think that one can get that as a writer, that one can get that accuracy of the inner voice. That's the hardest part of all, because you can think you are getting it. One is always being defeated in terms of what is the pitch of the voice. That is the biggest thing. It's the same problem that has existed for the American writer. An American sentence by Hemingway uses English words, but it is an American sentence and it is a very different sentence even, I think, from one by Graham Greene. The same words. It's the inside thing which makes that sentence by Greene a different sentence from one created by Hemingway. That's the toughest part, I think, for literature that is emerging with all the vehemence of wishing to express itself. Getting into arguments about what is and what is not.

Rowell: I was thinking that those two poems (*Another Life* and "The Schooner *Flight*") are examples of a certain kind of linguistic ability that. . . .

Walcott: You're not asking a controversial question. I know you're not. If I read "The Schooner *Flight*" aloud, and if I read parts of *Another Life* aloud—one would ask is this the same man reading in the same voice or is it somebody doing an act in either case. I think that at my age I have achieved an evenness inside myself that makes "The Schooner *Flight*" a dramatic poem. In other words, it has a voice in some way that a lot of Brathwaite's poems contain a persona or different people talking. Whenever a persona arrives, the expression of dialect is, in a way, an expression of different personae. The basic language, out of which that dialect emerges, comes out of a dramatization through the medium of masks or faces or characters. It remains that, because our thinking is not pitched on the level of dialect. I'm not saying that dialect is incapable of conveying intellectual subtleties; I'm saying that to be true to the interior tone of reflection you need to know the exact measure of the sound you are reflecting. If I become Shabine, then, there are passages, I think, in "The Schooner *Flight*" that seems to me a little too elevated. . . .

Rowell: I was going to ask you about that.

Walcott: When that happens the persona has not remained completely whole. There are parts of the poem I could say that about, but I also didn't want to restrict the possibility of man's intelligence at a pitch to exclude it. So I think it really is a matter of the measure of the language chosen to reflect what he is saying; it is not that the dialect poem cannot achieve syntactical subtleties or that you cannot have a great thought in a dialect poem. But we have to accept the fact that most writers in the Caribbean have been in a position of intellectual privilege in the society. In fact, I'm certain they are most in a middle class situation. The mind is continually refining itself in the process, widening itself, absorbing more things. In a sense, without any estrangement at all, one may be moving further and further away from the language of one's youth. There's nothing wrong with that. It's like Shakespeare's leaving Warwickshire and going to town. If Shakespeare had remained true to his countryside, we might have had great speech but how could that have been arrested? How could one simply expect him to talk in an incoherent language to other people in London—to write in an incoherent language that is totally thickened with provincialism. So what does one say? Shakespeare is a phony for writing *Troilus and Cressida*? Why is he not true to his roots? And of course he was attacked for that. He was attacked for being pompous and pretentious; Robert Greene attacked him for that. And then the people who envied him asked, "Who is this country boy?" To remain purely a country boy all the time is to deny yourself the width of ambition that Shakespeare, as one example, demonstrates.

Rowell: I want to go back to some of what we were talking about earlier—matters that are autobiographical or are related to your life as well as to the lives of other Caribbean writers. So many of the writers and other intellectuals of the Caribbean have gone into exile. One of the things that always fascinated me about the Caribbean writer is movement. In your case, it was movement from St. Lucia to some other island, Trinidad and Jamaica, for example. Wilson Harris moved to England during the 1950s. Then there's René Depestre who remains in exile in France. Would you talk about the writers' exile from the region? What is the source of that impulse? There seems always the impulse to travel.

Walcott: It's not an impulse in the same sense of travelling for travelling's sake. It's an impulse of the writer, and in each case the writer's situation is different. There are books being published in the Caribbean, but that is not to say there is a situation there in which a man can decide to be a novelist, although Earl Lovelace gets his books published now in America and stays in Trinidad. That's a whole generation later, after my generation of writers—simply because the forerunners established the idea of a body of Caribbean writing. It was created by people like George Lamming, Samuel Selvon, and other writers. These writers didn't have a choice about staying in Trinidad because they wanted to be novelists. Lamming began as a poet. Selvon also wrote poetry. One could publish one's own book. I did that. There were no publishers there. But if you are embarking on a novel the only thing you could do was to send your book away and hope that it would be published. Some of the writers left without knowing they wanted to be novelists. They left as poets and short story writers. Their books could not be published, because there were no publishing houses in the Caribbean—in the British Caribbean, that is. Now in Cuba—I imagine also in Haiti—books would be put out, but I am not sure how strong an industry that was back in 1947 or 1948. So that physical thing of going away differs in each case. In V. S. Naipaul's case—here is a young man who won a scholarship and left very early. He was a prodigious student. In John Hearne's case—he went to join the Royal Air Force, but he wanted to be a writer and get his work published. It was an environment that could not even materially support the idea of a publishing house; the machinery of publishing couldn't pay for itself. I don't think it would pay for itself now in the Caribbean. Books are phenomenally expensive now all over the Caribbean. You can't afford to buy a paperback book in the Caribbean, and a hardback book costs $50.00 sometimes. Well, it's like that all over. Way back then the need to leave the Caribbean was not only a feeling but chafing that happens in every young writer about home. That is normal—e.g., whether Ernest Hemingway leaves the Midwest, or somebody else leaves wherever. Or Shakespeare Warwickshire and goes to London. This impulse to go towards the city, the center, the metropolis, is just a part of the nature of the provinces. Now I didn't have that desire as strongly as say the novelists, because I thought—although there was a time when I would've wanted it—that the job I had to do was closer to painting. You can't paint a landscape overseas. There's too much in painting that is physical; I mean you can't do it by memory, you can't do light by memory. It's impossible to do it. I was doing poetry and painting. I thought poetry and painting were identical. It was an inconceivable idea that one could paint a western landscape from England or that one could depict it from England. Now I think a novel is different in the sense that it has all these qualities in it. It has the poetry. It has a total reality. It has its historical world in it. So you needn't actually be there when you're writing the novel, since most writers really mine their childhood or their boyhood up to about eighteen or twenty, when the formidable things happen and the shocks and revelations come. We don't freeze with the life's span of experience. The true experiences of writers form somewhere between the age of ten and earlier. So what happens to us in those years becomes very formative. It's like Graham Greene's essay about the lost childhood. The lost childhood is what every writer concentrates on. What happens to that

innocence? That is a part of it. I think it must have been for some
writers a devastating experience to leave the Caribbean—although for
others it might have been exhilarating, because at the time when the
writers were gone the British Empire finally decided that it was no
longer an empire and that just ordinary profit motives were from
reality. But there were a lot of people who could read about themselves. And so you had books being published by Caribbean writers
and by African writers and by Commonwealth writers. Not purely
from sentimentality. . . . For Caribbean and African writers, England
was exhilarating. It was not a matter of breakdown; it was a matter of
ventilation of things that were happening in England. The whole
beginning of the migration to London following the war, the shock
that the Empire was not so much crumbling as changing, the fact that
West Indian political emergence was without suffering . . . it was just
the air of independence . . . it was part of the excitement that was
there for young writers. Their going to England, too, was exciting in
the sense of discovery—whether that discovery was ironic to find out
that they were not really wanted, but that they were wanted and that
they were respected. It was working both ways. Their memory of the
Caribbean was very fresh, very close, and was ready to be put down.
I'm talking about the novelists. And what I think they also had was
this fantastic elation of realizing that they would be able to put down
sentences which would be words that had never been used before in
the context of print—whether it is a word like *breakfruit* or somebody's name. Or just the sentence itself conveyed that whole excitement of naming for the first time in prose. And so a lot of the fiction
of that time appears to be picaresque—that is, from a distance it
appears to be picaresque. There can be bitter picaresque, as well as
there can be ironic picaresque. And there can be comic picaresque.
The fiction was judged as picaresque—very poorly judged, because
the English critic began to get a little afraid of his ignorance. The
English critic had to confront the idea of here's a man writing about
Africa, and he, the English critic, didn't know shit about Africa. And
all the English critic could do was relate the African writer's fiction to
English literature, which is the safest, the laziest and the most
cowardly attitude to take, because then the English critic would have
to say, "What does Chinua Achebe mean by Nigeria?" And the critic
would have to say that that's the history of Nigeria—not only the

history of Nigeria but the history of the Ibos and the history of all the
other tribes. So the easiest thing was to make the fiction referential:
to say this is like a Charles Dickens novel, etc. Of course, there are
resemblances and that continues because it remains the safest thing
that any critic can do. So any writer coming from the Caribbean . . .
any book of his that comes out . . . the easiest thing is to make it
referential: to say, well, this is like Dickens; this is like John Steinbeck. That is so stupid and so lazy, because obviously, since the
language is English, the influence of any writer is universal. The
influence of William Saroyan on English is universal. On Hemingway.
On Steinbeck. It was equally a heritage of someone working in the
English language as much as anyone, even if you were Indian or
Black. We're talking now about a spectrum that would include the
terrifying spectrum to an English critic saying, "My God, here's a
novelist from Ife. Here's a novelist from Hong Kong. Here's a novelist
from Toronto. Here's one from Malaysia. Here's another from the
Port of Spain. What is happening? What is happening to English
literature?" It isn't that it is getting colored, whatever. It is suddenly
the confrontation of this dam that broke; this writing coming out is of
very fine quality. It became something not threatening, but it had to
be absorbed in the idea of English literature because it had to be
phased out as politically as the phasing out of the Empire. So you had
a status which would be as a colonial writer, a protectorate writer, a
dominion writer, and then, finally, an equal writer. It's the same way
as you would phase out a colony into a protectorate, into a dominion
and, finally, maybe into someone who would share the same status as
an English writer.

An Interview with Derek Walcott

David Montenegro / 1987

From *Points of Departure*, edited by David Montenegro (Ann Arbor: The University of Michigan Press, 1991) 80–104. Originally published in *Partisan Review*, Vol. 57, No. 2 (Spring 1990), 202–14. Reprinted by permission of The University of Michigan Press.

DM: Could we start with "Another Life," your longest poem, and, in particular, with Part One, "A Divided Child"? Would you talk about the divisions, beginning with painting, since, in the poem, you start with painting and, in a sense, end by choosing poetry as a vocation?

DW: I didn't give up painting. I do a lot of storyboards for my filmscripts and plays, and I do them in a lot of detail. I draw carefully, although a storyboard merely dramatizes an incident or focuses on a different angle, and so on. I still do a fair amount of watercolor painting from nature. I haven't done—as I thought I would have—much oil painting on canvas.

Last summer I strongly resolved that I'd go back to the rigidities of drawing and painting, and that I'd give myself a heavy schedule for doing them daily. But that got broken again. When I'm in the Caribbean, my prime attraction is towards representing it in painting. So I think there is still a dual attraction for me to painting and poetry.

The division one talks about I don't think is ultimately a sort of career decision between becoming a painter or a poet. You can't, obviously, put words into paintings, but, on the other hand, I had the absorption of the visual that is part of poetry and can be very strong, and I think that must be present in the sort of *frame* of work on a line or even a stanza sometimes. On the other hand, I have a quite different approach to what I'd like to achieve in painting. I think it's perhaps not as—I wouldn't say ambitious—not as arduous perhaps, not as sweaty or industrious as with the writing.

There's more to it than that, though. The older I get, I realize that I'm a pretty competent draughtsman, and I'll get better with practice. And the watercolors are getting better. But all I'm after really is a visual representation of a thing that I see in front of me. I am very

135

square when it comes to painting, especially watercolor, because in watercolor you can't really muck around with abstraction. It's too delicate a medium. Oils can be very rhetorical, in that sense, very pretentious sometimes, especially abstract painting. So I love watercolor because it's harder really than oils. It's less egotistical.

So I haven't given up the idea of painting. I suppose, in "Another Life," the section I'd refer to would be the one that talks about what exists in the wrist of a painter—the true painter—which is a very confident flourish, a feel for the weight of the paint and how it's confidently manipulated, that I didn't think I had. I don't think now that that's necessarily a condemnation. There are different kinds of painters. There are those who layer and build, and those who slash and mount and increase the surface of the canvas by strokes. There is a big difference between even, say, late Rembrandt and Degas. So, I may have said once that I don't feel I have the life inside my wrists to be a painter, because at the time I may have been comparing myself with other painters whose style was much more vehement than mine.

DM: Is part of your attraction to watercolor the way watercolor can catch nuances of light?

DW: Watercolor's an extremely difficult medium in the tropics. It's more or less a temperate medium, though not entirely, because you have obvious exceptions in Winslow Homer and Hopper, for instance. In the tropics, the dramatic division that exists between the horizon and the bottom of the horizon, in other words between the sky and the foreground, is extremely dramatic. It's almost complementary, in terms of the hues that are there. The incredible blue that is there in the tropics is almost impossible to get—the *heat* of that blue—in watercolor. And it may be silly to think it's because the paint is made in temperate countries. That's maybe a facetious attitude to have, but look at the palette that exists for watercolor in the tropics, where shadows are black, black-green, or contain black, which you can't really use in watercolor. And the fact that you saturate the surface of the paper sometimes with a tone on which you can dip the paint is not quite useful in the tropics. I mean here the lines are hard, but there the lines are hard-edged, and you have a very hard time manipulating them into any kind of subtlety. If you see a negative of the tropics, you realize why cameramen always find it much harder to photograph in tropic light than they do in the magic hour at twilight or right after dawn.

One other thing that astonishes and exasperates painters from the north is that what they see in front of them is a lot of green, basic hues of green, green and red. I remember I was going out to do some painting, and there was a German tourist in a small hotel where I was staying. He said he couldn't paint there because it was too *green*. I think it's the way he looks at the color. Obviously there is subtlety, an immense amount of variety in tones of the green that exist in front of you. And there is haze in the rain or early morning, and so on. But, in a way, forms in the tropics are almost emblematic; they're very hard and bright. I think that to try to capture that on paper means that the words have to be used almost as heavily as strokes are used in paint. Just to put down "blue" or "green" is not enough, because that's a postcard. What matters is how you manage to get into that blue whatever other variations and subtleties and orchestrations that one tries to get in the *words* so that you can feel the sensuality, the presence and the texture of, say, water and crisp sand, of going into cool water, that sudden change of temperature that exists between light and shade in the tropics.

DM: So it's a problem of very strong contrasts and maybe too much light?

DW: Well, if you say it's too much light, it means God has made a mistake, you know. There can never be too much light. It's the glare that is there. No one runs away from glare in terms of what's to be depicted. That's like saying in the Arctic it's all white. But it's all ice. I don't know, it leads to a kind of literature of indolence, a concept of lethargy, you know, of the siesta, of decay, of afternoon languor that is really more theatrical than real. It's just *literary,* that idea of the tropics, really.

DM: You mentioned different types of blue. Is it that there is not a language for the different shades of blue, or the *particular* shades of blue, and, in a sense, through words you are trying to identify those shades that have not been named?

DW: A passage I always quote when I'm teaching is the first chapter of *A Farewell to Arms* in which the model is really a combination of Gertrude Stein and Cézanne. Sometimes I point out to the class certain effects Hemingway achieved by watching Cézanne. One was to let the stroke of the word "blue" appear very late in the first few paragraphs. So that the first startling stroke of the word "blue" comes much later, after the dust and the leaves and so on, and the waters swiftly moving are blue in the channels. Now, *what* blue is not described, but the point is that the stroke is put down with exactly the same cubic area that a Cézanne stroke is put on a bleached background. Or, say, the rocks or trees are skeletally or sparingly indicated, and then that stroke appeared next to another hue—a blue or a lilac, and so on. Hemingway's technique comes from a scrutiny particularly, I think, of watercolor.

DM: What stereotypes do you have to break through in language to bring out the reality of the tropics?

DW: Well, you know, every truth becomes a cliché after awhile. I came on a break this summer from St. Lucia to Boston. On the first or second day, I thought my body would burst from the humidity. The acute, implacable discomfort that I felt in the house was nothing compared to the kind of heat that exists in the tropics. It can be fierce, scorching sun there, but you've got only to step into the shade to be cool. And that contrast is—in terms of temperature—melodramatic. So when people give an image of the tropics as a place of swelter and indolence and exasperation and languor and idleness and so on . . . well, I was devastated by the humidity of a northern summer. Now if we amplify that kind of cliché to say, well, in hot countries nothing is ever produced, we would have to say that for the bulk of time that summer represents in all northern countries *nothing* can be produced. And it should not be, if you're going by that kind of geographic description of what is expected of certain locales. Whereas more can be produced in the summer in the Caribbean because it's cooler. So that concept of the tropics being a place of intense heat where nothing happens and nothing stirs makes for good fiction, but it's not true.

But I'm going deeper than simply the climate. I'm thinking of an attitude that's both geographic and historical. Hot countries, until the emergence of the Latin American novelists and poets, were not supposed to produce anything. It's a sort of Graham Greenish fantasy about the tropics that was perpetuated. But Greece is a hot country, and you've got to ask: What has Greece produced?

DM: What other divisions have come into play in your life besides painting/poetry, light/sound?

DW: I suppose the biggest cleft, the biggest division, the biggest chasm is cultural, in a way. Obviously—however jaded a subject it is, and I do feel jaded talking about it—race is an enormous one. Not for *me*. I look at the chasm, I don't share it. But it's obviously here. And it seems to have widened every day in America. As an observer, I think the reality of saying this is a further fact that the Constitution of the United States is so democratic. Not only is the Constitution almost defensive in its democracy, it seems to say daily that *despite* this or that, people are equal. And it's the despite part, I think, that I experience as active day to day now. And that is quite frightening.

Not just racism. I think the examination that is required is to ask: Is one inhabiting a kind of fallacy or fantasy, a sort of suspended Constitution within one's daily life that is not enacted by various races, whether it's by the Italian or the Jew or the Black or the Puerto Rican? And what holds that fantasy together? It's basically fragile. It's more like a rotten string than anything that really binds all the various races around the concept of democracy. And that is, I think, perhaps the most frightening aspect of America. As absolutely beautiful and true as the ethics of the Constitution are, the reality of them moves further and further away daily, I think. And one must, of course, adhere to and believe in the principles that are there. But they have been turning into a kind of gospel as opposed to a reality. You read the New Testament and see the same thing, that men must love one another, and Christ is the example, and so on, but nobody lives the New Testament. And it may be that, in this democracy, the equivalent of the New Testament is in the Constitution. So one does not actually live it; one can only believe that it exists and pay homage to it, as a sort of inside faith, but not in practice. I've spent some years in America now, and that separation is as if the Constitution were a church that you go into from time to time and come out of. Monday morning you don't adhere to it; the citizens do not go by that faith.

DM: So a person pays homage but goes away without being held to practice?

DW: No, I'm not saying it's not practiced. There are some fantastically astonishing things in the practice of democracy in America that continue. Among them, the press's relentless, self-adoring idea of justice is useful. *Many* things work and keep the bonds strong. But it's the one constitution that says you must do *this*. It's the closest thing to the New Testament instruction that exists. But now, I think, it's become as remote, in a way, as the concept of brotherly love. It's not a *paradox,* it's just a frightening kind of fantasy.

DM: It seems almost as if, because of the diversity of cultures and races in this country, people have become gradually *less* tolerant of difference.

DW: You have to go into a very deep reason why that is so. It would have to do, perhaps, with the economic structure of the country, in a place where the width between those who have property and the people out in the street, the homeless, is staggering. The multiracial aspect of the society can be visually exciting, as it is in New York. But in a city like Port of Spain in Trinidad, you see a more active multiracial tolerance practiced in what is supposed to be a backward, smaller country than you would in any city in the States, and certainly in New York now. But I don't think it's simply because of the size; I don't think it's simply because of the hustle and the competition and the capitalism and all that. I think that there's a lot more to be said for the excitingly real variety of races from all over the world that exists in the concentrated place called Port of Spain. I'm not pretending that there isn't a lot of hostility and prejudice—if you wish to call it that. But I do not consider it to be really profound. I think the day-to-day exchange between the Indian, the Chinese, the Portuguese, the Syrian, the Black, and so on has historical depth and guilt attached to it, but the daily practice of that life in that city is not one that contains any threat of violence. You're always on the edge of violence in every city in America—of racial violence. And why is that? I think it's got to do with money: it's got to do with who protects those who have the money.

You can use the same argument, I imagine, in the ex-colonies. But there's also a way of life that is different. There's a sort of elation about life, I think, an enjoyment of it that is totally separate. And if you want to talk about division, *that's* a division to me when I come here. When I come back here I find that I'm clenching my teeth a little more, I have to shout a little harder, I have to keep pointing out that I'm not ready to take anything from anybody, and it's really a back-up attitude, you know. Not because I'm black, but because I think it's the average experience of anyone in the street.

DM: Your work is dominated by poems that are set out-of-doors. Much poetry in northern countries is indoor poetry. This suggests a different relationship to nature.

DW: No. I don't think that entirely. The closeted and hermetic poets that exist now in northern poetry may have as much to do with syntax as with climate. The sort of tight-sphinctered, monosyllabic thing that passes for good verse these days is not only a matter of weather, of people staying inside. The pages of a lot of great American poets like Frost and Whitman are ventilated by wind and by weather. And it's very easy to call them nature poets—any of these adjectives that come before poets just to be dismissive. *All* poets are nature poets—or poets by nature, which is the same thing really. But I know what you mean, that there is a kind of closing in of American poetry that I don't think has really to do with the outside or the inside because you can get stanzas written by people who may be in Montana, and the poetry still feels closeted, it still feels tight. It's some sort of screwing tight of the mind that has happened, I think, which may be derivative of a *mis*reading of William Carlos Williams, a misreading of Japanese or Chinese poetry. A lot of people who practice what they think is Chinese poetry forget the *width* of the thing, and think it's all minimal and modest. There's a great epic width to Chinese poetry. It's an immense country. And when somebody talks about a river in China, it's not a brook up in Vermont.

I *do* feel that American theater is closeted and chambered and dark and small and so on. But why is that? I think what's missing is a kind of width of the imagination that very few American playwrights have. Alien subjects aren't approached. They aren't wild enough, I find, for the size of the country. If you measured the height of American theater—when I say height I mean in terms of its concept and what it dares to do—you'd imagine that it was written in a country no bigger than, say, half of Wales.

DM: So it's almost agoraphobic?

DW: Well, it's enclosing; it is shuttered. There are a lot of themes that are just not approached by American writers. One of them, obviously, is the epic of the Indian or the epic—in theater—of crossing the country. I don't just mean the Western; I mean something with a scale and width to it like Whitman's poetry. You don't get that feeling of scale in American theater. And it doesn't have any *tribal* power.

It's all very hermetic and private and individualistic and diaristic. It's very prosaic and journalistic, in that sense, and very conservative in form. I suppose why I say that is to point out that when one talks about an outdoor theater, there's no outdoor literature. There's no reason why American literature shouldn't have that width to it.

DM: In northern literature, is there a feeling of having been pulled up by the roots?

DW: I speak from a position of luck and privilege, because I share two climates, but perhaps the fact that poets keep wearing shoes, you know, gives them small feet or tight feet and corns. A lot of modern poetry is like having corns. It hurts. It's tight and small.

And I don't mean just going barefoot up on the Cape. What I mean is to be barefoot in spirit. Maybe I'm being too Gravesian, but I think if that doesn't happen poetry dies. If a man keeps walking on leather, on concrete every day of his life, and if you take that to represent the spirit of poetry, then it's going to get corns, it's going to get withered and chilblains. I think the poet goes unshod, and that's for the whole feel of the thing. To walk about barefoot, as Whitman said, really is the first need.

And the shape of the human foot is not a matter of style. A lot of modern poets are stylists. It's French prose poetry or it's Williams or its southwest or whatever. It's like different cuts of shoes, styles of shoes.

DM: In *Midsummer,* you say: "No language is neutral." Could you expand a little on this?

DW: Well, I think the surrounding text may help. Obviously, when you enter language, you enter a kind of choice which contains in it the political history of the language, the imperial width of the language, the fact that you're either subjugated by the language or you have had to dominate it. So language is not a place of retreat, it's not a place of escape, it's not even a place of resolution. It's a place of struggle.

DM: So, particularly in colonial countries, *any* choice of words— this is an exaggeration—is, in a sense, a political choice, or there is a stance involved?

DW: Well, in a way, it's only the proportion of stress that matters. It's surely more theatrical for people to say to what is called the third world: Well, you have inherited this language and how do you feel *in* it, and that sort of nonsense. But obviously in a country of tyranny, there is a political choice involved. The next word you write could get you in jail, really. You avoid the next word or you put it down at the risk of whatever happened to all sorts of poets in that totalitarian regime. And, in a sense, if you expand that and intensify it within yourself, and you make yourself your own regime, when you're as dictatorial and as threatening to yourself as you are, it's the defiance of that inner regime that makes you choose, and not cower, in the courage of using the right word.

If you use a political metaphor, I would say that every poet is imprisoned in a system that is himself, that he is *jailed* in himself, and that that effort to get out of that jail is the struggle he has or the defiance he has in having the guts to use the next word without the safety or the cliché of repetition. And that inner political action of the choice of the next word, if it were broadened and taken out into a visible arena, is not any different from being on the witness stand in front of a regime. And the regime that is rigid is the one that says inside himself: Are you conforming to a tradition which is a regime or being *outré* and fake revolutionary to astonish the regime, or are you simply writing as honestly as you can without self-astonishment, without self-congratulation, without self-heroism or even martyrdom, and continuing by the process and the line that you think is true to the language that you are working in? The inner prison that exists is one that's outside and yet is inside the totalitarian regime. I consider that to be obvious in our time. And whether it's Mandelstam or Herbert or Milosz or even Seamus Heaney in the conflict in Ireland, there *is* an inner prison that one recognizes in oneself, and one is both judge and prisoner. But you don't plead and you don't whine; you state the condition.

DM: And, in a sense, you're always guilty.

DW: Well, guilty until the next time [laughter]. But, no, you don't stay in guilt. I really think that—not for the poet but obviously for the race in the twentieth century—poetry has never been more urgent than it is now. What we have are regimes that are not just opposed to the idea of poetry because it is seen as something effete, but as something that is really threatening. We're in a time of ideas, *heavy* ideas, not ones that are as emblematical or as simple as, say, the Church versus the State. We are in a whole area of conscience that is articulated, that has to be articulated within the regimes themselves. Looking at a poet like Seamus, for instance, it would be very easy for him not to concern himself or to concern himself on a level where his conscience is not so tortured. It would be very easy to write a kind of poem which is abstract and which is theoretical. But to share, to be involved in—take someone like Adam Zagajewski—is not only physical. There is a small community of conscience that exists all over the world now that brings poets closer together into a very small brotherhood. They may come from anywhere, from India or Poland or wherever. But it's like a concentration camp.

DM: Is there another danger of oversimplifying, of taking an issue at face value and writing a poetry that has a pro and con?

DW: Exactly. These choices are even more demonic than those raised by the average, say, nature poem—if you want to call it that—because the temptations are enormous. One can then move into being bard, spokesman, martyr, even coward as a role. And all of these are roles offered by the regime, by the *exterior* regime, and the poet can be tempted, without knowing that he has been tempted, to become any one of those. I think a lot of great poets at some point move into that kind of high flatulence in which they may be believing at the time that they are absolutely necessary, that their voice, that particular pitch of the voice is necessary for the time. It exists in all great poets, but it's just that part of the great poet that you turn from and say sometimes: Oh, give me a break, knock it off, cool it down, you know—whether it's the "prophetic" vision of a bitter prophecy or whatever it is. Unless it has that kind of *total* devastating light or blight that exists in Blake, for instance, who is talking the truth. You sometimes hear it in Yeats, you hear it in Virgil, you hear it in Frost. It is that bardic voice that, after a certain age, a poet is attracted to without knowing that he is on a platform bellowing.

DM: The theater gives you satisfactions that poetry might not, or allows certain parts of your voice to express themselves that poetry does not.

DW: Well, there's a bit of sadness about poetry. Once a poem is finished and it goes away, it's severed from you, it's not yours. Whereas in the theater, the playwright is the one who takes all the blame and the burden. And, of course, there's the sharing of that elation or that despair by several people. Twenty people, thirty people can be in that boat together. So, in a sense, yes, the personal elation, when it's multiplied, can be ecstatic. But also, by contrast, so can the personal despair for which you are responsible. Multiplied by twenty—right?—this makes you twenty times more depressed than if you wrote a bad poem [laughter]. If you write a bad poem, you just throw it away or hope you realize it's a bad poem. If you write a bad play, you never know it's a bad play until you really hear the groans.

DM: What about the line itself; when the actor begins to speak the line, does it lift itself off the page and change into something else?

DW: No. The poetry that survives in the theater survives by itself. It isn't *made;* it can't be *created.* If it's there, it's there; if it's not, no amount of lighting effects and terrific acting can make it happen. I sometimes give my students exercises in which they read their own lines. If you take a lyric poem and treat it dramatically, the embarrassment you can feel in reading a line that is not on the page but is coming out of the human mouth is acute. So I do a lot of that with the writers in the class. You learn a good deal either way. You learn that a line that may pass by the ear and be forgiven and slide by *grates* in the theater. Of course, the other threat is pomposity because you can elevate theatrical speech into making it sound extremely good, but that's the voice getting up on a platform, you know, and performing.

DM: In your poem, "Nearing Forty," you implied you were trying to strip your style: "the household truth, the style past metaphor." In your recent book, *Midsummer,* you seem to be more spare, almost impatient with artifice, almost impatient with poetry itself, and yet these poems are extremely concentrated.

DW: But there can be *clear* concentration. I mean a drop of dew is clear concentration, because it can reflect an entire universe. In the little window in a dewdrop you can have that. The clarity that one wants and never *will* get but one lives all one's life for is, I think, to become an element, if it were possible. To become water, you know, to have no coloring, no obvious source, no artificial source, no frame. And, in a way, as one who is dealing with time, you think of the component of water, the element of time in the stillness of water. In a sense, that's the kind of simplicity that one strives for. I mean you wish to live to be ninety so you can try to be as clear as that in the effort. Larkin has a poem that says: "If I were made to construct a region, it would be of water." Pasternak says it about water, about simple nouns. Or Rilke says it—just to put that word down as if it were the first time, as if it had an element of simplicity. And I think there are periods in the epochs of English poetry in which again one comes back, as Wordsworth did, at a certain point, to something that is—not illiterate and not dumb—but *clear,* a simplicity that may contain a lot of knowledge in it, like Blake's has. The simplicity of Blake is a profound simplicity that has all the cosmology and myth that is in his head. But when he gets to putting down his monosylla-bles, that's the clarity one is talking about, something that is an elemental, unmeasured, unscannable kind of clearness. And one is talking, I think, about memory, really. How direct is the word to human memory? The word put on the paper should be not *read* but remembered when it is read. The moment of reading is a moment of remembering, not a moment of learning.

DM: Distillation, in a way, and expansion at the same time?

DW: Yes, it's Blake's grain of sand.

DM: In your poetry some words seem to have a different meaning than in most poetry in English. Take the word "sugar," for example. The costs of sugar, the human costs are alive in the poetry, which makes the word new, in a sense, or reveals what the word really means.

DW: Well, the word "wheat" for me will always be a literary word. It's a word out of poetry; it's not a word out of agriculture for me. It's not a word that I know—it's not a *world* or word that I know. When you plant wheat, that's *work,* but wheat in tapestries, wheat in literature becomes a pastoral word that has no work in it, in a sense. I think that may be the difference, because sugar is not a pastoral, though it may appear to be a pastoral thing. The fields of sugar in the Caribbean are divinely beautiful, are supremely calm and so on, but there's a lot of blood and sweat in the earth for it. I think the same is true of wheat, and when a northern writer writes about wheat, he's writing close to the idea of bread, of survival. The wheat in the Bible is hard-work wheat; it's not a literary word. The same thing would be true, I imagine, of olive oil in Greece or, if you change places, the coconut. For one person it's picturesque and archaic and literary. For another person it's something that smells and grows.

DM: What voice leads you from line to line?

DW: I was thinking today, at fifty-seven I may have not wanted to be a poet but an anthology, which I don't mind, because I enjoy so many voices that my own is irritating. So what you ask, what leads me from line to line, I *hope,* is any poet who is inhabiting the next letter. If poets can shift like shadows and an *A* may belong to Dante, and a *J* to Homer or Pasternak, those letters aren't my property. And I just hope I don't have the vanity to believe that they are. So what leads me, I imagine, leads anyone who is serious and admits the generations that precede the word, and one is only adding, if one can, to that general sound, with a very small sound of one's own. I think every poet of any modesty hopes to make just a small contribution to the sound of the world's hum, and does not by any means wish to be individual or be praised for his style or whatever.

Just to come to a conclusion, and not because he's my friend, I think Seamus Heaney, for instance, could have done a very nimble thing. He could have danced away conspicuously, with great levitation and skill, from the haunting shadow of Yeats, and turned into something very aggressively different. But he knew that gradual absorption *would* lead to his own voice. And, for instance, in the phase that he's now gone through in his last book, *The Haw Lantern,* his use of the abstract noun as a whole territory and not just as an abstraction is very different from the way Yeats emblematically used abstract nouns. Seamus uses a language now that is not concentrated and fine and provincially exquisite or right, but one that is passing into a language of understanding, of exchange in a territory where the *blocks* of the polysyllables exist as solidly as if they were nature. And how does that happen? It happens because Heaney allows the voice in.

Poets who frantically try to escape any accusation of sounding like anyone else, who bloat themselves up, are the ones who have eventually sort of floundered.

DM: In your earliest poems, there's already a maturity in the voice. Somehow your poetry doesn't evolve, in a sense, as if you were whole at the beginning. And yet there are many changes. What would you say the changes are over the span of your poetry?

DW: I agree with that. I'd say only the suffering is different, the quality of the suffering is different. You see, one can have an unembarrassed conversation and say at fifty-seven, without any fake humility, that I was a prodigy in the sense that I wrote very well very young. *Tonally,* it sometimes amazes me that I don't seem to be any different from when I was eighteen. You know, it seems to me to be the same person talking. Now that may be an imitation, because there may be no wisdom there. But it may be in my nature, and may be in the nature of the eighteen-year-old writer, to *avoid* wisdom. There's a kind of prerogative attached to wisdom, which has to do with style. There are certain great poets who achieve wisdom, and it's very inseparable from style. Yeats and Eliot are two who are full of wisdom, but you can't separate the wisdom from the style. The wisdom of Eliot is the style of Eliot; the wisdom of Yeats is the style of Yeats. But the wisdom of the Bible is wisdom; the wisdom of Isaiah is wisdom, and so forth.

I think that that openness is what I've always had. I have been very flattered, as opposed to being insulted, when I've been told that I sound like someone else who was great. I always considered that to be an honor and not an accusation. You see—and maybe I have a medieval mind—I'm really part of a *guild*. I don't consider myself to be an individual. And if I were working as a stonemason in a guild, that would be my contribution to the cathedral. If I was an apprentice to Leonardo, I would feel terrific if someone said, this is as good as Leonardo, or you got this from Leonardo. Obviously, I'd say, yes, thanks very much. But the twentieth century—and especially in this country—is obsessed with the idiosyncratic genius, the doing your own thing, having your own style. It's like the movies. It turns everybody into a movie star. Television extras—there are no extras in American poetry.

DM: In "Sea Grapes," you say: "The classics can console but not enough." Does this need any explanation?

DW: Well, I don't think so. All of us have been to the point where, in extreme agony and distress, you turn to a book, and look for parallels, and you look for a greater grief than maybe your own. You can immerse yourself for awhile in that tragedy, and hope there will be some elation, as tragedy's supposed to provide. And it does. It provides a distance—the distance of character, of experience, and you can distance your own experience through this. But the truth of human agony is that a book does not assuage a toothache. It isn't that things don't pass and heal. Perhaps the only privilege that a poet has is that, in that agony, whatever chafes and hurts, if the person survives, produces something that is hopefully lasting and moral from the experience.

DM: You've never had to deal with any type of censorship, but is the lack of an audience—aside from other poets—a type of, not censorship, but of silencing by neglect or indifference? What does this do to the voice, the silence of not being heard, in a sense?

DW: Well, I've always wondered about the sense of isolation of the American poets that is *so* acute in contemporary American poetry, especially the generation of Lowell and Berryman and Jarrell and the others. How come there was such adulation and yet such isolation at the same time? And how come so many made almost a frantic claim to the right to be poets in a culture? I'm not an American, so I don't go through that. I really, in the Caribbean, am not treated like a literary figure. And it's extremely healthy because, in a way, I'm really left alone. It makes you very much your own judge and your own applauder, unfortunately your own audience. At the same time, it also does not make a social crisis out of the idea of being a poet, as it does here.

I think the thing about being a poet in America, or even a young poet in America is the poet is almost crying out for the society to be hostile to him—or her, I mean both him and her—to repress him, to take notice, to imprison him, to pay attention in a sense. But what happens is suddenly or quietly there is a very wide blandness that occurs, in which the poet is subtly absorbed and given a name and a trade *separate* from the society, maybe because of that naming. You are a poet, you write poetry, you get your books published, you're in magazines. And you don't go around with a cape and a rose, so you can't tell in this democracy how different being a poet would be. And I think that it is this real unnavigable but hospitable space ahead of the poet that finally makes a lot of them say, I'll just do something else. And that is another kind of death, really, that happens. It's not some big dramatic thing. It may not be like breaking your pen and fleeing into the jungle or something. But there's something that just quietly absorbs and deadens the spirit. And it's not inertia, because Americans are vigorous, industrious, honest—that's the quality of American activity—direct, forthright. Pay you what you deserve, reward you with what you get, etcetera. It's a just society, and not a cunning one. And it isn't that you want more evil, but it may be a

very, very spiritually satisfied society—or apparently spiritually satisfied society. It can't be disturbed. It's like making a lot of noise in a
void room. And I think that when that voice begins to sound as if it's
being raised for effect or lowered so that attention can be paid to it,
that middle ground is not found, you see. And then, in a way, the poet
goes into a kind of isolation. He may be on the Pacific coast, or he
may be alone on a farm in Iowa, or he may be in a loft in New York,
or he may be teaching in Boston, but there's no *necessity* in him.

DM: Communication?

DW: Yes, he doesn't feel needed. By luck, by blessing, I feel
needed. I feel very needed. In the Caribbean, meeting people anywhere, on a beach somewhere, talking to poor people, to fishermen,
a guy in a store, anybody, I feel as if I could speak for them. When
that is missing, it's deadening.

DM: I think I'll leave you in peace.

DW: Deadening is a terrible word to end on [laughter].

An Interview with Derek Walcott

J. P. White / 1990

From *Green Mountains Review,* Vol. 4, No. 1 (Spring-Summer 1990), 14–37. Reprinted by permission of J. P. White.

JW: Both you and V. S. Naipaul felt an early calling to be writers. Your fathers were both writers. But his path led him away from Trinidad almost completely. What is your relationship with Naipaul and other Caribbean writers? Where do the paths meet and separate?

DW: If you took an anthology of photographs of Caribbean writers—and we are talking about a small place—you would see faces of various mixtures. You would see white faces, Indian faces, Black African faces, and then the combinations that exist in these portraits. For instance, Naipaul is what we call an Eastern African writer, John Hearne a writer of mixed blood, Wilson Harris a mixture of African and Indian, etc. The portraits are multi-racial. One of the most promising young poets I ever saw in the Caribbean was a Chinese boy; I've forgotten his name. As I said before, the great West Indian writer might be a Chinese, he could be a Lebanese, he could be anything. Now this is true of America as well, but the point is, we are talking about a very concentrated area. The Caribbean can produce any kind of good writer, not necessarily relegated to one particular class or color, and that's what is fascinating about it. The more the whole Caribbean ethos coheres, the more varied it will become, because each writer, each artist, will see how complex and interesting and exciting that very variety is. For that variety, the artist would normally have to go to sources in China, India, Africa, the Mediterranean, and Europe. But that vitality and richness is all there in the day-to-day presence of simple exchange, found in places like Port of Spain and Kingston.

JW: To what extent did the lineage of mixed blood compel you to become a poet of mixed languages with a musical tone? I wonder if you would talk a little bit about your commitment to give full flourish to the languages you love.

DW: I may have contributed to the illusion that there is such a

151

division of language in me that I came to English painfully and slowly. The reality is I grew up in two languages, Creole and English. And, of course, tonal English with a Creolized inflection. So there were actually three languages or even four. There was French, which was not spoken too much on the island, French Creole, English and then French Accent. I could move among any of these. Writing in Creole was much more exciting than writing down English, but at the same time, I was growing up in a tradition of English, and I was trying to learn the craft of English verse as well as I could. So in a way I may have not developed all the languages open to me. I could have quite comfortably and justifiably written in French if I had learned French properly or practiced it sufficiently. Because in a way St. Lucia is not different from Martinique. It is only different because of a political treaty between France and England. By temperament and linguistically, St. Lucia leans toward the French, not the English.

JW: How would you characterize your early poetic apprenticeship? How did you go about learning to write the strong iambic line and who were your first literary models and teachers?

DW: Very, very early, I was encouraged by my mother and by very good teachers in elementary school and even primary school. The fact that one was Protestant and one went to a very simple wooden church in which the hymns that were sung had the design of quatrains had something to do with it. The word became more important than the ritual, it was not in Latin, but rather in Elizabethan English or Victorian English. Some of the hymns must have entered into me quite early, because the whole conduct of the Methodist service is really based entirely on the word. Between the sermons from the Bible and the oratory of the preacher and the hymns themselves, what one had was an English that was rigid in its design and in its meter. Also, in St. Lucia, one of the benefits of what is called backwardness is that the librarians are very good. Because one has to be ordered, and economically justifiable, you can't order trash. So there was a good library there, and at home there was a book case with some good writers, like Scott, Dickens, Sabatini, the adventurous Italian novelist. I had access to those books, so the choice was really between comic books and the classics, without too much trash in between. The well-bound novel, say the average American novel, was too expensive, so it was an object of admiration just as if it were an

American shirt or something. Plus, of course, the secondary school training in the Caribbean is molded very much on the English public school system of education, in which the discipline was extremely strict. It had a hierarchy of obedience through the monitor and prefect and the assistant head master and head master. But also, what you were taught was the same syllabus as all the colonies and protectorates of the empire and England itself. You sat for the Cambridge exams, for London matriculation and so on. But in addition to that, it was not, for some reason, incongruous to do Latin in a place where you could look outside the window and see bananas. It was just taken as part of one's education, and one didn't have a choice. I think education is not a matter of choice. It should not be inflicted, but I think that one should entrust oneself to the wisdom of teachers and the curriculum of teachers. With all that behind one, it was easy to enter and take pleasure in the discipline of poetry and the delight of writing about a place around you that had not really been described before. So there was that double kind of excitement—the one that existed in the classroom in English poetry, and French verses, and the one outside the window. A whole life outside waiting to be described. And I think that is the same excitement that exists in the Western Indian novel of the generation of Lamming, Hearne, Reid, and so on. There is a very strong sense of exploration and discovery and delight, not only of sociology and language, but of the landscape itself. The influences I had in the beginning were the best influences, because I immediately knew that there was no one better than Shakespeare and if one wanted to be good, one would have to write like Shakespeare, which is a good model. One had to write at the highest possible level, because there wasn't too much trash in your mind. I think the climate cleans out the trash too. If you finished school, and you came home and suddenly it was very cool in the afternoon, it would be like putting aside one kind of life and taking on another, not necessarily opposite. What was good was the two lives were real. Of course, you could see a demarcation between what you learned at school and what was outside you. The poverty around you and the barefoot, poor people around you. But there was never a sense of any superiority in terms of feeling that we were privileged or that we were depriving other people of things.

When I began to write, I hadn't read too many modern poets. But once I was led into modern poetry by a friend of mine, Harry Simmons, and another friend, James Rodway, who lent me books by Eliot and Auden, I just modeled myself on those writers, poem after poem. I would write one poem in the style of Spender and one in the style of MacNeice in the same exercise book. And yet, because I treated them as if they were poems I was recreating, I never felt that they were anything else but original. I knew they were imitations, but I had a sense of original excitement in the imitation.

JW: You've said in your essay "What the Twilight Says: An Overture," that the goal of theater and poetry must be to explore the origins of aboriginal calamity. But more important than this is to search below these origins for the deeper questions of who we are and what our nature is, what mix of good and evil we are capable of? Does the meditative streak one finds in *Midsummer* and elsewhere come from this quest?

DW: The phrase aboriginal calamity is from Cardinal Newman, who said mankind is involved in some kind of aboriginal calamity. I suppose you could say it means original sin, but it goes beyond that idea. It comes down to a question of whether one considers human nature to be intrinsically and irrevocably evil—and certainly there are many statements made by poets who have come at some point to that conclusion. Homo lupus homini, man is wolf to man, or in Larkin, "it deepens like a tidal shelf" in terms of man's sorrow and the suffering he inflicts on others. If one comes from a history in which the background is genocide and slavery, poverty and colonialism, and one still sees it around, not only residually but almost actively, then you ask, of course, is one race alone capable of genocide, capable of enslaving another? And you know this is not true. Every race is capable and has had slaves and has had tyrants. Now maybe that's just sociological, but the deepest question of the 20th century has to be the question of the Holocaust. I still think that there is no historical event equal to it. I'm not talking only about the extermination of the Jews. I'm talking about the kind of reason that scientifically, not ethnically, justifies the experiments of extermination. And whether that is not the depth of corruption of the human mind. But then, as profound and as shattering and unanswered as that question is, at the same time that this is happening, there may be a larger number of human beings doing good. The four or five doctors or generals smoking behind glass and watching Jews being gassed is not multiplied by every single individual in the world. You can ask, how can such a thing have happened? But no question is ever asked about good. Nobody ever asks, why do men do good? The act of doing good, of being charitable does not have a question attached to it. The act of evil has a question attached to it. Perhaps one settles too much on the idea of the question, which may be the whole point, because the question exists in the figure of Prometheus, and it exists in the figure of Cain, and it exists in all of the emblematic characters of pride or deceit found in mythology. It's not benign to say that while evil is happening, good is also being done perhaps by even more people than those four or five very cool, calculating men who go home to their wives and children and have dinner after watching people being gassed. The question then travels to the furthest point possible, *which is love*. Which is embodied in the figure of Christ. Or it takes you as far as Dante, because the horrors through which Dante goes are finally sublimated in love, a radiant light that swirls backward into a center. There is validity in that progress. It is not apparent, and it certainly is not apparent in the cycles of history. But the cycles of history are repetitive, they do not resolve anything. What remains unresolved is the *is,* the light, the *is,* the thing that is at the heart of being. Now I don't embrace this notion of love in some evangelical way, I just know that individually one endures things for the sake of love. I think any average parent is capable of that, and the child who becomes a parent inherits that possibility. While love lasts in two human beings, if it is not simply sexual longing, or need for company, or loneliness, yes there is that force. It is a force not reached or contained by prisons. It cannot be contained by any kind of siege. And that love can be manifested in a situation in which a man may love his country and suffer for it—such as a poet like Mandelstam. Even if that person perishes, the tyrant can't touch him. And therefore, what had to be touched by those people behind the glass is that idea. And that's stronger, it is ultimately stronger than the victims who are lying around. It may sound very silly, but I think that the whole history of the Afro-American has been redeemed by a very strong love of the idea of worship, which continues today in the churches, in the storefront churches. It continues in the idea of endurance, it even continues in the idea of a sublime gaiety that goes

beyond suffering. I think that is the greatest contribution the Afro-
American has made to America.

JW: In that same essay, you oppose a theater and a language born
of political revenge or despair or cultural nostalgia—what you call
"mimicry." On the other hand, you favor a language that reflects the
diversity, the "schizophrenia" of your Caribbean inheritance. Is the
articulation of that favored language what you intended by the phrase,
"The future of West Indian militancy lies in art"?

DW: Schizophrenia—I use that word too casually. The idea of
division is permanent in all countries that have been colonial. It is a
shadow, a kind of meridian, a crossing that has to be examined. What
I believe is that there can be a mimicry of despair as well as a mimicry
of prophecy and political hope. There can be even a mimicry of
slavery, if one can perpetuate in the slave's child the idea of being
delivered from slavery, but it is still slavery. It is still the thing that
encourages gratitude—that's a technique of South Africa. To gradually liberate, at their own pace, generation by generation, law by law,
concession by concession. It appears to progress, but every time it
gets one step forward it takes two backwards, and therefore it gives
you the illusion of continuing. The same sort of thing happens in this
country. It continues in the colonization of the Afro-American, in
which certain things are handed out, in which the Afro-American says
"But look how we are doing." If you took the instant in which the
Afro-American in 1988 is saying "Look how well we are doing," and
you went back a 100 years, there could be a slave who is saying
"Look how well we are doing, 50 years ago they used to beat us.
Now they don't beat us, now they don't sell us." If you take the idea
of time as chronological time, everything looks as if it is progressing.
Everything seems to be in advance. In reality, of course, it is simply
how that technique is measured by who is in power. That is the
technique of Glasnost. But the idea of the domination of the Russian
citizen has never disappeared from the grip of the Russian comman-
deer. You measure the freedom until little by little if you take one
manacle off, you can move one hand; if you take the other one off,
you can move two hands. You can take a chain off so you can move
one leg and then move another, but you still are within walls. You
might be able to take a walk, but outside there is another world. When
all the walls are not there, then one can talk about freedom. But what

society in power does not make walls for the downtrodden of its class. There's none that does that. Therefore, when you have Black political groups saying that if they were in charge there would be complete deliverance, you have to mistrust them, because that leads to ideas of revenge, which is futile. It also leads to the illusion of freedom, in which one person is freer than the other. When I talk about the mimicry of the idea of slavery, it can always be a shadow ahead of us if we continue to think of the past as something like a light behind us by which we move. What happens in the Third World in the colonial imagination is acceptance of the idea of history as a moral force. That notion is what paralyzes and leads to mimicry of action or bitter memory.

JW: The word exile turns up throughout the poems. The feeling of homelessness, of not quite belonging to the culture, is a quality that describes many of the characters in your plays—Claudia, Sheila, Makak, Jackson. But even homelessness is not quite right. It's more like someone on the periphery of empire—of looking in and out simultaneously. How would you describe this double vision, this seeking of your characters?

DW: In a very simple way, it is extremely physical. One has grown up in a certain climate from childhood, and that climate is built into one's body, into one's temperament. So every year, as I get older, it becomes more intensified, this physical nostalgia for simple things like warm sea, sun, a certain kind of food. It may in fact simply grow stronger in all writers. And it may be that in the childhood of every writer there is a taste of a certain fruit, a slab of light in a certain field, a color of the sky. All of these things are instinctive in a writer and they may be clouded over by a lot of experience. But the taste on the exile's tongue is the taste of his childhood. The taste cannot be washed away with a different wine, with the best sort of food, for beneath it all, the travel, the politics, the sociology, there is a simple food and fruit of his region, the place he has come from. So there is an interior exile, however sublimated, in every writer who is not in his own territory, who may even be superficially enjoying the absence that he is either celebrating or lamenting. If you expand that into a wider sense of culture, this sickness increases in proportion to time, and obviously it must, because in the old idea of banishment for life, you find an unendurable idea. It means never will you, not necessarily see this temple or that palace and the faces of your loved ones, but rather you may lose the particular and simple things in your memory. It may be a bird that one never sees on a particular shore in exile. It may be a smell, it may be a smell of wood, somewhere suddenly. All these things are part of a kind of displacement. Now if you amplify that displacement to say, as a phrase in the Bible says, "And Man goeth to his long home," then the long home may be heaven or it may be the grave. But perhaps the idea of heaven is created from this idea that we are in exile on earth from a place to which we really belong and this period of time is simply a passing. That may be the root of the concept of paradise, that we have an interior heaven in our own heart. This idea certainly is in the heart of poetry, because poetry is a situation of divine discontent. It is a blessed discontent. It is a discontent that says there is more than this. There is more than me, there is more than what's immediate and what's temporal. That discontent is part of the beat and spirit of poetry.

JW: In *Midsummer,* the "tropic zone" section, you write . . . "my own prayer is to write / lines as mindless as the oceans of linear time, / since time is the first province of Caesar's jurisdiction." In this poem, there is a belief that the manifestations of empire will eventually erode. Everywhere you acknowledge the ruins of empire in an elegiac tone, yet you are careful in assigning blame or guilt. What is your thinking behind this emotional reserve?

DW: The element I know contains an enormous lesson. And it is not a lesson of emptiness, because in St. Lucia the presence of the sea is bigger than the land in your own sight. There is a horizon; it could be totally empty—the waters of the bay could be empty of boats. Then you'd have an immensity between the sky and the sea. Obviously, there is the usual thing of creating a sense of insignificance compared to that immensity, but it has something stronger than that to say. Nothing can be put down in the sea. You can't plant on it, you can't live on it, you can't walk on it. Therefore, the strength of the sea gives you an idea of time that makes history absurd. Because history is an intrusion on that immensity. History is a very, very minor statement; it's not even an intrusion, it is an insignificant speck on the rim of that horizon. And by history I mean a direction that is progressive and linear. With the sea, you can travel the horizon in any direction, you can go from left to right or from right to left. It doesn't

proceed from A to B to C to D and so on. It is not a rational line. It's
a circle, and that's what you feel. You feel that first of all, that if you
weren't there you wouldn't be missed. If you are on land looking at
ruins, the ruins commemorate you. They more commemorate than
lament the achievement of man. They may contain a moral lesson but
underneath that there is still praise of the tyrant or hero. There is still
awe at the immensity of the ruin. And that's what the ruins of any
great cultures do. In a way they commemorate decay. That's the
elegiac point. The sea is not elegiac in that way. The sea does not
have anything on it that is a memento of man. Somehow the motion
of the sea enters the motion of the mind. The mind itself tries to
absorb part of that immensity, and realizes that its own contributions
to immensity of that thing are simply a bubble, one of many bubbles
in an infinite area. There is a strength that is drawn from island
peoples in that reality of scale in which they inhabit. There is a sense
both of infinity and acceptance of the possibility of infinity, which is
strong. And in a way that provides a kind of endurance. It provides a
kind of settling of the mind that is equal to the level of the horizon.
That is what I have learned from growing up on an island.

JW: In the poem, "The Star Apple Kingdom," a Black woman
whispers to the speaker through a keyhole, "Let me in, I'm finished
with praying, I'm the Revolution. / I am darker, the older America."
Here and in "The Schooner Flight" you reject Revolution and yet it
is unclear what new vision of democracy replaces that whispering
through the keyhole. Do your characters place any faith in political solutions?

DW: As a writer of verse, it is not my business to offer political
resolutions. If someone came to Christ with this question, his answer
would be "Render unto Caesar the things that are Caesar's." If you
render to Caesar what is Caesar's, you are saying, "If Caesar wants
me to be a slave, then that is what I'll do"? No, if you scan it, if you
pause it exactly, then you say, "Render unto Caesar the things that
are Caesar's." If you stress "that *are* Caesar's," that do belong to
Caesar. What belongs to Caesar? Does Caesar own my spirit? Caesar
does not own my spirit. Can Caesar tax me? Yes, he can tax me. But
then, the deepest political answer is the one that becomes banal and
impractical allegedly. If you take Gandhi, if you take Christ, or
anyone who simply says, "Love one another," that is a political

answer. And that is the answer of the poet, "Love one another."
Now somebody says that's impossible, that's not human, that is not
practical, human beings are not like that. How can you legislate love,
how can you design governments with love? But that *is* a political
answer. It is a political answer in Dante, it's a political answer in the
gospels. That is a political answer for a human society that listens to
its poets.

JW: Shabine, the speaker of "The Schooner Flight," is a seaman
and poet and a reprobate. He says, after being forced out of Trinidad,
"I had no nation now but the imagination." As a Caribbean writer
living in two worlds, do you think of yourself as an intermediary
between first and third worlds, with poetry your only language.

DW: In the case of a character talking, on this particular point, by
imagination he also means memory of what could happen to only
himself from his experience. Or you could take this to mean that the
nation of the imagination would be a nation in which the temperament
and the spirit of the poet would enter the spirit of politics. It is the
same kind of thing that Joseph Brodsky says in the Nobel lecture: if
politicians read poetry they might be better human beings. Sometimes
politicians write poetry and they are terrible tyrants. But certainly if
poetry could inform the state, it would be the same answer as if love
could invest the state with its power. Now again, for the politician,
the rational man, the man who believes that human nature, by its very
conduct historically, repeats itself, repeats its errors, repeats its
prejudices, repeats its persecutions and its masochism, poetry becomes simply a homily, a doormat emblem, something you have at
certain occasions. This other nation we are talking about is the nation
that acts imaginatively in the higher sense of the imagination. And in
the way that the imagination creates a work of art, a nation's ideal
should be to be a work of art. Now you can say that is impossible
because no artist ever thinks he completes a work of art. Whether it
is Shakespeare, Dante or Joyce, no artist is ever satisfied. Even if
some of the works appear to us to be perfect, for the artist it is always
flawed. And, therefore, it is inevitable to have a flawed nation, but the
effort to create a nation as if it were an act of imagination would be
more creative than the repetition of the usual cliches and conduct.
Shabine is not going that far with his statement. I am simply saying
that if I have no nation but in imagination, the artist is left out of the

nation and therefore his recourse is to an imaginary nation which is
his nation, his imagination. So by disaffection, he has become an
artist.

JW: I've heard you give a public talk about the role of the epic, and
I have a couple of questions along this vein. You said the epic not only
records the memory of the tribe, but also the faith and joy that bind
people together. Given America's fascination with a self-created
destiny apart from divine intervention, do you think an epic poet is
likely to emerge from this continent? Do you think of Whitman, Crane
and Neruda as epic poets?

DW: No, I think I said that the epic poem may have been in the
Navaho poetry. Because epic does not have self-conscious width, it
has natural width. And the Navaho hymns have natural width, not
because they're all pastoral and primitive and polytheistic, but simply
because you inhale and exhale an epic as naturally as if you inhale the
air. And that's what you find in the Navaho poetry, natural width and
air. Now, even *Moby Dick* is a sort of short circuit epic and a very
literary one. When the whale is all damned and the guy is all damned,
and they are working like hell, you find a sense of epic struggle and
so on. To me, *Moby Dick* seems so overloaded with symbols, the
freight is too much. *Ulysses* is an epic because it breathes. It's an
urban epic, which is remarkable in a small city. It's a wonderful epic
in the sense that the subject is lyrical and not heroic. The subject is a
matter of a reflective man, not a man of action, but a sort of wandering
Jew. That's the width of that epic, that Bloom is the wandering Jew.
With Whitman, the exhilarations are specifically aimed at the pioneer;
I don't see any obstructions. I don't see the Indians coming in the
opposite direction. I don't see Indian massacres. I don't see brutali-
ties, scalpings, and burning and torturing. It's a sanitized version of
infinite wheat fields. I think a great poet has a deeper sense of evil, a
wickedness of malice and malignity. You say, where is it in *Ulysses,*
and it's there in *Ulysses* because Bloom is tormented. He is tormented
by an allegedly gentle-hearted people which the Irish are supposed to
be, but they are his tormentors. They may be minor tormentors, but
they are crucifying Bloom.

JW: You've made the argument that in the true epic, the individual
is absorbed by God. Do you feel that your own work expresses the

view of the individual absorbed by God or at odds with the inventions of man?

DW: I'm reviewing Les Murray's new book and we were in a taxi going somewhere and I asked him, who is your new book dedicated to, and he said to the "Glory of God." And that's what Paradiso says. What is swallowed up in Paradiso is Dante himself; everything becomes translucent or it becomes the center, and the work goes to an irradiance. So, in a sense, if the page itself had become white, like a white light, then Dante would be swallowed up in God, and the poetry would be swallowed up in God. And I think, yes, I would like to be swallowed in that if at all possible. But you don't write poetry to God. He doesn't need poetry. You write poetry for human beings. You write poetry in praise of God, but you don't write poetry for God. He's a better poet than anybody. Also, that whole idea of being absorbed in and taken up by God is so un-20th century. But it's there in Rilke, it's the whole idea of swirling up and away into some kind of final radiance in which you don't count, and your work certainly doesn't count. Or that the work of the world revolves backwards, as it does in Paradiso, with Sybil's leaves reeling backward, all memory gone. They are bound in one volume, and that one volume is a poem, which may be Dante's poem, but it is also the poem of the world. It is the poem whose pages cohere and finally turn right back into the light at the end. I wouldn't say all this if I was an American or British poet, but I'm from the Caribbean. I come from a very simple society of apparently simple beliefs. From childhood, this has been my belief, what I wanted to happen to me. If one could shed ambition and shed craft and suddenly be an element, it's not that the self is dissolving, it is joining something larger than itself. This feeling is there in every poet; I think it is there in Wordsworth; it is there in the radiant ending of Shakespeare's *Tempest*.

JW: In the poem "North and South," you take a good shot at the free verse poets: "the free-verse nightingales are trilling 'Read me! Read me!' in various meters of asthmatic pain," and in your Auden elegy you say, "but you, who left each feast at nine, knew war, like free-verse, is a sign of bad manners." What do you see as the limitations of the prevailing free-verse poetics, both in form and content?

DW: I think it is a blight now. I think most modern American and

British poetry is stricken by a blight of modesty and a blight of muddle and obliquity. Most free verse does not write from memory. It writes for reading, it writes for the appreciation of its design on the page. It writes as if it chooses to evaporate the moment it is finished. I'm getting older, so I can talk like that. Sometimes, I can even feel a great distance between my students and myself when I talk in this particular way. I'm not saying the only answer is to write everything in rhyme, but I have encountered situations in which rhyme is sneered at or people ask, "do you write in forms?" When I hear there is a particular rhythm to American breathing that is different from Roman breathing, then I get exasperated. I have come to the point now, not so much where I want to proselytize the idea of structure, but I'm exhausted by the quiet hostility one encounters in regards to saying simple things well. Poetry is communication and communication is memory. There is a lot of waste in most contemporary poetry. It is not intended for memory; it is not intended to last beyond the book that comes out, the page it is on, or the magazine it is in. If that continues, memory can decay. If you encounter persistently the kind of convinced hostility that everything in rhyme is old-fashioned and free verse is the only way to write, then this position carries its own penalty. And the deliberation in technique that was supposed to come through W. C. Williams, the great disciplinarian, has become the rhetoric, but it is still rhetoric.

JW: Many critics believe that Lowell's *Life Studies* is the most influential book of English poems since World War II. After years of enjoying the reputation of a strict craftsman, Lowell suddenly began to open up the line and the subject of his poems. How do you feel about Lowell's attempt to open the line? Do you think it gave him access to a certain kind of experience that he might not otherwise have been able to describe?

DW: I don't think that Lowell opened the line so much. The classic tension never disappeared in that book. I think he tried very hard to affect a casual tone, like throwing a jacket on a chair. It's the kind of poetry that sounded as it were being spoken. It was a rhythmic and mellifluous and casual line he created, not only in *Life Studies,* but throughout his work. The Lowell line was metered in his own voice, in his own conversation. And this is true of a lot of other poets I know—you can hear the rhythms of their speech in the rhythm of their verse. So that I never found *Life Studies* to be such a pivotal example, a turn of influence, as you say. The art of having a slack line and then a tight line and then long and a short one only comes from a total comprehension of the linear tension that exists in the poem. And that understanding is as much in *Life Studies* as it is in the other Lowell poems. People who praise it do the wrong thing. They begin with *Life Studies* as a vested model, and nobody remembers the fact that a couple of lines of Lowell's *Life Studies* get their origin from "The Quaker Graveyard in Nantucket." The classic Lowell derives from Milton or Gerard Manley Hopkins, and they don't study that part of the man. It's just like beginning with James Wright. Everybody wants to write James Wright poems, and they don't recognize that Wright earned that liberty. He earned that freedom. He earned that apparent tension there in the work. It is a penalty that disciples pay for an example. They perpetuate the wrong aspect of the example.

JW: When we talk about contemporary poets in America since World War II, we routinely talk about them in terms of content, what they choose to write about. And yet your own poetry comes to the reader more as a musical interpretation of the world. Does the music, the form precede the content? How does a Walcott poem begin to take shape?

DW: Well, it would have to take shape the way any other poem does, which is in a phrase rather than a sentence. The musical structure of poetry doesn't come with a sentence that starts on the left-hand side and goes across—that is the structure of prose. The meter of the poem would be dictated by the extent of the phrase that comes to mind—how many beats it has past the caesura. The poem doesn't begin in front of the caesura, it begins in the second half of the caesura. If a poem is moving from left to right, then it is going to make an artificial caesura. What is audible in a line is a remembered half of a forgotten preceding beat. One does not know preceding that pause what one has finally hooked into. When the beat finally clicks, then the poem can do its work and cohere. If one little thing may be true about poetry, it's that it doesn't come like prose, it doesn't come from some sequential ordering of events. In poetry, a phrase may come out of the air, or out of a collected memory, and from that phrase, the beat begins to dictate itself.

JW: How would you characterize your major theme—your poetic obsessions, if you will, the subjects that you must keep working through?

DW: When you talk like that, you talk in capital letters, right? But this thought here is in lowercase, and it's true. The Caribbean people have a dignity, a suppleness and a beauty that I would like to articulate. I really mean that. And I don't think I have done it. I wish I could do it as well as I might.

JW: The issue of race is treated quite differently in the islands than it is in the states, and you have not explored the race issue in America at great length. However, "Arkansas Testament," the title poem of your new collection, does explore your fear that racism is a haunting, abiding presence here. Is this theme one that you would likely to turn to again? Could you see a new play emerging from this subject?

DW: I think that racism is on the increase in America to my great sadness. You look at something like the Morton Downey show, which I do. As rabid as it may be, it's popular. As thick-necked as it is, it's supposed to be the voice of the people. There is more conservatism, and with conservatism there is bound to be more guarded judgment, guarded offerings, guarded gestures. I never thought I would see the day when America (which is based on the idea of liberty, from which the word Liberal comes) would become so self-centered and hypocritical. I mean if a democracy considers liberal to be a term of abuse, then we should be terrified. A liberal is someone who believes in liberty. And if it is wrong to be a liberal, then the other side has to be fascist.

JW: You come from one of the most racially mixed countries, and yet you presently live in one of the most racially separate cities in America. How do you identify with the Black cultural experience in Boston?

DW: I'm aware of it. The simple fact is I've lived in this city for six, seven years. I teach at the University here. Most of my plays have been performed throughout this country—in Los Angeles, Washington, and Chicago and Hartford, wherever, but I've never had a play done here.

JW: Why?

DW: I don't think they want Black people on stage here. That's it. I'm talking about Anglo-Saxon New England. I'm just saying, I don't give a damn. Because I have some Black actors calling me up right now. I didn't know there were so many. I told them on the phone, I

didn't know all you guys were here. I said to one of them, this is the
toughest city in terms of Black fear. I hate the word Black fear, but
there's a fear of using Blacks in the theatre of this town. It's not true
in the Midwest, it is not true in the South. But it's damn true of
Boston. But who gives a shit, because when you encounter it, you are
encountering a mediocrity of a very high order, so it is no compliment
to be performed by any of these people.

JW: In *Dream on Monkey Mountain,* you suggest that history is a
series of absurd misunderstandings, betrayals and tribunals, where
the peasants become the authorities and the authorities become the
barbarians. What remains at the end is a small victory: Makak's
kingship is finally accepted in relation to something greater than
himself, a kind of spiritual renewal. And yet, when that play was first
performed in the States it was heralded as a call to Black power. Did
you anticipate the political ramifications of the new African king
killing his white goddess?

DW: I think it was hysterically judged by both sides because it's
West Indian. And therefore, from an American or African viewpoint,
it's very different. It is a West Indian experience. In other words, an
African would be so secure in his identity that that scene would be of
no real consequence to him—it would be a metaphysical thing. From
an American point of view, during the Black power time, it was seen
as a symbol of Revolution. The scene does contain the fact that the
man's mind has been white-washed. The name he is given is Makak,
the monkey, and he is following the moon as it goes in a circle, and
he is following the moon as if that is going to be the thing that takes
him back to himself, and back to Monkey Mountain. So there is a
circle that's completed. And when that circle is completed, what
happens is that he is stripped of all illusions. And one of the illusions
is the substitution of Black power for white power and the continuation of the same legacy. In other words, if Black power oppresses the
white victim, it is no different from a white power oppressing a Black
victim. Now you can say that it is justified on the basis of revenge and
it is justified on the basis of history. But it is the very idea of history
as revenge that does nothing for humanity. If South Africa were taken
over by Blacks, the terror would be in whites that the Blacks would
do the same thing to them. Such is the law of history—revenge. But
if, for instance, you consider Gandhi's or even Martin Luther King's

idea of history as not containing revenge, then you have change. And that's why King got killed, because he was not offering revenge. People who are offering revenge, they are just an enemy. But when you offer peace and love, that infuriates people. And you get killed for that. That's why Christ is killed, that's why King is shot, that's why Gandhi is killed. The idea of a man believing in the universal brotherhood is totally unendurable to someone who would prefer to have that man talk about revenge. One may say that the over-all experience of slavery is common to the Black man, but the consequences can be different. The Black American is still enslaved. There is an immense colony of the Afro-American that exists in this empire and the struggle rages wherever you look. But this is not the form of address that goes on in the Caribbean, even though the preponderance of people there are Black. The difference has to do with the reality of the geography of the islands, the sense of freedom, of possibility, of just the simple reality of air, sun, light, grass, fruit, beauty. This is not true in the ghetto. It is not true in the slums of Philadelphia. You can't go anywhere. You get out on the pavement and you go home. So what else is left but some other kind of adventure on the barrenness of the pavement. It is a kind of boredom, a desperation that happens not so much because of the poverty, because the Caribbean is poor. But because there you step out of hut, you step out of shack, and you inhale these things. You feel good. And therefore the conditions of slavery vary according to geography. One Black critic, reviewing *Monkey Mountain,* asks, what has Makak achieved? I say, he goes back to his mountain. When he goes back to his mountain, it's his mountain. It belongs to him. He has another name and now he can say it. He can get up tomorrow morning, who gives a shit that he is poor? Okay, a Marxist gives a shit if he is poor, a politician gives a shit if he is poor, and therefore a poet should give a shit if he is poor. I'm not talking about poverty, I'm talking about the sense of ownership that allows him to feel that when he walks on that road, it belongs to him. That is a condition of the West Indian. That sense of finally putting your foot down on a piece of earth that is yours. All right, somebody says, that's not his. It belongs to United Fruit, it belongs to Texaco. The point is that is what he feels. The people who walk the streets of this city, or back of Columbia University, or back in the blight of Philadelphia, they don't belong to the earth they are walking on. They don't believe in the concrete. There is a great difference between that kind of situation and the Caribbean experience. And those very Black people who may have a television set and a refrigerator also may have the same prejudices about poor islands as white Americans. One has seen Black Americans come to the Caribbean with the identical criticism that white tourists come with. They are not different. They are Americans. Black and white, they come with the same attitude. That's the shape of the country that made them what they are. So it is not just universally common to say that everybody was a slave and everybody has the same experience. The man from the *Dream of Monkey Mountain* achieves nothing, but he completes something. What he does is he sheds an image of himself that has been degraded. When he thought he was white, he did what the white man did. When he thought he was Black, he did what he thought the Black man should do. Both errors. So that moment of cutting off the head is not a moment of beheading a white woman. It is a matter of saying there is some act, some final illusion to be shed. And it is only metaphorical anyway—it's only a dream.

JW: Your friendship with Brodsky and Seamus Heany and in the past with Lowell is well known, but what is your relationship with other poets in America and other Black writers?

DW: Are you asking if I only have white friends?

JW: No.

DW: Michael Harper is a good friend. These poets live in different places, you know. I mean, Seamus is here and Joseph is in New York. My friendship with them has been strengthened by the sense of foreign geography we share. Is that an answer for you?

JW: Well, I guess I was also inadvertently trying to ask about your relationship with Black writers.

DW: Let me tell you something. Black writers in America are Americans. All right. That's important. They quarrel a lot. It's not my quarrel. I'm not taking part in a universal quarrel among all Black people all over the world. I am not interested in that; that is too noisy and is very tiring. I know that they wrangle. But it may be good for them because they may be looking for something in which they want a common bond to be realized. I have my own quarrels at home, I can't take on American quarrels. I sit back from it. But I do not sit back from the reality of the theater in this country. In terms of making its minorities visible, it's contemptible. What's on the stages of America is not America. Mamet is a particular writer writing about what he knows. Shepard is writing about what he knows. But where is the Black Mamet, the Puerto Rican Shepard? Where are these people? Where are those Americans? Is that the multifaceted, multiracial reality of this country, and its theatre? It is a chamber exercise concentrated on one or two aspects of American experience. It is calculated and measured by the box office. The same people who talk about what's wrong with the theatre are the same ones who do nothing about it. They make sure that they get a grant and do a Black show from time to time to keep the crowd going, but I'm not fooled by appearances of apparent vigor here and there. The theatre is a temple preserved by whoever can gain access to that temple and bar people out. So when I have a play done, I don't give a shit where it's done. I do theatre in the Caribbean with as much validity and sincerity as I can. What is done here I consider to be translations of what I do in the Caribbean—adaptations, not the real thing. I don't mind that, because I bring the accent, melody, and experience of a foreign playwright. There's a process of translation that goes on that can be good translation. But the problem is deeper than translation. It is not perverse, it is not spite, it is not prejudice, it's just that cool patronizing attitude that says, "there should definitely be more shows done here about Black people."

JW: There is a sense throughout your plays and poetry of keeping a pledge to be an artist, to nurture your gift, to approach the act itself as divine vocation. What is your sense of what it takes to write great poems?

DW: I don't think anybody sets out to write a great poem. I mean, you do, yes, you do. Otherwise there's no point in undertaking it. I think sometimes one confuses greatness with honesty. And that's our trouble when we get older as poets. We get a lot of great technique, but some kind of innocence is lost. That notion is in Wordsworth, in the Intimations ode. It's a great ode, but the ode is all about the loss of that informing innocence that was there. And that is an ode greater than anything he could have done in his innocence. And Blake shares that feeling. It's more critical in Wordsworth, more clarified in Blake. It's a kind of tragedy in writing poetry as you get older. A tragic sense that you wish that you could keep the exhilaration and the innocence of apprenticeship, but you can't sacrifice some kind of technical mastery that really fuses the poem.

JW: In your plays, you are more clearly funny, satirical, angry, bawdy, tender and loving than in the poems, where you always exercise such great control and compression. Is there ever a time when you would like to achieve this same openness of feeling in the poems that you have accomplished on the stage?

DW: I don't think comedy is an element of poetry, not because it's beneath poetry, but because there's something beyond comedy, and that's the sublime. The sublime is neither comic nor tragic. The idea of tragic comedy, of life being a tragic comedy, is an inferior idea in terms of poetry simply because it's inconclusive. For poetry, life is neither tragedy nor comedy. Life ultimately becomes sublime. It becomes sublime through faith, which may be faith in God or faith in poetry, and the ways are inseparable, even if one may appear to be an agnostic poet or an atheistic poet. Now, you can make jokes about God, certainly. One presumes He has a sense of humor. But ultimately, God is not a joke, and poetry is not a joke for that reason. Theatre is a joke because the theatre is artificial, and in a way tragedy is a joke in the theatre, because when you describe the great plots, they are comical. I mean, how can a guy not know that he went to bed with his mother. How can a guy kill a woman for a kerchief that she has lost. Ultimately tragedy, when compared to poetry, is a farce. Tragedy is, by its nature, farcical, but a great poet will make that farce sublime. Othello becomes a sublime character. In the same way that Oedipus obviously becomes sublime. But if the plot of Oedipus were comedy it would be hilarious. What redeems it is the sublime— not the comedy, not the tragedy even. The clarification of the pain becomes a moment of sublime vision. That's the cathartic thing. So it isn't because I feel like such a sublime being that I don't make jokes in the poems, but I do feel that it's not the instinct that lies in poetry, because it absorbs both the pathetic and the comic. Comedy is ready pathos in most cases because there's always somebody you're sorry for in comedy, or somebody you refuse to be sorry for. That's what comedy is. You're not going to be sorry for Chaplin, right? He's been through hell. You're not going to be sorry for Abbott because he doesn't understand what Costello is saying. You refuse to be sorry for

people, that's comedy. That's not true in poetry. Because generally
there's not a character in a poem that one is finding comic or finding
tragic. What Shelley is saying is true of me when he writes about
himself, whereas in comedy I don't identify with the victim. I laugh
at the victim in comedy and I can identify with the victim in tragedy,
but at the same time I am not as elevated as a Greek tragic figure, so
there's a distance that occurs that does not happen in poetry. Poetry
is a much more immediate dialogue. On the other hand, however, in
terms of being West Indian, this idea can almost be contradicted.
Because of its endurance, the Caribbean spirit can be comic. It's
amazing. The race that has suffered the most is obviously the Jews in
the holocaust, and Jewish humor is very much a part of suffering. The
kind of comedy that is in the Caribbean is also mixed with tragedy.
There is a combination of the African melodies behind the Caribbean.
The melodies are so upbeat, and they are there in Gospel music as
well. It's an uplifting thing to find the melody of celebration persisting
through the tragedy of slavery, so that the music is stronger than the
experience. Black people don't clap and sing because they are subli-
mating; they do it because they are Africans. That's their music. It's
not that they have to escape into an ecstasy of unreality, believing
that some day there is going to be a chariot coming down. The
reinforcement of the experience has come from the force of the music,
which in its original location is happy. And the happiness of that
music has come through the Western side of the world, this part of
our world, the new world, with the same upbeat melody. Calypso has
to be upbeat. People have to dance to it. It can be about the most
tragic situation. It can be satirical, but it can also be very sad. If it is
sad, you have got to be able to dance to it, otherwise it is not a
Calypso. So it is not so much a contradiction as a reality of the power
of music within the race, within the tribe. That's part of the comedy.
Because part of the element of Calypso is to be farcical, to laugh at
oneself. The ritualistic thing in Calypso is comic in its drive, even if
you have a tragic content. Now that is what I would like to accom-
plish. I won't consider myself to be a fulfilled West Indian artist until
I have written something in poetry with that kind of spirit.

   JW: How does your role as a playwright affect the way you build
drama into a poem? How generally do the two genres feed or fight
one another?

DW: Frankly, I think one weakens the other. I'd rather bring all the poem I can to a play than bring all the theatre into a poem. I think the one is artificial and the other one is more natural. You have to be a great poet/playwright to make a speech come out of Prospero or come out of Coriolanus, in which the drama is within the very phrases themselves. I'm still green in terms of the ambience and vitality of poetic vigor that can be there in Caribbean theatre. And perhaps being in America has made me a little deficient, because it's amazing how pragmatic Americans are. They are very Teutonic in terms of their thinking, very rational. And it's part of a rationalist society that it wants something to happen in a particular way, from A to B to C. It's part of the promptness of American efficiency, to want a scene to work well. This scene must not be too long. This must not be complicated. And that's what makes American theatre so mechanical, and American films so mechanical, and American novels so mechanical. They are designed by engineering. I wish we could have a more self-contradicting theatre, one that doesn't provide answers, one that is chaotic as an Elizabethan play is chaotic. Disorganized like life.

JW: In his tribute to W.H. Auden, Brodsky says that every poet should know at least one other poet's work inside and out. Do you have such a poet mentor or a group of poets whose work continues to be instructive?

DW: The poet that I find inexhaustible in my delight of his work is still Philip Larkin. I really enjoy Larkin. The poet I cherish to the point where if anybody says a single shadow of a word against him I will leave the vicinity is Edward Thomas. He's absolutely clear water.

Technically, I think that as you get older and you are still writing, you see all the tricks fall away. You can see who is doing what number. Everybody is doing something—the old suspended simile, the parenthetical balance. You see all the technique. It's all very transparent to you. You see through the skeleton of the poem, and then it becomes less great. By contrast, you come across something that is clear air, clear water. I don't necessarily re-read them, but I think that Dickinson is like water. I don't think Frost is like that for me any more. Stevens has long since faded out for me. Auden flatters my intelligence. He makes me feel bright. He makes me feel like I know it all. Then again, I read Edward Thomas for a breath of air. I don't give a shit anymore about what poetry is to anybody else. It's my private, personal heirloom. Nobody can touch it and nobody can take it from me. I cherish a lot of poets, and poems that to some people may be passe. I cherish a lot of Graves. I think he is beautiful.

JW: Your poems have sometimes been criticized for being too finished, too much concerned with artifice and not enough engaged with the natural convincing speaker. Do you feel that the literary traditions that you've mastered allow you to reflect all the things that you want to say?

DW: The only thing I can say to the critics is, go talk to Edmund Spenser, or talk to John Milton, or talk to Hopkins. Nothing I can do about a finished quality to the poems. Or go talk to Christopher Marlowe. Not to me.

JW: You have produced a tremendous amount of material in 40 years. When does the pace catch up, or do you feel like your character Sheila at the end of *A Branch of the Blue Nile* when she says, "Get up, do what you have to do for all our sakes, I beg you please. Continue to do your work."

DW: Over here in front of you, this is a 200 page poem that I have nearly finished.

JW: Can you tell me anything about the poem?

DW: It's finally called *Omeros,* which is the Greek name for Homer. And what this poem is doing, in part, is trying to hear the names of things and people in their own context, meaning everything named in a noun, and everything around a name. You see maybe the whole West Indian experience is not itself—it is translated. There is a film over the name, Caribbean. You can see the object, but between the object and you there is some experience, some artifice. We look through a glass in which the noun on the other side has not yet been named. It's the origin of the real Caribbean nouns that I'm after. As a narrative thing, the poem is not like a rewrite of the *Iliad*. I don't know the *Iliad* and I don't know the *Odyssey*. I've never read them. The only thing I know about those passages has to do with weather. I'm not boasting about it; it's ignorance not to have read them. I always found it hard to penetrate past all those gods, and all those endless battles and who did what to whom. I have a character whose name is Achille, and another guy called Hector, but Hector is a guy who drives a public taxi, and there's Helen. The connection is, we were brought up to believe that the Helen of the West Indies is St.

Lucia, because it was fought over 13 times. And there's Elena, a Black woman, much like the one on the bus in "The Light of the World." Those things are fed by very ordinary emblems. I'm taking these people as if they were fragments or shards washed up on this shore and looking at them for the first time.

JW: Is this an epic poem?

DW: Yes. I would think that the design of it, yes. It's not like one long poem with a hero. In an epic, you presume that there is no narrator, but I am in this, coming in and out. The book leaves the Caribbean when Achille goes to Africa. For a moment he is in his canoe and he is stunned when he thinks he sees a wrapped body. He gets sunstroke, and in that one moment is contained five centuries. He thinks he sees a sea-swift pulling his canoe across the Atlantic right up into a river into Africa. So he goes back in time up the river and sees the people who are his ancestors, who are also his children, because time is getting reversed. So there is a duality of meeting his father, who is also his own son, etc. Another book takes place in the Dakotas, where there is the Ghost Dance of the Sioux. In the epic terms of it, there is also a battle. The Battle of the Saints, which is a naval battle, fought between the French and the English—a crucial battle in history. The narrator travels to Europe, by crossing the meridian in the same way Achille gets back. I go to Lisbon, Ireland, London and feel some kind of reversal, something in time is happening, new into old and old into new.

JW: Is there a metrical form for this epic?

DW: Yes. Roughly hexametrical with a terza rima form. It's like a combination of a Homeric line and a Dantesque design.

JW: How long did it take you to write it?

DW: I think I began it about a year ago. I just found myself doing it. I had no intention of setting off to write such a long thing, but it just kept coming quite flexibly. Quite easily. With luck this has been going very, very well. And luckily I've done a whole draft and a second draft now.

Thinking Poetry: An Interview with Derek Walcott

Robert Brown and Cheryl Johnson / 1990

From *The Cream City Review,* Vol. 14, No. 2 (Winter 1990), 209–33. Reprinted by permission of *The Cream City Review.*

The following is the result of an interview with Derek Walcott, one of the leading poets writing in the English language. He has received many awards, most notably a five-year MacArthur Foundation Grant. His most recent volumes of poetry include *Midsummer* (1984), *Collected Poems 1948–1984* (1986), and *The Arkansas Testament* (1987). *Homerus,* a long epic poem, will be published by Farrar, Straus, and Giroux later this year. Walcott currently teaches creative writing at Boston University, while maintaining residences in both Boston and his birthplace of St. Lucia. Before teaching in Boston, Walcott served as founder and director of the Trinidad Theatre Workshop. In Milwaukee to give a poetry reading (courtesy of the UWM Creative Writing Department and an NEA Grant), Walcott generously consented to give this interview, which ranged from the shortcomings of the American Empire to racism to the blossoming of Caribbean arts. This material, a transcription of the oral interview, has been slightly edited.

Q: Which poets have influenced you the most as a writer?

A: Only because I lived in a small place—there was very little trash in public places—libraries became more important. In my time, there were comic books. We never really had stuff like paperbacks. It was either the classics or comic books. That's the jump. The influences, the great literature was there, throughout my house. Dickens was there, and Scott. And then of course the kind of school system that I went to was based on the English public school system, which was doing Latin and French and so on. This provided a kind of a scholastic background. I really began to look at modern poetry when a friend of mine, an older man who was an inspector of schools, brought some editions of Auden and Eliot. There was another friend of mine, a painter, who had collections of Dylan Thomas, and so on. The object, the book itself, the modern book of poems, was very exciting to hold, because you have the classics printed in one kind over here, and then you have this object. I don't want to make it sound like a kind of primal society in which there were no books. But, I think that the range of the influence was simultaneous. It didn't matter if it was Shakespeare or Dylan Thomas or anyone else. Of course, an anthology influence is different if you are living in a certain hierarchical kind of tradition in which you meet one writer earlier than another, so these served as models.

I also think that the idea of time affects study. If you are living in a "university" town, your faculty have a kind of laddered idea of what literature is; you go from Spenser down to whoever is next, Milton or whatever. It was called, if you will, the colonial society. Both the geography and the idea of time in the Archipelago was totally different. You don't have this kind of laddered idea that what happens, happens instantly and simultaneously. *Literature* influenced me, not one particular writer. Every day I used to do a poem in the manner of Eliot or Auden. In this country that's looked on as imitation, non-individuality, non-originality, right? I mean the idea of originality—

Q: The cult of originality, some people call it.

A: No, I think the young craftsman is thought to be original only half, and that's because you can't learn to write, unless you learn the shapes.

Q: That's the way the old poets all learned how to write: they'd imitate the masters or translate them. Do you think that in creative writing classes you should teach people to do imitations?

A: No, that's up to the writer. The way time is taught here—history has taught us literature, literature has taught us history. It's not a simultaneous experience. It is taught academically in the sense that you divide it into epochs, and there's this democratic idea of poetry that everybody is entitled to be original, which is ridiculous. So living alone, doing what I was doing, I didn't feel clouded or haunted by anyone else's ideas of being my own kind of writer. I didn't want to be my own kind of writer; I wanted to write as well as people whom I admired. The last thing I wanted to be was original.

Q: Last night, as I listened to you read, I noted certain juxtapositions you made which were just magnificent. They sent my mind in one direction, then, when I thought I could rest easily there, you would spring to something else. I was wondering about influence in terms of an oral tradition. Was the rhythm in your words affected to some extent by hearing and feeling how words fit together in voice and tone and rhythm? Did an oral tradition affect that at all, inform that, or titillate that?

A: You have to take somebody on the opposite side, somebody in England at my age, seventeen or eighteen, a young English poet of that time, say a contemporary, an exact chronological contemporary of mine in England, writing, with an English accent. In theory, that's his tribal accent. There is this whole question of heritage and inheritance. In terms of claiming what you know is yours, the language belongs to you; it belongs to you as long as you work in it. So that whether you are an African or a Ceylonese or a Burmese at the time of the Empire, you grow up speaking the English language without any signs of alienation from the language. In other words, people spoke English. Nobody was astonished by the fact that they were speaking English; they studied English or wrote it as you read it. But, for instance, if you were teaching, which I did in class, the language tended to make you go towards the accent.

I think that's why a lot of West Indian children were so badly taught. If they left home speaking in one way—forget the Creole language itself, but just the accent—they came to class and began to read, and felt they had to recite that language. The teacher and the child were made to believe that this poetry required imitation of the accent of the original tongue. Poetry became something that the child felt was beyond him in a socially structured way: it was something else. It was English. But if you did read in your own voice, with your own melody, the temptation to become English was simply resisted by the fact that you wanted to make it breathe as naturally as you were speaking. Not only did it sound all right once you said it, but it enriched the language; it gave it extra melody.

The melody that is written in the Jacobean melodies, as with Webster or any of these writers, is barbarian, really. It is a still-surviving accent. Barbarian speech is absolutely closer to Jacobean speech than it is to contemporary British speech; that's just a chronological fact about tone. But what I'm saying is that I never—even if I was imitating and trying to learn—I never thought of myself as being English. I never thought of myself as a young English writer. An English writer is immediately entering a tradition in which he just hears as he writes. It's not new to him. It's new, very new, to a young Caribbean person reading it, and I think that's true of the entire Archipelago and the Caribbean basin, including the Latin American writers, like Gabriel García Márquez. Spanish literature for them is not an inheritance, really, it is something that is brought to them fresh. *Don Quixote,* read in Mexico, is far more exciting, and is equal to the time of reading it when it came out. But a Spanish writer, living centuries after Cervantes, thinks in terms of the hierarchy of Cervantes. You don't write like Cervantes any more. You don't talk like they did in Cervantes' time. I'm not saying it's true of a Protestant America, where simply what happened was all the baggage was carried over, in this case, to New England.

Q: Gayle Jones defines the psycho-historical as the relationship between one's consciousness and one's personal experience. I was wondering if history has affected your kind of poetic perspective—I am thinking here of your reference last night to slaves and to the blacks in England. How does your own history, as a West Indian, in addition to language and rhythm, influence your work?

A: I think that's a very dangerous position, black history, because it only continues to segregate. There are traps of segregation that are self-inflicted by the black. They are the same traps as "feminist" fiction and "British" fiction. People are laying their own traps and putting their own feet into them. These labels, which may appear to be self-defining labels, are very satisfying to the other side. It's a pattern of ghettoizing that continues, on the part of the woman, on the part of the black woman, on the part of the black. Because it becomes OK if those labels are self-applied; the other side is very happy, right? Because the other side says, well, they've got their own definition, and it's perpetuating itself, and so that's good.

Q: As long as you are prepared to make certain historical stereotypes.

A: There is really a fallacy of oppression. The whole idea of oppression is a fallacy, right? Including slavery. It's a fallacy that's imposed at the point of the oppression. If the fallacy is believed, you're a slave; if it is not believed, you are not enslaved.

Q: But that distorts the historical—

A: That's the history of the oppressor. The definition of African slavery would be one of exploitation, with the total cooperation of Africans in selling each other.

Q: Not the ones, of course, who were put on the ships. They didn't cooperate.

A: Oh no, the whole idea of slavery was that you caught people and you sold them to the white man. Black people capturing black people and selling them to the white man. That is the real beginning; that is what should be taught. So what do you say? Do you say slavery is wrong regardless of its color? The people who sold African and West Indians as slaves were Africans. That's a reality that is not often told. We dramatize the idea of slavery by saying there's a slave ship outside and somehow these guys get out into the jungle or whatever, and then they capture these poor people and put them on the ship. That is not true. We have to face that reality. What happened was, one tribe captured the other tribe. That is the history of the world.

Q: I see what you are saying, I guess what I'm trying to get at is something just a bit different from that: the history of blacks in this country.

A: It is in parentheses. That's what I'm saying. It is put in parentheses and those parentheses are accepted by the black, and that is absurd, because there are no such parentheses. It is a parentheses of history that somebody captures slaves and sells them to other people, and we know it still goes on, right?

The parenthesis is preserved. It is preserved day by day in this country. When I see on television, everybody clapping and saying it's the achievement of a black governor, I really feel like saying, oh fuck off, because to me that's not an achievement. That one man should be elected governor is not progress. It is only in this country that the attitude makes you furious. I don't see a compliment in being the first governor of Virginia. But is this the attitude of the media? What is the attitude of the historians? We're caught in another parenthesis—on X date in 1989, America had its first black governor. I find that so secondary, so second-rate, of the culture, that it is not worth the anger.

Q: Are you against things such as affirmative action?

A: Am I against affirmative action? Yes, I'm against the idea of something called affirmative action, because it is patronage. It is the same idea of doing something and saying, well, look at how they're

doing—it is the whole parenthesis concept again. The subtleties
continue. You see an interview with Phil Donahue, and you see a
bunch of guys sitting up there, and nobody quite says, "Oh, there's a
good looking black guy up there with the other guys." But everybody
is paying themselves a compliment because the guy is up there. That's
the parenthesis that perpetuates itself throughout every moment of
experience on the part of the parentheticalized person who's up there
with the other white guys. It's a continuation.

Q: How do you eradicate the parenthesis?

A: I don't think you can. I've come to the conviction that America
will remain a second-rate civilization because of its one-up obsession
as a race. It will remain so, and it's getting worse.

Q: Racism is an arbitrary designation that's set up to do particular
things but, in reality, it always brackets.

A: The reality of it is that there are no large issues in America apart
from race. It preoccupies this country. And therefore, you cannot
begin to compare it with any of the previous empire cultures. Simply
because America does not wish to be, in its heart, a world-conquering
empire. You judge the American citizen as a citizen of that empire.
You don't judge Bush or whoever else is up there; you judge the intent
of the average citizen, and the intent of the average citizen—black,
white, green—in America, is not world domination. I think it was a
normal, accepted pride of any previous empire of the French, the
Spanish, the Dutch, the English to say, "We have colonies. We have
colonies in Sumatra. We have colonies in India. We have a dominion
in India." That's not an American attitude, which is great. But,
what's the alternative? The alternative is a kind of cultural empire.
I've no objection to America becoming a cultural empire, simply
because America is multiracial; if that were fused, this would be a
great empire. But, it is not fused. It refuses to fuse.

Q: You often hear that the tragedy of American culture is that it has
not really defined what American culture is.

A: Well, it can never define it while it is circumscribed by the idea
of race. It's like people objecting to Miami, you know. Miami is
probably going to be the most important city in America, simply
because the Spanish influence in Miami is entering to the point where
people are not even speaking English any more. Naturally people are
hostile. Blacks are hostile, because they're Americans—they've be-

come Americans, the very blacks that would talk about slavery. This is a pattern of immigration. The blacks of Miami look at all these Spanish people coming in here now, and taking our turf. These same things were said about them when they moved into a ghetto some-where. The same thing was said about Jews. You know, it's human stupidity. It's human stupidity and hostility, shared by every race.

I believe that the average Spanish person contains a presence of a culture in him. Certainly they are closer to their poetry, certainly they are closer to their daily arts, in the performing arts, much more than the average person, black or white, walking in the modern streets of America. There is something festive and something creative and something excited in them. The idea of excitement, now—everybody has become very square in this country because the idea of excitement sounds like vulgarity, including for a lot of blacks. Gospel singing has become just another part of entertainment. That faith, the faith that's contained there, diminishes under the glare of television lights. It is lurid. It's become another aspect of entertainment, so as long as this whole thing continues on television. On the Archipelago and up around Miami and on the fringe of the Caribbean, what is happening is exactly what should begin to happen in America, which is the interchange—no matter who resents it—the interlocking of the races. That's going to happen more in Miami, even if they're quarreling now. It's a phase that will pass. I'm simply saying that I've lived here for seven years, and seven years ago, I never expected racial tensions to increase in this country. I never expected it. And it has to be blamed on the administration. It has to be blamed on the government. It has to be blamed on "screw you" Republicans, on welfare, on all of that.

Q: To change the subject somewhat, do you consider yourself a poet in the classical tradition or the Caribbean tradition?

A: How could I wish to join a classical tradition when where I was had nothing to do with the vegetation, people or anything remotely referential to Greece or Rome? The Caribbean creativity is phenome-nal. It is an astonishing phenomenon. The kind of writing that has been produced in these islands is such elaborate work. It was inevita-ble historically and culturally. But it is still as astonishing. Now you're talking about writers of equality, of Jean Rhys, Saint-John Perse, Aimé Césaire, V. S. Naipaul. And these people are different colors and different races. Jean is white; Naipaul is Indian. The next great

writer of West India could be Chinese, because there are a lot of
terrific Chinese painters in the Caribbean. The proportion of Caribbean output in relation to the output of another geography, say
Arkansas, is entitled to equal recognition, right?

If Arkansas produced Jamaica Kincaid, hurray. You're talking
about writers coming from an area no bigger than 300 square miles.
Now the reason this happens is because of the ferment of all these
different continents, the cultural continents of the world, represented
in small, almost hot-house kinds of spaces that make things sprout.
That's the phenomenon. So if it is purely a Caribbean literature, it is
astonishing in terms of the quantity of output. Then, if you think in
terms of the entire Caribbean and its own culture, it means that nearly
everyone is an artist of some kind, because you're talking about
music. There is solidly a Caribbean art—not a culture, I don't need to
call it a culture—but literature is a particular aspect of it.

Q: How would you distinguish this culture?

A: I think it has to do with the sensation of freshness. I will try to
make one of those arty similes: you're stepping outside into the
streets without monuments, without cathedrals, and museums. You're
stepping outside your house into nature, or into the town. Therefore—
this is the crappy, pompous part—to read a page of Shakespeare is as
fresh then, as to look at a mango leaf. It's the same to you. There's
no difference between the freshness of the day, and the freshness of
the poetry that you are reading. In other cities where there is a sort
of weather that is historical, then you read Shakespeare as a product
of a continuing chronological process called English literature. But
the Caribbean experience of history is simultaneous.

Q: How would you relate this sense of history to your own work?

A: I know what's going to happen with this book. People are going
to say, "Oh, Walcott, now he is going for the big bucks. There's the
Iliad, there's the *Odyssey,* there's *Ulysses* and now he figures, well,
I'm ready now—here's my big one." OK? I call it a shield because I
want critics to get the references. And the guy is called Achille, the
woman is called Helen, and another guy is called Philoctetes, and so
on. So what's going to happen? The parenthesis, the large parenthesis
will begin. Everybody will put in a bracket—now he is trying to do
Ulysses. The freshness, the truth of the Archipelago, the weather of
the Archipelago, the perpetual freshness of it, the immortal freshness

of the Archipelago, has nothing to do with the figure that we call Homer. He is put into the form of the bleached marble busts that you see.

Part of what I'm saying in the book is that the Greeks were the niggers of the Mediterranean. If we looked at them now, we would say that the Greeks had Puerto Rican tastes. Right? Because the stones were painted brightly. They were not these bleached stones. As time went by, and they sort of whitened and weathered, the classics began to be thought of as something bleached-out and rain-spotted, distant. People who praised classical Greece, if they were there then, would consider the Greeks' tastes vulgar, lurid. The same thing is true of looking at art as exotica. They would not be looked at as stately classical painters, but as exotica, barbarous exotica. All the purple and gold—that's what I'm saying is very Caribbean, that same vigor and elation of an earlier Greece, not a later Greece, not the sort of Romanesque Greece, the Greece of Greece. When people start to look at it, they are probably going to look at it as if I was trying to recapture, *faux* Caribbean. But that is humorous for me to try to recapture, or make a parallel of the Caribbean prior to Greece. They're not the same thing. Everything is reduced, as soon as a comparison begins. An almond leaf is not an olive leaf. The only thing that makes an almond leaf or an olive leaf important is literature. It is art that makes the olive leaf significant.

Q: Why did you choose the figure of Homer?

A: A slave is captured: he has a certain name. The physical beauty of these men working on their own boats and ships relates to the Caribbean. Their bodies are astonishing, right? So, if you think in terms of them as classical statues, if you want to see those ligaments that way, then you'll see them as Africans. African painting is not representational. It is not three-dimensional. It is emblematic. Nobody does the figure. The African identity does not come into African work. The individual artist would blaspheme if he was signing a totem to a god. Same with Indian work, because then you say, "I'm creating a man": that's humanism.

Q: I was just looking through some of the poems this morning. You have one line, "You had losses enough, you can't hold them all in your arms." That seems like sort of a stoic attitude. Are you stoic? Is that your way by nature? Or is it out of necessity?

A: I think that—not to escape this question directly—I think that I'm by nature romantic. If I've been driven to that position, it is because the noises out there are very seductive, in a sense, and therefore you can become some kind of statue of yourself.

Q: The biggest question in the room is really a question of culture and what culture is.

A: I think culture separates itself from art after a while. When art becomes culture, it's dead. It enters museums; it becomes "culture."

Q: Is there any way to avoid that as an artist or writer?

A: Particularly in the Caribbean, it becomes very involved. I am reading a book of essays by Gleason on Caribbean culture. Now why are these things opposed? Why does a study of Eliot seem to be a different subject from Gleason's essays? Well, the subtle difference is because the metropolitan center culture considers opinion outside the center to be provincial. The provincial is only accepted by the metropolitan when it seems to take on the qualities of the metropolitan culture. This is the terrible irony that has happened in my own case: one is praised for acquiring those attributes that convey some kind of benediction.

Q: Do you think that people put you in parentheses?

A: That is the instinct, the nature of the empire, an empire of opinion: whatever Gleason says about the Caribbean cannot be impor-tant because the Caribbean is not important. There's that split be-tween writing about colonial literature and writing about the real center of things. Writers like Eliot or Henry James, and everybody who left here and went to Europe—were happy to continue the idea of a focal, central, civilization. It is a way of seeing literature and literary criticism as an iceberg, in one continual motion, a motion of history, a motion of literary criticism, and so on.

Q: Your whole idea of time is very different.

A: Nothing greater than going into a place, not because you're a hermit, or because you're in exile, but going into a place in which what you feel continually is a daily erasure of what was yesterday. Simply from the sunlight, simply from the sea. Yesterday is erased.

Q: That's the way you feel?

A: Yes, absolutely, so every day in the Caribbean, when I get up, is a date that I have to start working. I'm not continuing—I love to start to work.

Q: That's a wonderful attitude.

A: You see, it is the Caribbean, and it has never been accepted by people who make opinions. I'm talking about a much bigger thing than an individual reputation. I'm talking about the fact that a landscape and a people are simplified by saying, "Well, there's nothing down there!"

Q: Do you think that's true about the Spanish cultures? Are they more like the Caribbean?

A: There's a very strong African presence in Márquez, because he's Caribbean. People are disturbed by agitation: if a tree makes a sudden noise in the wind, it is disturbing, it is nice, but then you get used to the idea of what happened. The sound of Márquez is like a lot of leaves in a tree.

Q: When you read last night, there seemed to be echoes of Eliot in your work. Is that deliberate?

A: You're talking parenthesis now. Any English sentence is going to sound like another English writer. And again, I'm being compared to somebody who achieved the glory of sounding like somebody else.

Q: But doesn't that happen to all poets? They're always being compared to their forefathers, their ancestors.

A: I don't think there's anything that sounds like Eliot in there.

Q: Really?

A: No, God, I hope not, not at my age. If somebody told me it sounded like Dante, I'd say, well, thanks. But even then, that's not true, because it's not the same language. This is supposed to be a great compliment, "Well you're the inheritor of—." It's the same sort of patronage and benediction as saying, "Well now, you're no Eliot." I'm amazed at critics who say, "Obviously you learned from X or Y." I don't feel any echo in anything. I have a passage in the book in which there's a volcano, a standard plot of any epic. It's just a big poem, this dread of the idea of visiting, going back with, the dead. That dread is just normal human nature. The volcano, which is there, out of which steam comes, is a natural metaphor for that kind of apparition. But once you write that, you are going to find yourself sounding as if you were copying Dante. You are bound to. But if you went to the average person, who had never read Dante or Homer, and spoke of a dream, or vision, or retrospective thought, the image that would come up would be of a cloud, of mist, of people emerging, or shadows. It's a normal thing, as common to Stephen King as it is to Homer.

Q: What about Harold Bloom's work, *The Anxiety of Influence?*

A: I don't really read criticism. Sometimes I read the journalism people who are not poets, who review and appoint and crown and uncrown. But they have nothing of any merit to say to people who are working in the craft. Eliot and Coleridge do because they are poet-critics, not critics.

Q: Did you ever feel like you suffered anxiety of influence? Do you ever feel that past poets have been pressuring you?

A: I'm ashamed of you, using a phrase like that. What does it mean? I've heard the phrase; I don't know what it means.

Q: Well, that you feel like you're belated, that you're working under some pressure to outdo your poetic ancestors. It is a Freudian thing—the poet wants to kill off his poetic forefathers.

A: Well, you know, it's an ambitious, careerist phrase: "If I invent a phrase called the anxiety of influence, then I'll be a hot-shot top dog in literary criticism." It means nothing. I could reverse it and say the influence of anxiety. What does that mean?

Q: Well, I guess, not very much. In the "Arkansas Testament," there are several quite short-lined rhymed poems. Why did you use that form? There are usually about two or three beats a line, and the rhymes are very close together. Why did you choose that?

A: You write a line that is long, expansive, such as in *Midsummer,* which is reflective, and contains a lot of indirection, and psychology and self-analysis and connotation. But I thought that it was an antagonistical meter in a sense; it is a meter of evil. I wanted to do something in which the idea remains, and my instinct was rhyme. To have to say anything about instinct, and to define instinct, is like defending breathing. I found that the most pure kind of meter was one that simply went to the length without a breath—you know, like "a ballad is a truth" in a sense—along a pentameter, a collective pentameter, like blues. But this is not active work, this is like thinking.

Certainly blues is work-thinking, that is, working meter. And then you have the psychologically reflective, meandering kind of thing that is not working. In other words, the meter of contemporary poetry is of people who are unemployed. They don't have a job, really. The job they have is writing. But I was thinking of someone who, perhaps, if he was exhaling in and out, and wanted to create something, he would go to that beat. It seems to me it's the right span, throughout. I was trying to think of the metric in which the meter would be very acceptable to the breathing of somebody up on a hill in St. Lucia who was working there.

Q: One thing that's really amazing as we are reading the poems out loud, is how quiet and settled the rhymes are. They're fit so closely together.

A: I didn't want the rhyme to come to a bump at the end; just breathe in and out, it will come right through. Of course, that didn't last, because now the opposite has happened. In my new book, the larger, twelve foot narrative line happened instead. I certainly don't want to use pentameter. That's too heroic now. It's like heroism in Italian. It could have worked in a sense in the Caribbean, because it's a beat of the calypso, a rhythmic beat, a percussive beat. It's legitimate in the Caribbean. Not that you have to legitimize it, you see. That is such a pain in the ass, to say, "Why are the calypsoians working in pentameter, why are they not working in stressed free verse?"

Q: Do you have much faith in free verse?

A: Less and less. I think it's too egocentric. It's egotistical, free verse.

Q: You don't like, then, a lot of American poetry, probably, especially the narrative, flat-voiced poets?

A: Exactly. I read them, but I find them so egocentric, so vain in their modesty, that it's very boring. It's really like listening to my thoughts.

Q: So you probably think that sort of poetry is a dead end.

A: It's already dead.

Q: Earlier we were talking about T. S. Eliot. Many contemporary critics are devaluing his work.

A: I know, but Eliot is solid. Why are you knocking Eliot? The real way to knock Eliot is to look at Auden. Now that's a great twentieth-century poet.

Q: Do you really think that?

A: Oh absolutely, definitely. In scale, in subject, in skill. Absolute deftness, absolute. A wonder.

Q: That's interesting. I guess in the universities he's not taught as much as Eliot and Pound, or even someone like Robert Lowell.

A: They don't believe in intelligence. They believe in something called poetry that has a lot of shapes. The universities encourage laziness in the sense that they encourage the individuality of the young writer, and they don't include the scholarship and history of poetry. There are no young American writers who are interested in anything that wasn't in *The New Yorker* last week. So a writer like Auden looks like another aspect of academia. And the people who teach probably would have to be heretics to teach that he is a very shapely poet. Of course, they begin with James Wright. The man would be horrified that the work he achieved was taught as a beginning to an apprentice.

Q: Since we're on writers, which contemporary writers do you admire?

A: Well, they are many. I think Mark Strand is writing extremely well now. I still like Ted Hughes and Thom Gunn a lot.

Q: What do you think of Josef Brodsky's work?

A: Josef Brodsky does his own translations, and they're terrific. People like Dick Wilbur and myself, when we get the drafts that Josef does, we put them into a certain shape. In a translation, Josef is willing to change a metaphor for the rhyme. That's very gutsy. When his last book came out, there was a lot of criticism of his work, because people were saying that it was not English. But that's the point of it. It has to be read as the intelligence of a Russian entering English. And if it is seen as that, it does a lot for English poetry, because one of the things that's there in poetry is that poetry's intelligence. How to think is as much part of a poem as describing a tree or what you admire about it. What there should be more of is thinking. Most poets don't really think. Thought is supposed to be for the philosopher, for the essayist. But you know, if you read John Donne, what astonishes you is how he is thinking. It is not a very common quality.

The Man Who Keeps the English Language Alive: An Interview with Derek Walcott

Rebekah Presson / 1992

From *New Letters*, Vol. 59, No. 1 (1992), 7–15. Reprinted by permission of *New Letters*.

Derek Walcott's emergence as an extraordinary multicultural talent perhaps owes to his own divided nature. Born in the West Indies to an English father and African mother, Walcott's plays and poems are distinguished by the tensions between the European and African/Caribbean cultures, and by the resolution of those tensions. In play after play, poem and poem—and especially in his recent epic poem *Omeros*—Walcott explores the burden of cultural pasts (*Omeros* is itself Walcott's Caribbean *Odyssey*), and how those pasts contend within his heroic, if all-too-human, characters. Playgoers and readers alike respond enthusiastically to Walcott's incandescent style. Walcott's vision is perhaps best summarized in his statement, "There's an immense amount of danger out there." In 1992, he was awarded the Nobel Prize for Literature.

New Letters: The last time we talked you made much of what *Omeros* is not, and so what would you say it is?

Derek Walcott: It's long. I don't know. In the reviews that have been coming out, they've been using the word "epic" a lot. I just reread it again, and I suppose in terms of the scale of it—as an undertaking—it's large and does cover a lot of geographic elements, historical ground. I think that's the word. I think the reason why I hesitate about calling it that is I think any work in which the narrator is almost central is not really an epic. It's not like a heroic epic. I guess that's what I think of it, that since I am in the book, I certainly don't see myself as a hero of an epic, when an epic generally has a hero of action and decision and destiny.

NL: The hero, I guess, is the whole village.

Walcott: There are different characters in the book who have elements of the heroic in them. I think even a character like the retired

English sergeant major is a heroic figure, even if he's slightly ridiculous.

NL: Is that because he's at least making an effort to record what's
happening?

Walcott: Well, no. He was in the war; he was in World War II. World
War II was probably the last war that had a sort of moral reason, in a
way. He served and retired and was wounded and has a memory of a
wound. So in action he was heroic, not more than anyone else, but
certainly in terms of the fact that he served in a war. The endeavors
of Achille, the day-to-day fisherman, are heroic. I don't put myself in
that company, that's all.

NL: So the story in *Omeros* starts out with a picture of this village
and of these fishermen and their canoe that they fish from, which has
the name "In God We Troust"—sort of a variation on trust.

Walcott: There's an actual canoe like that that I saw spelled like
that—T-R-O-U-S-T—and I thought, this is very touching, because the
ordinary thing, "In God We Trust," you would have just passed by,
but the error was interesting; I mean the spelling was interesting and
personal, and perhaps more devout than the regular spelling.

NL: Your poem *Omeros* follows the form of an epic in some ways.
It's written in hexameter, but it seems to me that you pull out your
other writing tricks, too. There's actual dialogue, as in a play, and
needless to say, you are a prolific playwright, and you vary the
passages between lyric passages and dialogue passages and action
passages. Is this a pull-out-the-stops kind of thing?

Walcott: No. I didn't know what I was going to encounter as the
poem proceeded. I was aware in the beginning that there would be
voices; I didn't know about the dramatic encounters that would
happen. But also, I had been working on film scripts as well, and I
think that there's an element of a scenario of a film script in there,
certainly in terms of the width of the thing and the possibility of a
cinematic version of some aspects of it. In a large poem, though, the
writing is like a novel, and as in a novel, everything is in there—
geographic description, the weather, the characters, and the action,
and so on. So, what was exhilarating was to widen yourself to such
an extent that you could just bring in everything that you wanted to do.

NL: It is interesting that you'd been working on a film script,
because another cinematic aspect is that you cut quickly between

times and places. Achille is in his journey to Africa and suddenly you cut to Helen, or cut back to St. Lucia, or cut to a different time.

Walcott: That kind of editing keeps the story going, because about four or five of them going at the same time help the propulsion of the narrative, as you edit and jump and cut back to another and continuous story. It's the same technique as film, right?

NL: Some of your plays have a fairly large cast, but it seems like there are a lot of balls in the air here, a lot of people to keep track of. How much of a challenge was that?

Walcott: I don't think there are that many. There are certainly the principle characters, and their lives, and so on. Sometimes I wish I'd gone into the lives of one or two of them a little more deeply, but then the narrative goes on, and it pulls people along with it. But each domestic situation has its own drama, as in life, so that Achille and Helen and Hector is one kind of play or drama or story, and then Major Plunkett and his wife is another story, and Philoctete with his wound, and so on. So it was exciting to live one life one day, and go to another life another day, and connect them. But I didn't have a plot design as such, saying, today I'll do this; tomorrow I'll do that. Whatever seemed to be needed, I would do. Then, when it needed to be arranged in a kind of a sequence that would build the momentum, I sometimes drafted the chapters in a line and then needed spaces to connect. It would make a mural, in a sense.

NL: Do you feel like you were writing a novel?

Walcott: Not a novel, but I have felt for a long time that poetry has surrendered too much of what it used to do. The novel used to be an epic poem, and it's sort of withering and withdrawing into small, personal, diaristic considerations that a lot of lyric poetry has. Everybody has an ego, and nobody's ego is interesting, none. Art is interesting, but not the person who makes it, really.

NL: What is your obsession as a writer? Are you primarily concerned with giving a clear and accurate picture of life in the Caribbean?

Walcott: That's certainly what I had in mind. It is a votive act. I feel grateful for the kind of life that's down there. It's simple. The rhythm of life there, the beauty and simplicity of the people. All of it sounds patronizing and sort of wrong, but those values are there. Certainly the values are there in the beauty of the islands.

NL: And I suppose what all this leads to is the middle passage of the book in which Achille has a sunstroke and takes an imaginary, spiritual journey to the Africa of his preslavery ancestors.

Walcott: In this section, Achille the fisherman, for a moment that contains all of history, staggers and has a sunstroke. Within that moment he goes back to Africa, and time is concentrated in that. I mean, it's longer than just a second; it does go beyond that. When he gets on this imaginary journey, which is led by a sea swift up the river, from across the ocean, he sees someone whom he recognizes as his father, because the man walks like him, looks like him; and he stops and searches in the face of the man for the features of his father and it is his father, from generations back.

NL: The segment in which the protagonist, Achille, meets up with his preslavery ancestor is the pivotal scene in Achille's growth as a character. Could you talk about what it means to Achille to question finally what his name means, and who he is?

Walcott: I think the condition of colonialism, or of any first migration of people who were given another language, means the erosion of identity and the desperation to preserve their identity, which can sometimes be punished or banned. But even deeper than that, in adjusting names, somebody from Europe comes over here and changes his name. Something goes into that, in the process of adapting to the name that you've been given, because as an immigrant it's better to call yourself Smith than some unpronounceable, apparently Czechoslovak name, or something. What happens in the process of that naming? If someone is called Achille, what is he? You have to go through a whole process of becoming a name that you have been given. It's the process and technique of removing identity and altering identity so you can rule or can dominate. There must be a moment in a woman's life when she changes her name, like in marriage—if women are supposed to change their names—when that person becomes Mrs. X. Yet, who is Mrs. X?

NL: I'm talking about Achille himself, his personal decision. His decision is that he is Achille the fisherman from St. Lucia; he is not an African, because he's not happy in Africa.

Walcott: Who's happy going back to that scene? That's not his home. That's another point in the book. You talk to a third-generation American, and you say, Why aren't you Russian; why aren't you

Japanese; why aren't you Czech? And the person says, well, I'm American. The whole idea of America, and the whole idea of everything on this side of the world, barring the Native American Indian, is imported; we're all imported, black, Spanish. When one says one is American, that's the experience of being American—that transference of whatever color, or name, or place. The difficult part is the realization that one is part of the whole idea of colonization. Because the easiest thing to do about colonialism is to refer to history in terms of guilt or punishment or revenge, or whatever. Whereas the rare thing is the resolution of being where one is and doing something positive about that reality. And this would be true of the Caribbean, where all the races of the world are central, are collected, like in Trinidad, for instance. Syrian, Indian, Chinese—they're all there. Of course, it's wonderful to keep the heritage and even the distinction of identities in terms of culture, but when it's ultimately said, that is the composite nature of Trinidad. It has all these various things. That is what it means to be Trinidadian. If I lived in Trinidad thoroughly, I would have to understand Chinese culture; I would have to understand Indian culture, African culture, Middle-eastern culture, as well, because those realities are there.

NL: You anticipated my question. I was going to ask you what all this means to Derek Walcott, because you don't fit in one world. Achille has a niche in the world, but you fit in many worlds.

Walcott: Not really, I don't think.

NL: You're a professor at Boston University.

Walcott: All the time I'm teaching I want to be on the beach swimming. That's what I want to do. But, I know what you mean; one can adapt to situations, and you can have a function. My ideal is not simply to be on the beach swimming. I would really prefer to be working and writing and painting in the Caribbean; so I know exactly where I want to be.

An Interview with Derek Walcott

William Baer / 1993

From *The Formalist*, Vol. 5, No. 1 (1994), 12–25. Reprinted by permission of *The Formalist* and William Baer.

In 1992, Derek Walcott was awarded the Nobel Prize for Literature. As Peter Balakian has written in *Poetry* magazine, Walcott's verse "has already taken its place in the history of Western literature."

Derek Walcott was born in Castries, St. Lucia, in 1930, and he was educated at St. Mary's College in Castries and the University College of the West Indies in Mona, Jamaica. His first collection, *25 Poems,* was published in 1948 at Port-of-Spain, and his first produced play, *Cry for a Leader,* was performed in 1950 in St. Lucia.

From 1947 to 1955, he taught at various schools in St. Lucia, Grenada, and Jamaica, and he also wrote articles and drama criticism for *Public Opinion.* In 1959, he was co-founder of the Trinidad Theatre Workshop. Seven years later, he became a fellow of the Royal Society of Literature, and he received a Guggenheim Award in 1977 and a MacArthur Fellowship in 1981.

Since 1985 he has been a Visiting Professor at Boston University, and he's also taught at Harvard and Columbia. He currently lives in Trinidad. His numerous poetic works include *In a Green Night: Poems 1948–1960* (1962), *Collected Poems 1948–1984* (1986), *The Arkansas Testament* (1987), and his long poem *Omeros* (1989); and his many plays include *Dream on Monkey Mountain* (1970), *The Joker of Seville* (1978), *Remembrance* (1980), and *Three Plays* (1986).

This interview was conducted on August 1, 1993, during the Sewanee Writers' Conference at the University of the South—William Baer.

I'd like to ask you a few questions about your excellent and powerful poem "Eulogy to W. H. Auden," which you first read at the Cathedral of St. John the Divine in 1983. Were you commissioned to write this poem by the church?

Derek Walcott: No, not by the church. What happened was that Joseph who was a friend of Auden's—Joseph Brodsky—wanted a commemoration of Auden in New York City. I remember him telling

me at some point, this is going to be done in the church, and that I
had to write something. So I said, "Joseph, you're crazy, I can't do
that," and he said, "Well, no, you *have* to." So I did it, under
great—with a great deal of concern. And I remember when I showed
him something close to a final draft—or what I thought was a final
draft—and he said, "Well, you know, it's okay, but it has to go 'up'
at the end." Meaning it had to get, at some point, a bit seraphic at the
end. Which I did. Not making it too sublime—but trying to balance
something between the sublime and the ordinary.

*How long did you have to do it, since it was being done for a
specific event?*
Derek Walcott: I don't remember exactly, but it was quite difficult
in terms of finding the appropriate structure—as well as the responsibility of actually doing it. I decided to use a model—Auden's tribute
to Yeats—and I think that's what happens in all eulogies or tributes to
poets who are master poets and whom one admires. For instance, if
you take Auden's tribute to Yeats, it's very Yeatsian. Even in Shelley's
tribute to Keats, Shelley picks up some of the flavor of Keats.
Something unique happens, I think, in the writing of the actual tribute.
You get absorbed in the person whom you're paying tribute to, and
you also get absorbed into the sound of that person. Thus Auden got
absorbed in the sound of Yeats because that's part of the tribute—the
surrendering of oneself to the melody of the person whom you're
commemorating. So the design of my own poem is obviously
Audenesque. And the less one's presence is there in the poem, the
better. You must accept it as a sort of acknowledged debt, especially
with a master like Auden.

   Then, once the shape is settled on, the tribute also acquires the
diction of the poet. I don't think of it as pastiche, I think of it as
homage. I think that what, in our time, a lot of people call derivative
or maybe pastiche or imitation, is not something that bothered people
in previous centuries. There were guilds of painters who were not
really imitators—but who were continuing a kind of a style. And I
think it's only the success of the identification of individuality in the
author that makes people rear up at the idea of say, writing in the
same tone of someone to whom you're paying tribute. Yet even in the
little tribute of Eliot to De la Mare, there's an attempt to try to

express the quality of what De la Mare is all about. So the writer of a tribute must subdue his own style and individuality to what the sound of the person is. For instance, Joseph's poem on Lowell is very much like a Lowell poem.

Yes, it enhances the tribute.
Derek Walcott: Yes, and I think any other way means that the ego of the person mourning is superior to the subject.

Did you know W. H. Auden?
Derek Walcott: I didn't know him. I only met him once—very, very briefly. It was outside an elevator in Berlin, and I thanked him for his poetry, and he accepted it very graciously. Of course, Auden didn't know Yeats very well either, but I think the proximity of Auden and Yeats was something much closer. Even though I know an enormous amount about Auden—who doesn't?—there wasn't anything personal or close about it, but I did know how much Auden had done for Joseph. When Joseph had to get out of Russia, and, later, when he had nothing, he turned to Auden, and Auden was extremely kind to him. Thus Joseph's affection and respect for Auden is a very personal one. So when I was asked to do the poem, it was a personal request, and I felt extremely honored that Joseph would ask me to do it for a writer of that stature. That he should think that I would in any way do justice to Auden's memory was a tremendous burden. And a tremendous honor.

A lot of poets have difficulty with occasional poetry. They feel uncomfortable having to write for a specific event. How did you feel about that?
Derek Walcott: Well, I wouldn't want to turn into a sort of MC, or a guy, you know, you could book him for a eulogy—a sort of George Jessel of the cemetery, or something like that. And I don't think I'd do it again. The thing about eulogies and elegies is that they're sometimes very suspicious because they so often focus on the person writing them rather than on the subject. "How do *I* feel about the subject," that kind of thing. But I remember when Joseph asked me to write the poem, and I thought to myself, this is a tremendously painful responsibility because I—as an admirer of Joseph—needed to somehow translate his gratitude and love of Auden into the poem,

even though I don't mention Joseph within it. So it was more than an occasion, and it was not a typical occasional poem in that sense. It was something much more responsible, I think, than that.

And very personal, even though you only met Auden very briefly.
Derek Walcott: Yes. And I do mean really briefly. I'm talking about a nod, you know.

Yes, I see. In Section II of the poem you talk about reading Auden's poetry in your youth: "when strict as Psalm or Lesson, / I learnt your poetry." Do you remember those early encounters with his work?
Derek Walcott: Yes, I remember Auden being revealed to me through a man who died, a beautiful man called James Rodway—I've, just recently, given a memorial prize in his honor in the Caribbean. And Rodway had a collection of a lot of Faber books, a lot of modern poetry, and I'd often show him my work—my poems. He was an education officer from Guyana who lived in St. Lucia and also wrote verse. And I remember, during that period, reading Auden with a tremendous amount of elation, a lot of excitement, and discovery— everybody knows what I'm talking about. And some of the stimulating aspects of his work were there in Eliot before, but they became much more immediate in Auden—expressions like "arterial roads," or even a line like—and maybe it hit me harder than most readers—"August for the people and their favorite islands." That sort of thing. The freshness of his poetry was tremendously exciting, and it induced you to model yourself on Auden, or on the other Pylon poets, but obviously they themselves had been influenced by Auden, whether it was MacNeice or Spender or Day Lewis.

What one heard reading those books—even in the Caribbean, in another climate and another culture—the distance doesn't count, really—was the vigor and wit and freshness that was there in those poems. They were really tremendous. You see, I think Auden actually dared a lot more than either Pound or Eliot. I think that his intellect was far more adventurous, far braver, far stronger, and far more reckless than either of them—plus, of course, there was also that tremendous intelligence behind the poetry. There was so much to amaze you: the casual astonishments of certain descriptions of things that were happening, the strangeness of some of the words, the Anglo-Saxon derivatives that he used, the landscapes as they were described,

and so on. It all created a new vocabulary. In a way, Eliot's vocabulary felt—as poignant as it was—it felt a little jaded in the sense that
it seemed as if it were looking at the world much more wearily and
warily. But Auden took on the challenge of the phenomenally ordinary. In the vigor of Auden's work, there was no sort of poignancy or
nostalgia. And there was no elegiac note. If it was elegiac, it was
politically vigorous, it wasn't simply elegiac. And that was very exciting.

Even the books themselves made a tremendous impression on me
at the time—the actual physical book, the Faber editions of Auden.
You can't overestimate how a characteristic print—or font—affects
you. When I first printed my own books, I modeled the print on the
Faber type, because I felt, well, I'd like to have a book that looked
like Auden's. It gave me the confidence of feeling that I was also, in a
way, though not their equal, a contemporary poet. There was something in the actual font of the print that made it feel as if it were up to
date, as if it were immediate and fresh. It didn't have that cursive,
authoritative kind of lettering found in other, older editions, so you
felt like it was fresh off the typewriter. You could hear the clatter of
the typewriter in the language. And there were so many great poems.

Auden is a poet you go back to all the time, and, especially as you
get older, you look and admire him more and more, and you see how
tremendous his technical skill really was. That's what I mean in terms
of the daring—the technical daring that goes beyond, I think, Eliot
and Pound.

*I have another question about the form of your poem. Edward
Baugh in* The Art of Derek Walcott *suggests that the meter and
quatrain structure of Section II is based on the Wesleyan hymns that
are mentioned in the poem. Did you have a sense of that, and keep
that in mind?*

Derek Walcott: Definitely. When you think of the experience of
reading Auden, you think of a sort of fountain sound—of something
that's like a very cold mountain spring. That's the feel of it: something
way back in time. It comes out of the poetry itself, or the sound itself.
And that sound, that kind of running clarity that's there—it's as if the
line is also moving over the stones at the bottom of the stream, very
fast, but you can still see the stones as the stream—or line—moves

past. This is very much like the King James version of the Bible because the rhythm of the King James has a phenomenal clarity and still a tremendous depth. So when I'd go to church, the Methodist church, I'd hear those passages of Elizabethan poetry—which is what it really is if you're listening. And then, by the time I got to Auden, I could again make the same association to the sound of that running brook. Auden's work had the clarity that I'm trying to describe and even the same kind of language, plus the rigidity that's there in the design of the Methodist hymns—in the great poems by people like John and Charles Wesley, Bunyan, and others. The Methodist hymns were also sung in a very clean manner—there was no adornment in the chapel—just some flowers and a very simple altar. So the concentration was on the words and the music and not on the ritual. The whole experience was essential, and very clear. You directly addressed the very rigid stanzas of song that were there in the hymnbooks. Finally, there was also the pastoral aspect of the hymns that often occurs in Auden—pastoral in the sense of a pastor talking. Auden's poems often reflect the fact that he sometimes thought of himself as some kind of old vicar somewhere. That might seem slightly comic, but it's still perfectly appropriate.

As you've been discussing, your tribute to Auden—like other poets in The Arkansas Testament—*is very concerned about the craft of poetry. Edward Baugh in the collection of essays mentioned earlier says that, "Walcott's sustained engagement with the quatrain in* The Arkansas Testament *is an expression of his insistence on the notion of poetry as discipline, a craft which one has to learn, and work at, and 'get right.' " Given these concerns, do you feel that younger, contemporary, aspiring poets work as hard as they should at learning the fundamentals of their craft?*

Derek Walcott: No, obviously not. I'm a teacher, and I find it very irritating that so many of the younger poets just read their contemporaries' poems. It's a dangerous and terrible thing in this country that poetry has become a very competitive and "contemporary" business. It's become a kind of career. It's become emphatically so in some young women who think that to be a woman now—to be a woman poet—means that you have the right to utter all kinds of dangerous things. It can happen to any group. It can happen to young black

poets, and it can happen to feminist poets. It also astonishes me that
in this country the usual complaint is that anything before William
Carlos Williams is dated—or that American verse is something emphatically different from the world tradition. And not only are so
many young writers ignorant of the tradition, but they've also been
taught to write verse which takes total anarchy with the individual
imagination—which, at *any* age, you really can't do. In truth, all you
can really do at a young age is apprentice yourself to the craft. And
the total absence of that apprenticeship in this country has made most
of the verse unbearable.

And the young are constantly being misadvised. The greatest horrors in my teaching life have occurred when young students have
repeated what other teachers have told them: "this thing has too
much melody," "this thing has too much rhythm," "you shouldn't
use rhyme," and so on. I mean, I don't know *any* other culture in the
history of the world that has ever said that to anybody—that poetry
has too much melody! I don't know on what basis this is founded. I
think when a democracy gets over-assertive it becomes very fascist.
It turns authoritarian in its insistence on freedom.

That problem doesn't seem to be going away.
Derek Walcott: Yes, and I think that there are a lot of people,
especially young students, who would have liked to have learned the
craft, for *all* the difficulty that the craft presents. I try to explain to
students that the difficulty *is* the joy, and that if you don't find the
difficulty an elation, then there's no point in trying to write poetry—go
and write something else, or do something else. But you can't separate
the two. Just look at the terribly mediocre consequences, including
the books that are published, one book after the next, like a little
factory.

That reminds me of Larkin's little essay "The Pleasure Principle."
*That concept's certainly been lost. People don't think of poetry as
something that should provide pleasure; it's just something that if
you write it and you're "sincere," that's enough.*
Derek Walcott: Yes, but I had a nice experience last night. This
house I'm staying in is full of books, but a library can be like a morgue
sometimes, with all those names up there. So I'm looking through the
books and I'm getting more and more abashed staring at all these

books that I've never read. And I'm thinking, "What would I *really* like to read." Then I saw Betjeman, and I thought, wait a minute, don't tell me I'm going to pick this book up, above all the others that are here, whether it's Melville or Hemingway or anybody else. Why am I picking up Betjeman? But I picked the Betjeman, and I began to read it, and I was reading it with *complete* delight and much more respect and fun, you know, than all the other guys on the shelves—very few of them have any fun . . .

Yes, he's remarkable . . .
Derek Walcott: And Auden also had a lot of fun. That's the great thing about Auden, there's a lot of humor, a lot of wit, and a lot of fun.

Yes, always that wit. Some of those ballads are very serious, but they're also very funny at the same time. Your own poem seems to reflect Auden's clever lines, "I cannot settle which is worse, / The Anti-Novel or Free Verse." In your poem, you say . . .
Derek Walcott: I don't know that couplet. What did you say?

It's from one of the late poems, "Doggerel by a Senior Citizen." It goes: "I cannot settle which is worse, / The Anti-Novel or Free Verse."
Derek Walcott: I didn't know that. That's very good.

You seem to echo it . . .
Derek Walcott: But I couldn't really echo it because I didn't know it. That's hilarious, that's wonderful, funnier than anything I've ever said.

But what you did say is very excellent and interesting: ". . . but you, who left each feast at nine, / knew war, like free verse, is a sign / of awful manners."
Derek Walcott: Yes. I think it's very Audenesque to think of war as bad manners, which it is in a way because war is based on a disrespect for another religion, culture, identity, race, whatever, or even territory. And in a sense, wars begin with a kind of indiscipline. They begin as a concept of some kind of indiscipline, with the promise of a reward of some kind. Some order is disestablished, to be reorganized aggressively. Thus the poem makes an analogy with free verse, which is sort of an expression of unrestrained free will, as opposed to subjugation to a kind of order superior to the idea of the individual artist. But that order really exists.

Yes, and it comes out of a long and valuable tradition. I also wanted to ask you about one of the most famous phrases in Auden's "In Memory of W. B. Yeats." He writes that "poetry makes nothing happen," yet, in the same poem, he concludes with a plea to Yeats to "persuade us to rejoice" and to "Teach the free man how to praise." What do you make of Auden's remark about the limits of poetry?

Derek Walcott: You know, I've heard Joseph talk about it, and I've heard various interpretations of it, and I think that people are often too quick—we always quote half of the phrase—and forget that it continues into an image of poetry as a river which "flows south / From ranches of isolation." And I think if you said to a river, "What do you do for the world?" the river's answer would be, "I don't make anything happen." Nature doesn't make anything happen. As human beings we've certainly suffered the loss of awe, the loss of sacredness, and the loss of the fact that we're not here—we're not put on earth—to shape it anyway we want. So Auden's comment is actually an urgent reprimand, and not a resignation. It says, you want something to happen with poetry, but it doesn't make anything happen. So then somebody says, "What's the use of poetry?" Then you say, "Well, what's the use of a cloud? What's the use of a river? What's the use of a tree?" They don't make anything happen.

So it's more a description of its fundamental nature?

Derek Walcott: That's exactly what it is. It goes beyond the simple, ordinary, human temptation of saying, "Well, you'd better *do* something, poetry." And those who demand it are tyrants—tyrants would naturally demand that it do something, right? They always do.

Let's take a parallel idea in Aimé Césaire when he talks about the black raising himself up, and he says "Hooray for those who have not invented anything." So if the accusation is, "What have you invented?" and the answer is, "Nothing," that's a profound answer. Because nothing that's ever been invented has ever cured a single evil. Perhaps the highest tribute that one could pay to one's creator would be to do "nothing." Maybe the beginning of trying to do "something" was the cause of the fall of man—doing something different than simply being in Eden, you see what I mean? That "do something" attitude leads to all kinds of consequences, so I think that Auden wanted to put poetry in another category—in the same category as, well, not exactly prayer, but beyond that. And I think that to take his phrase as a cynical comment of resignation—which people often claim it to be—is not enough. As a matter of fact, poetry *does* make something happen because in the flow of the river which he talks about, the river touches many things as it passes by.

Yes, and then the poem ends by asking Yeats to show us how to "rejoice" and "praise."
Derek Walcott: Exactly right.

In your collection The Arkansas Testament, *the eulogy to Auden is the initial poem in the "Elsewhere" section which represents European culture, as opposed to the earlier poems about Caribbean culture that comprise the "Here" section. The eulogy refers to both the "Empire" and the "colonial streets," and it also talks about reconciliation. You use terms like "communion," "one mouth to speak for all," and "the gift of peace." These ideas relate directly to your long poem* Omeros, *and also to a comment you made in your* New Letters *interview with Rebekah Presson: ". . . the easiest thing to do about colonialism is to refer to history in terms of guilt or punishment or revenge, or whatever. Whereas the rare thing is the resolution of being where one is, and in doing something positive about that reality." Do you feel that this sense of a hope for some kind of reconciliation is one of the predominant themes in your writing? In other words, people always talk about your personal "search for identity," but it seems to me to go beyond that—that there might be one voice "to speak for all."*
Derek Walcott: Yes, that process of a search . . . it's not really as simple as just a search for identity, but let me begin there because I think the process is an important aspect of English literature right now—whether it's Ondaatje, or Rushdie, or Naipaul, or anyone. It's a process, a post-empire process, which has to be historical, and which also has to be, eventually, spiritual in a sense.

For example, say you're not English but you're working in the English language, and you're writing in the best possible way you can. And though the language belongs to England—still there's no distinction between someone in Ceylon who's a young poet, and someone in England who's on the same level of talent or whatever, enjoying the language. But what tends to happen is that things get divided up politically. An English critic might say, well here's a young guy from Ceylon who's certainly learned something about the English language and is doing "very well." Now that's a patronizing attitude that never goes away because people are protective about what they think is their language. I once had an Italian ask me, "What are you doing messing around with Dante?" As if to say, "He's *our* poet exclusively." I mean you often get that kind of stupidity. On the other hand, you can get the local stupidity which says that you must stick to local subjects and expressions—so you get into a battle on either side. And if you're not careful, you find yourself drawn in two—and a target for both sides.

And that's not to deny that there are real crises of resolution, and conflicts and ironies, about the fact that you're writing in English. For example, you can't just think of Sir Walter Raleigh as someone who was simply an adventurer, some who exploited—even if you're inclined to use that kind of historical post-mortem on Raleigh. You can't let it cloud the fact that Raleigh is a superb, a great poet. A more recent example is the Larkin controversy. Whatever his prejudices might have been, his poems remain pure because real poetry doesn't permit such prejudices. It purges itself of that. It's a kind of a grace that's bestowed on the serious and talented poet. Now one could, for example, write a kind of verse that might be very vigorous about, let's say, get the "niggers" out of Britain, and he could make it rhyme, and it could be funny, and it could be skillfully done. But then you ask yourself whether such a vitriolic, bitter—even anti-Semitic in the case of Pound—effort could really be poetry? No, I don't think so. I think that poetry—no matter how well it's done—must still achieve a supreme compassion and tenderness.

Now if that's the center of real poetry, then it really doesn't matter what the time or place or race of the writer. So no matter what the clever arguments, the English critic has no right to patronize somebody on their "efforts." And the local critic has no right to accuse someone of "betrayal." Unfortunately, all these various problems can exist inside the writer himself, and are externalized by these conflicts. And this complicated process affects writers from India, from Canada, or from anywhere else. But it's a conflict that makes a drama, and it's a conflict that makes the exercise, you know, the endeavor, dramatically and historically interesting. So, I guess, I've drifted away from a direct answer to the question, but I don't think that the options for the contemporary poet should be so harshly dramatized: that he *has* to make a choice, one or the other. That's what tyrannies say, vote for me—you can't choose. But that's not the territory of poetry.

Well, you did get to that important notion about the heart of poetry being compassion, and that leads into my last question about the "Eulogy" being a reaffirmation of the need for human kindness, as in the hopeful lines, "that the City may be Just, / and humankind be kind." Do you think that contemporary poetry deals enough with this concept? In other words, are we too afraid to come out and talk about charity and compassion and so forth? We certainly make a lot of noise about it, but does poetry really deal with it as much as it should?

Derek Walcott: My answer to that question is this: aren't you, yourself, astonished, and in a way, disappointed, that the rein of American verse is so tight, that it's so small, so provincial, and that all it takes in is the neighborhood, the next farm, or the next street? Especially for a country of this size, whose responsibility in the history of the world is, as you know, the greatest responsibility any country has ever faced, in terms of conscience, and in terms of justice. Yet its poetry . . . if you looked at it generations down the road, you would say, "What the hell were those people thinking about?"

Do you see what I'm saying? You pick up a contemporary poem and you say—apart from certain poets—that it's diminished; it's something so small and positively boring to hear about—all the little, anguished egos that are represented in all those little poems. No one dares to write a capital letter word like Pity, or Love . . . contemporary poetry doesn't exalt, it doesn't condemn, and it's all very muted. The limited scope of contemporary thought, and the narrowness and the confines of even young poets is astonishing. In the past, the average young poet was someone who was shouting inside himself. There was an exaltation, and there was a sort of daring. But today in America what you get is such timidity that it's astonishing. It could have come from a corner of the most remote little village somewhere. But it's what comes out of New York, and out of Boston, and out of Chicago.

It seems that to exult is to be embarrassed. Who can write something in the pitch of exultation like "The Windhover" or Dylan Thomas's poetry—because it becomes embarrassing to sound so . . . well, happy! I mean a lot of great poems are happy poems, poems of joy.

Well, "Eulogy to W. H. Auden" is a beautiful and masterly poem that's not afraid to remind us about Hope—one of those capital letter words—as in the last quatrain:

> *and the mouths of all the rivers*
> *are still, and the estuaries*
> *shine with the wake that gives the*
> *craftsman the gift of peace.*

Derek Walcott: I should end by saying that the figure that one has of Auden at the end of the poem—keeping in mind that Auden was a religious poet in the nature of Herbert—is of this guy shambling along somewhere down lower Manhattan, almost looking like a bum in the way that he's going by, but containing within him a tremendous concern for others. All those *big* words. Auden could write them because he was a great poet. He could write Pity with a capital "P," and he could write Justice, and the Just. Maybe the authority to write of such emotions and qualities with a capital letter is gone now. But Auden was entitled to do it, and he believed in doing it. So the final scene of the poem highlights the fact that he contained so much love and concern within him—and also within an industrial context, not simply in a pastoral setting, not sitting outside the city brooding on the rocks, but in New York City.

Your own poetry has the same power to express the large and significant aspects of our lives. Thank you very much.
Derek Walcott: Thanks a lot. I enjoyed it very much.

Index